Critical Voices In
AMERICAN
CATHOLIC
ECONOMIC
THOUGHT

John J. Mitchell, Jr.

New York   Paulist
Press   Mahwah

ACKNOWLEDGEMENTS

The articles reprinted in *Critical Voices in American Catholic Economic Thought* first appeared in the following publications and are reprinted with permission: "The Long Loneliness" from *Loaves and Fishes* by Dorothy Day, Harper & Row; "What is Capitalism" by Virgil Michel, *Commonweal,* Vol. XXVIII, April 23, 1938, p. 6; "The Layman in the Church" by Virgil Michel, *Commonweal,* Vol. XX, June 4, 1930, p. 125; Excerpts from *By Little and By Little: Selected Writings of Dorothy Day,* Alfred A. Knopf, Inc.; *A Long Time Coming* by Anne Loftis and Dick Meister, copyright 1977, Macmillan Publishing Company; *Three Theories of Society* by Paul Hanley Furfey, copyright 1937 by Macmillan Publishing Company; *Fire on the Earth* by Paul Hanley Furfey, copyright 1936 by Macmillan Publishing Company; *Mortality Gap* by Paul Hanley Furfey, copyright 1969, Macmillan Publishing Company; *Rebel, Priest and Prophet* by Stephen Bell, Devin Adair Publishers; *Houses of Hospitality* by Dorothy Day, published by Sheed & Ward; *American Catholics and Social Reform* by David O'Brien, published by Oxford University Press; *Piks Dietz, Labor Priest* by Mary H. Fox, published by University of Notre Dame Press; "Five Hard Sayings Repugnant to Natural Man" by Paul Hanley Furfey, *America,* 4-3-37 issue; *A Popular History of the Archdiocese of New York* by Florence Cohalan, published by the Catholic Historical Society; Quotations from *Orate Fratres* published by *Worship* magazine.

Book design by Ellen Whitney

Library of Congress Cataloging-in-Publication Data

Mitchell, John J., 1944–
    Critical voices in American Catholic economic thought.

    Includes bibliographies.
    1. Economics—Religious aspects—Catholic Church—History. 2. Sociology, Christian (Catholic)—History. 3. United States—Economic conditions. 4. United States—Social conditions. 5. Catholic Church—United States—History. 6. Catholic Church—Doctrines—History.
I. Title.
BX1795.E27M58   1989   261.8'5'0973   88-28895
ISBN 0-8091-3029-7 (pbk.)

Published by Paulist Press
997 Macarthur Boulevard
Mahwah, NJ 07430

Printed and bound in the
United States of America

Contents

⌒

REMBERT G. WEAKLAND
Foreword vii

JOHN J. MITCHELL, JR.
Introduction xi

ORESTES A. BROWNSON
Building a Christian Economy 1

EDWARD McGLYNN
The Fatherhood of God and
the Brotherhood of Man 30

PETER E. DIETZ
Christ-Consciousness in the Economy 55

VIRGIL MICHEL, O.S.B.
Eucharistic Economics 77

PETER MAURIN
Apostle of Christian Personalism 106

PAUL HANLY FURFEY
Personalist Economics 130

DOROTHY DAY
A Catholic Worker 153

CESAR CHAVEZ
Economic Justice for All 174

Acknowledgements

No author writes alone nor in isolation discovers the inspiration for a book. *Critical Voices in American Catholic Thought* owes its life to a community of friends and colleagues.

I owe a special debt of gratitude to the Seton Hall University community (South Orange, N.J.), especially Msgr. John J. Petillo, Chancellor, Dr. Bernhard Scholz, Provost, the University Research Council which provided a research grant, my faculty colleagues at Seton Hall, especially Dr. Richard Adinaro, and the members of the Department of Religious Studies, especially Rev. Richard Nardone, chair, and Rev. John A. Radano. All offered continued encouragement.

The seeds for *Critical Voices* were planted long ago by my friend and mentor at the University of St. Michael's (Toronto), Gregory Baum, a prophetic voice in twentieth-century Catholicism, and Rev. John Haughey, S.J., a voice for justice.

The people of the Archdiocese of Newark provided special inspiration. I have long drawn from the pastoral concern of Most Rev. Peter L. Gerety, former Archbishop of Newark, especially in his leadership role in the Bicentennial Liberty and Justice for All Program, and the subsequent Call to Action Conference in the mid 1970s. I owe a particular debt to the members of the Archdiocesan Justice and Peace Commission, especially Bishop Joseph A. Francis, chair, and Sr. Suzanne Golas, Patricia Natale, Fr. William Reilly, Kathleen DiChiara, Marie Varley, Steven St. Hilaire and the others who encouraged me.

Seton Hall University librarians, Sr. Anita Talar, R.S.M. and Anthony Lee deserve special thanks for their invaluable research assistance.

Special gratitude is owed to my mother, Helen, and my father, John Sr., who have always cared and shared. They taught me the first lessons about faith and justice.

My three children, Jessica, Cathleen and Mary Elizabeth were always supportive in their questioning and encouragement.

And finally, my wife and best friend, Mary Lou, was ever the quiet encouraging voice. She believed in *Critical Voices* before pen first touched paper. Without her it would have remained simply a good idea without reality. I thank her today and every day.

FOR THOSE WHO DO JUSTICE
IN WORD AND DEED

REMBERT G. WEAKLAND

୵

Foreword

When the first draft of the Economic Pastoral Letter of the bishops of the U.S.A. appeared in November of 1984, many were surprised, if not startled, by its contents. Catholics were high on the list of those so reacting. One asked, naturally, if they were aware of the many members in the history of their own Church in the United States who had treated similar issues. These precursors are just not as well-known as they should be.

The beauty and usefulness of John J. Mitchell's book is that it brings together under one cover the thinking on the relationship of the Catholic Faith to economic attitudes of so many who formed an integral part of the history of the Catholic Church in the U.S. We need more knowledge of these voices and how they relate to one another. Professor Mitchell has not tried to give us biographies of the authors he treats, but only deals with such material as is needed for a fuller understanding of the positions taken by each author. His work is, rather, a history of ideas—and the people he presents come alive in their ideas.

In our day there is a renewed interest in all of the figures here presented, perhaps stimulated by the Economic Pastoral Letter. Brownson, McGlynn, and Michel for instance, are the subjects of recent biographies and reassessment. Some others are better known because they are more contemporary figures—Peter Maurin or Dorothy Day, for example—but even these are being studied again under new lights. For some time they were considered as peripheral to the mainstream of American Catholicism, but that attitude is changing as one sees the influence they have had both before and after their deaths.

One of the aspects of the writings of so many of the figures in this book that may surprise the reader is the vehement opposition many showed toward capitalism itself. At first the bishops, too, were criticized for being opposed to capitalism as such, but their Letter is indeed mild in its criticism compared with the writings of many of the authors here treated. Some even raised the basic question of whether or not capitalism can in any way be reconciled with the Gospel. Virgil Michel or Monsignor Furfey would have said that the two were irreconcilable; their words are harsh and uncompromising. The bishops did not take that extreme view but had to admit that in reality, as capitalism has worked itself out in history, there are some grounds for skepticism. If one defines capitalism as an economic system based on greed, self-interest, or profit for its own sake, then the negative judgment, naturally, follows. It is impossible to reconcile such a theory with the Gospel. On the other hand, theorists of capitalism would deny that these elements are intrinsic to the definition. They see instead a system of checks and balances created by the realities of supply and demand.

Perhaps the most devastating arguments center around the accusation that capitalism reinforces the individualism inherent in our society, and leads to such self-centeredness that it is harmful to the common good. Virgil Michel was certainly of that opinion. He also was negative toward the effects of competition on the well-being of society. I leave it to the readers to form an opinion of the convincing quality of the argumentation of Michel by reading the excellent summary Professor Mitchell presents of it. One thing is certain: Michel and other Catholic critics like him force us to juxtapose the biblical vision of a Christian society as presented in the Sermon on the Mount, in particular, against the actual capitalistic society in which we live and to examine our consciences concerning the results.

One of the most challenging but incomplete parts of the Economic Pastoral Letter of the United States bishops, ECONOMIC JUSTICE FOR ALL, deals with a Christian lifestyle based on the Gospel values of social justice. We Catholics today are searching for models or examples of those who have wrestled with this issue in their own lives and have come up with personal solutions. Among the individuals presented here by Professor Mitchell are many to whom the social teaching of the Catholic Church is not an economic theory for the whole of society, but truly a personal challenge for each believer. It was, thus, perceptive on the author's part to include people such as Peter Maurin, Dorothy Day, and Cesar Chavez, because they are living examples of those who took the Beatitudes seriously in their personal lives. Most often their actions speak louder than their words. They call us back to an attitude concerning the teaching of Jesus that is both simple and convincing.

The task of relating the long tradition of the Catholic Church on social doctrine to our U.S. scene has just begun. Perhaps it is the first time in the history of the nation that Catholics have been in a position to ask the question about the relationship between the Gospel preached by Jesus and the way in which our consumer society presupposes other values and places other demands on us. It is a crucial moment for us, because we want to do our best to help the poor in our own country and around the world to lift themselves out of poverty, and we realize that this can only be done in cooperation with all other peoples on this globe. It is important, therefore, to articulate what the goals and aims of our economic system really are. We must do so in a way that is convincing and attractive; but we cannot hope to win in this aim if we project in theory or in practice a system that is self-serving, oblivious to the poor, or founded on any form of exploitation.

The critical thinkers in the Catholic tradition that are presented in this book can be for us models and exciting prophets. They will force us to sharpen our own concepts and integrate our biblical and ethical demands with our daily conduct. We all need a book of this sort, and the examples described here enable us to enter more fully into the Catholic tradition of social teaching and to respond more adequately to the responsibilities of our own day.

Most Reverend Rembert G. Weakland, O.S.B. is Archbishop of Milwaukee and served as Chairman of National Conference of Catholic Bishops' committee which drafted Pastoral Letter on Catholic Social Teaching and the U.S. Economy—"Economic Justice for All."

JOHN J. MITCHELL, JR.

⌐

Introduction

The recent publication of *Economic Justice for All* (1986), a pastoral letter of the American Catholic bishops, represents a significant moment in the history of American Catholicism. It invites the Catholic people of the United States and all people of good will to reflect on the relationship between the American economy and the values of the Judaeo-Christian tradition. Not since the publication of the *Bishops' Program for Social Reconstruction* (1919) have the Catholic bishops of the United States engaged in such a comprehensive moral analysis of the American economy. The pastoral offers a variety of specific recommendations designed to enhance the moral fabric of the economy and advance the American promise of economic justice for all.

Many of the recommendations of the 1919 pastoral letter of the Catholic bishops, written in large part by the legendary Msgr. John A. Ryan, eventually earned the endorsement of President Franklin D. Roosevelt. Throughout the 1930s Roosevelt incorporated many of the bishops' proposals into his New Deal policies as he led the nation out of one of its most severe economic depressions. It is too soon to say what impact *Economic Justice for All* will have on the American economy, or if it will give birth to a new commitment to improving economic conditions in American society for the millions of men, women and children who are impoverished and marginalized. Thus far the response to *Economic Justice for All* has been predictably mixed.

The critics of the pastoral, including a number of prominent Catholics such as William Simon, former Secretary of the Treasury and Michael Novak, theologian-in-residence at the conservative American Enterprise Institute, have accused the bishops of harboring a liberal bias in their approach to economic issues. These critics have been particularly displeased by the pastoral's criticism of American capitalism, which they consider the most morally viable economic system available today. Simon, Novak and others argue that the existing inequities in the American economy are not the fault of the capitalist system per se, but either the failure to properly apply the principles of the free enterprise system or the result of human failings. The conservative critics of *Economic Justice for All* will undoubtedly continue to voice their criticisms in the years ahead.

The enthusiastic supporters of *Economic Justice for All* have warmly applauded the moral courage and vision of the American bishops. Many of these advocates, such as Michael Harrington, author of *The Other America* (1962), which awakened a nation to the existence of a culture of poverty in a land of affluence, welcomed the Church's willingness to play a more active role in the continuing struggle for economic justice in America. They have applauded the willingness of the bishops to raise serious moral objections about those aspects of American capitalism which generate human brokenness and alienation both at home and around the globe.

A third reaction to *Economic Justice for All* has also been heard. This reaction may well represent the feeling of a majority of American Catholics who have wondered aloud why the bishops have suddenly taken an interest in economic issues and affairs. Unfortunately, many of these men and women are not aware of the tradition of Catholic socio-economic thought, the social encyclicals of Leo XIII, Pius XI, John XXIII, Paul VI, John Paul II, the social teachings of the Second Vatican Council or the past involvement of the American bishops in the national debate about economic justice. For these men and women, including many priests and religious, the Church's social message has not been a keen interest of theirs in the past. Consequently, *Economic Justice for All* is experienced as a totally new dimension of their participation in the life of the American Catholic Church.

Critical Voices in American Catholic Economic Thought is not written primarily for either the vocal critics or the avid supporters of *Economic Justice for All,* but for the large number of American Catholics who are unaware of the Church's commitment to the cause of economic justice. Hopefully *Critical Voices* will help to provide some background to the Church's historical concern about economic justice in America and offer some insight into the motivation which inspired *Economic Justice for All.* It is my conviction that *Economic Justice for All* has grown out of a living tradition; a tradition which, theologically and pastorally, has often found the American Catholic Church allied with the poor and dedicated to the struggle for economic justice. This tradition needs to be better understood and appreciated today.

Some commentators have suggested that the publication of *Eco-*

nomic Justice for All, as well as the active involvement of the bishops in the American economic policy debate, represents a new stage in the development of the American Catholic Church. A number of historical factors, both social and ecclesiastical, lend credence to this assessment. From the mid-nineteenth century to the mid-twentieth century the Catholic Church in America was continually called upon to respond to the immediate needs of waves of immigrants. This often diverted its attention away from broader national policy issues, including those pertaining to the economy. The Church's interest in dispelling a variety of anti-Catholic sentiments in society also contributed to prudential decisions to avoid public criticism of American institutions including the economic order. The Church's harsh condemnation of socialism and communism was often erroneously interpreted as a blanket endorsement of American capitalism. Finally, the increasing privatization of Catholic belief tended to minimize the importance of the relationship between the Church and economic affairs. The most significant exception to this was the Church's active involvement in the labor movement in the late nineteenth and twentieth centuries. However, much of this involvement was rooted in the Church's interest in advancing the economic rights of Catholics rather than a broader interest in the moral foundations of the economy.

A variety of developments in recent years within the Church and society have contributed to the Church's renewed interest in the relationship between Christian faith and the American economy. The Fathers at the Second Vatican Council enriched the social conscience of the Church by pointing to the need to carefully read "the signs of the times" in order to properly proclaim the message of the Gospel. This task requires a new attentiveness to the impact of social structures and institutions, including the economy, on both personal and social life. Catholics in America are challenged today to examine the impact of the economy on human dignity, justice and social solidarity. Pope John Paul II has played a particularly significant role in awakening Catholic men and women to the need to examine the relationship between economic systems and the principles of Catholic socio-economic philosophy. His social encyclical *On Human Labor* offers a comprehensive and highly critical analysis of the failure of contemporary economic systems, including capitalism, to nurture human well-being and foster justice. The American Catholic Church's renewed interest in the relationship between the economy and Christian faith has also been fueled by the fact that the gap between the rich and the poor in America has increased dramatically in recent years. Although the gross national product may have increased, there is little evidence to suggest that this has enhanced the lives of the millions of men, women and children who live on the fringes of the American economy, often deprived of the very basic economic necessities. Conditions like these in a land of affluence cry out for justice, and the American Church has expressed a new willingness to put her voice and her energies at the side of those who are victims of economic injustices.

Renewed interest in the relationship between the Christian Gospel and the economy has given new life to the rich social tradition which has been a part of the American Catholic experience since early in the nineteenth century. Unfortunately this tradition, which adopted a critical posture toward the American economy, is neither well-known nor properly appreciated. Historically it has raised serious and troubling questions about the nature of capitalism and its compatibility with the Gospel and Catholic economic principles. Because this critical social tradition is not well-known, American Catholics today have experienced some difficulty in identifying with a tradition which questions the moral foundations of American capitalism. Unhappily, this lack of knowledge can easily lead Catholics to a naive and uncritical acceptance of capitalism which fails to adequately recognize the discrepancies between the actual consequences of capitalism and the demands of economic justice.

This critical social tradition is not known or appreciated today because it was never presented in a highly theoretical or systematic form. It is available primarily through the stories and the struggles of courageous men and women who recognized the need for a proper relationship between the Gospel and economic realities, and who identified those aspects of the American economy which violated the tenets of economic justice. Even a cursory reading of *Economic Justice for All* draws the reader's attention to some of the major themes which have occupied the attention of this critical social tradition. Together with the American bishops, these men and women have asked these probing questions: What does the American economy do *for* people? What does the American economy do *to* people? Do the workings of the economy foster community and human solidarity or do they generate social divisions between individuals and groups? Does the economy and the nature of capitalism enhance and protect the dignity of workers, or does it lead to human exploitation and alienation? Does the profit motive in capitalism contribute to a materialistic ethos which undermines peoples' responsibility for one another? How does the American economy treat the poor? Does it work to empower those who are marginalized or increase their anguish and misery? Do all members of society enjoy the same economic rights, or are there classes of people who are relegated to second- and third-class citizenship?

These questions need to be raised again today by those who are committed to a better understanding of the relationship between the economy and the Gospel. Perhaps this can be more easily accomplished by examining the lives of those Catholic men and women in America who raised them in the past. We need to appropriate this critical social tradition and use it as a foundation for our own efforts. In *Critical Voices in American Catholic Economic Thought* I have tried to give new life to this tradition by exploring the lives of several American Catholics who understood economic justice as a constitutive dimension of their own Christian lives and a necessary part of the life of the Church. Their struggles can challenge us today if we listen attentively to their prophetic voices.

In the mid-nineteenth century, Orestes Brownson foresaw the inherent contradictions in industrial capitalism as it was developing in the United States. His writings provide a vivid description of the social fragmentation which results when individuals are encouraged to pursue their economic self-interest regardless of its consequences for other members of society. The collapse of community, which he considered synonymous with the rise of capitalism, set millions of men, women and children adrift in society. Brownson looked to the Catholic Church to proclaim anew the rights of persons and the need for social solidarity in economic affairs. In his writings he placed special emphasis on the need to understand the social significance of the mystery of the incarnation. Christ's presence in human history should be seen as the foundation for the creation of a socio-economic order giving form and focus to the values of the Gospel. The privatization of Christian faith tended to limit the meaning of the incarnation. If the social meaning of God's incarnation was more adequately understood, Christians would better understand the need to create socio-economic structures which protected human dignity and fostered communal bonds among people.

Edward McGlynn was the pastor of a large parish in the lower east side of Manhattan from the late 1860s until the 1880s. The human poverty which afflicted the lives of his parishioners shaped his Christian social conscience and gave rise to his famous rallying call proclaiming

"The Fatherhood of God and the Brotherhood of Man." McGlynn rejected the popular wisdom of his day which argued that the economic disparities in society, including the enormous gaps between the rich and the poor, were inevitable and beyond human control. He contended that the economic conditions which accounted for much of the human misery and poverty were human creations which had to be reshaped in keeping with the values of the Gospel. McGlynn believed that all people had a moral right to share in the bounty of God's material creation and that economic policies should be established to achieve this goal. He likened the economy to a banquet table set by God and intended to be enjoyed by all.

Few Catholics in the United States have made a greater contribution to the American labor movement and the cause of economic justice than Peter Dietz. His efforts shortly after the turn of the century led to the establishment of the first official relationship between the Catholic Church and the American Federation of Labor. Because he was keenly aware of the economic injustices in American society, he repeatedly called for the need to replace "class-consciousness with Christ-consciousness" in economic affairs. His leadership role in the formation of the Militia of Christ, the Social Service Commission of the American Federation of Catholic Societies, and the Academy of Christian Democracy, provided the foundation not only for the Bishops' Program for Social Reconstruction in 1919, but it awakened the American Catholic bishops to the leadership role they were being called upon to play in advocating the cause of economic justice in society. Despite all the setbacks he experienced during his lifetime, Peter Dietz never waivered in his belief that the Gospel provided the moral vision for the creation of a cooperative economic order in the United States, which could protect and enhance the economic rights of all the citizens.

Virgil Michel, OSB is well-known for his pioneering work in the liturgical movement in the United States. Unfortunately, his work as a social reformer and harsh critic of America's brand of capitalism are not recognized or appreciated. Michel continually spoke about the intimate relationship between the liturgical life of the Church, especially the Eucharist, and the transformation of socio-economic conditions in society. He promoted his theology of economic justice as founder and editor of *Orate Fratres,* now *Worship,* throughout the 1930s. In his book *Christian Social Reconstruction,* Michel brought the economic thought of Pius XI to American Catholics. Throughout his brief lifetime his personal dedication to economic justice was evident in the support he gave to the Catholic Worker movement, migrant farm workers struggling for economic justice and industrial workers who were organizing labor unions across the United States.

Peter Maurin, co-founder of the Catholic Worker Movement, is one of the most fascinating individuals in the history of American Catholicism. Maurin's repudiation of industrial capitalism in the United States was absolute. He contended that the basic tenets of capitalism were so far removed from a Christian economics that only the collapse of capitalism and the rise of a new economic system could provide the foundation for economic justice in America. Although he repeatedly pointed to the presence of the poor as evidence of the moral failure of capitalism, he was equally concerned about the "bourgeois culture" created by capitalism and the enormous hold it had on all Americans, including Catholics. Bourgeois capitalism had an insidious power to subvert human compassion and community and promote a materialistic philosophy which contradicted the Christian Gospel. Throughout his life Peter advocated a new Christian personalism linking personal transformation with the eventual transformation of the American socio-economic order.

Paul Hanly Furfey promoted the cause of economic justice in the United States as a teacher, writer and social activist throughout a lifelong career at the Catholic University of America. The starting point of his work was the admonition that "Catholics had to acknowledge that capitalism was evil." Once the moral failure of capitalism was recognized, Catholics could align themselves with other men and women of good will in the work of building a new economic order. In the 1930s Furfey rejected the argument that the Depression, and the human havoc it caused, was an aberration in an otherwise morally acceptable economic system. The Depression was the logical consequence of an economic system which placed a premium on profits at the cost of personal well-being and social solidarity. Throughout his work he promoted the Mystical Body of Christ as the model of a new socio-economic order shaped by the social vision of the Gospel.

Dorothy Day's contribution to the social conscience of the American Catholic Church is unparalleled. After her conversion to Catholicism in the early 1930s, Dorothy embarked upon a fifty-year struggle to awaken American Catholics to the moral failings of industrial capitalism and the need to embrace the struggle for economic justice as an essential obligation of membership in the Church. In addition to her personal life of voluntary poverty for more than fifty years, Dorothy pledged her talents, time and energy to a variety of economic reform movements from those concerning industrial workers to farm workers in an effort to give expression to her commitment to economic justice. The simplicity of her message, especially the need to see Christ in the sufferings of one's neighbor, was often unsettling to more affluent Catholics, and yet it remained the essential insight of all of her labors.

Cesar Chavez continues today as the leader of the United Farm Workers Union, the first successfully organized labor union for farm workers in the United States. After more than four decades of struggle, his message remains what it was when he first began his efforts with a band of poor and powerless migrant workers in the fields of southern California. Cesar has repeatedly proclaimed that farm workers, as sons and daughters of God, deserve to be treated with justice. No economic system, whether on a farm or in a factory, which violates the tenets of economic justice is deserving of support. Through his program of nonviolent civil disobedience, Chavez helped to awaken a nation to the human exploitation and misery which characterizes the lives of migrant farm workers. Central to all his labors has been his conviction that the creation of a just economic order which respects the rights and dignity of all workers was indeed the work of the Lord entrusted to the hands of men and women of conscience.

Although as I indicated earlier that the critical social tradition in the American Catholic experience did not develop or find formal expression in a highly theoretical or systematic form, it does embody some central and unifying themes which are reflected in the thought and work of Brownson, McGlynn, Dietz, Michel, Day, Furfey, Maurin and Chavez. Some of these themes center on common economic assumptions while others focus on shared theological assumptions about the relationship between Christian faith, the economy and economic institutions. A brief summary of these themes can provide a helpful introduction to the chapters which follow.

The treatment of the poor is the measure of the moral quality of any economic system. The American Catholic social tradition has consistently understood that a variety of factors account for the presence of the poor in society. It has maintained that the treatment accorded the poor is an essential measuring rod of the quality of economic justice in society. When the economy works in a way which empowers the poor and includes them in the economic processes of society it is deserving of support. When, however, the economy marginalizes the poor and renders them powerless to effect the social conditions which envelop their lives, it violates the moral principles of human dignity, justice and social solidarity. Economic justice requires actions and policies which assure that the poor enjoy social development and access to the social goods which society has to offer.

In a democracy economic rights are akin to political rights. In *Economic Justice for All* the bishops look upon the American experience as a continuing process for extending to all citizens those fundamental rights which are essential to human dignity and social justice. This theme is reflected in the thought of Brownson, McGlynn, Dietz and others who recognized that Americans cannot really enjoy their political rights unless they enjoy economic rights. A denial of fundamental economic rights subverts the democratic processes of society and renders some citizens powerless to exercise real political participation in society.

Respecting human dignity and fostering social solidarity must characterize economic systems. The American Catholic social tradition rejects the premise that economic institutions are first created and then infused with moral values rooted in the Judaeo-Christian tradition. On the contrary, the tradition has consistently maintained that respecting human dignity in all its manifestations and fostering social solidarity must be the starting point from which economic institutions are created and policies developed. Maurin, Furfey and Michel point to the economic injustices which result when moral values take second place in the creation of economic institutions. The American economy must flow from a moral vision which gives primacy to human dignity and the fostering of cooperative relationships.

Capitalism harbors inherent moral contradictions which place it at odds with a Christian understanding of the economy. Although many Americans, including many Catholics, assume a naive compatibility between American capitalism and Catholic economic philosophy, this is not the position which is presented in the critical Catholic social tradition. Brownson, Michel, Day and others have raised serious and troubling questions about the inherent inability of capitalism, and the bourgeois mentality it generates, to nurture those moral values which are essential to a Gospel vision of the economy. They repeatedly point to evidence which suggests that the individualism, materialism and competitiveness which characterizes American capitalism pose an insurmountable obstacle to reconciling capitalism and the Gospel.

The creation of a new American economic order must be grounded in the Gospel. The voices of the social tradition within American Catholicism presumes the eventual collapse of industrial capitalism because of its inherent inability to advance economic justice. Maurin, McGlynn and Michel pointed to both the signs of this collapse as well as the growth of new trends in society, foreshadowing the emergence of a Christian cooperative economic order. Although they may have been unduly optimistic in their forecasts, they consistently maintained that a new economic order would have its foundations in the Gospel values of compassion, justice and community.

The Eucharist provides a model for a new economics in America. The proper role of the Eucharist in the transformation of American socio-economic institutions is a theme which runs through the social tradition of American Catholic thought. Virgil Michel pays special attention to the social consequences which flow from understanding the Eucharist as the model for the creation of an economic order intent on advancing the cause of economic justice. McGlynn tells us that the Lord's eucharistic must be the model for economic institutions, policies and decisions which seek to extend the bounty of God's good creation to all people.

The transformation of the American economy is an essential religious work. The critical tradition rejects a privatization of Christian faith which reduces the saving power of the Gospel to personal life. This tradition holds that the struggle for economic justice in America reflects the presence of Christ's continuing redemptive activity in history. To cooperate in building a just economic order represents participation in the ongoing work of Christian salvation.

Finally, Brownson, McGlynn, Dietz, Michel, Day, Furfey, Maurin and Chavez understood *Christ is present in the poor.* In their writings they offer reflections on the final judgment as presented in Matthew's Gospel. Their reflections are as simple and straightforward as Matthew's. When we feed, house, clothe and heal the poor, we feed, clothe, house and heal the Lord Jesus. And when we refuse to feed, clothe, house and heal the poor, we turn our backs on the Lord Jesus. When we participate in the struggle to transform the economic order so that it serves the needs of the poor and protects their rights and dignity, we are acting to free the Lord Jesus from the bondage and indignity of economic injustice.

In his very gracious Foreword to *Critical Voices,* Archbishop Weakland of Milwaukee has observed that the publication of *Economic Justice for All* has already fostered a renewed interest in the work of the authors represented in this volume. Hopefully what follows will make some small contribution to uncovering the critical tradition in American Catholic economic thought which deserves special attention today. I have written a simple book about a small group of courageous Catholics who demonstrated an abiding commitment to the intimate relationship between the Christian Gospel and the struggle for economic justice. With equal vigor they dedicated their lives to the Gospel of Jesus Christ and the American promise of economic justice for all. As prophetic voices and prayerful people, they continue to challenge us today.

ORESTES A. BROWNSON

Building a Christian Economy

Orestes A. Brownson was one of the most significant American converts to Catholicism in the nineteenth century. Unfortunately his thought has not always received the attention it deserves. Perhaps the volume of his work which included philosophy, theology, economics, politics, and education has frightened away many students. He was thoroughly involved in the life of the Church and the nation during most of the nineteenth century. Few issues escaped his attention. His conversion to Catholicism in 1844 represented the culmination of one religious quest and the beginning of another. Although he found a home in the Church, his conversion did not end his pilgrim journey. Until the end of his life in 1876 Orestes Brownson continued to grapple with many of the fundamental questions which are equally important today. How does the Christian attain salvation? How do men and women create community? How can social and economic reform be achieved? What is the relationship between Christian faith and the creation of a just social order? Do Christians have an obligation to alleviate the plight of the poor?

Brownson's lifelong dedication to economic reform in the United States is especially interesting. Because of the complexity of his thought some critics have relegated this interest to the earlier stages of his life. Others do not share this view. Brownson's concern for the victims of industrial capitalism in the nineteenth century did not diminish in his later years. His economic thought is especially interesting because it was never divorced from his religious and theological concerns. He continually worked to build community and thought in terms of relationships. Christian belief and the creation of a just economic order were intimately related. Belief in Christ obliged the believer to practice Christian charity and to participate in the creation of a social order foreshadowing the coming of the kingdom of God. Of special interest today is the relationship we find between Brownson's dedication to economic reform and his understanding of the meaning of the Incarnation. His thought here deserves particular attention and examination.

1

The importance Brownson gave to economic reform was central to his desire to better understand the nature of his Christian vocation. An appreciation of his economic thought cannot be pursued in isolation from his other interests. It requires attention to the earlier stages of his life when his religious quest was most turbulent; an analysis of his criticism of industrial capitalism; an examination of his assessment of the destructive consequences of an economic order steeped in individualism and materialism; and, finally, a review of his analysis of the relationship between economic reform and the role of the Church in society. Brownson was not a secular reformer motivated by a marginal Christian impulse. The need for economic reform in society was at the heart of Brownson's understanding of God's entry into human history in the person of Jesus Christ.

Orestes Brownson formally entered the Roman Catholic Church in October of 1844. It is more difficult to say when he became a Catholic in his heart. An examination of his writings between 1836 and 1844 indicates that he was moving toward the Church for several years. During this period Brownson at times sounded more Catholic than after his conversion. These years were a period of enormous intellectual and religious ferment for him. He struggled with a variety of fundamental questions both religious and social. At the heart of it all was the question of the relationship between a just social order and the mystery of God's redemptive presence in human history. During this time Brownson vacillated in his understanding of the best strategy for achieving a just social and economic order. At times he sounded like the American Marx; at other times he epitomized the privitization of religious belief.

In the years preceding his formal entry into the Church Brownson became cynical about the ability of the Protestant Churches to make a meaningful contribution to the creation of a just economic order. Protestantism provided religious legitimacy to the spirit of competitive individualism and secularism in American society. Economic life had become fragmented because the prevailing religious ideology promoted individualism at the expense of community. As he moved toward Catholicism, Brownson became convinced of the need for a new organic unity in society which could provide the basis for a cooperative ethic in economic affairs. His work after 1840 has led some of his critics to argue that his thought became increasingly conservative as he approached the Church. However, his constant call for a fundamental reordering of the social order based upon the principles of unity, community, solidarity and concern for the poor can hardly be interpreted as a blessing upon the industrial order in mid-nineteenth century America. Brownson believed that industrial capitalism was the work of the devil. Although he eventually modified his thinking about the appropriate strategy to follow in achieving a new social order, he never abandoned his convictions about the evils of capitalism and the need for fundamental economic reforms.

In the following I want to move through Brownson's thought between 1836 and 1844. My primary interest is in outlining the relationship Brownson saw between Christian faith and economic reform. I begin with a review of his essay "The Laboring Class" published in 1840. Here he presented his most scathing attack on industrial capitalism and its consequences for the poor and the laboring class in the nineteenth century. Then I will look at an essay he wrote in 1842 entitled "The Church of the Future," a summary of his book *New Views of Christianity, Society and the Church* which he published in 1836. In this essay he offered his views on the relationship between the mystery of the Incarnation and economic reform. In "The Present State of Society" published in 1843 Brownson reaffirmed his conviction about the need for the reconstruction of the social order. Economic reform was impossible without the establishment of a new organic unity in society providing the foundation for cooperative relationships in socio-economic life. Finally, in "No Church, No Reform," published shortly before his conversion, Brownson claimed that without the Church no meaningful economic reform in society was possible. Only the Church could adequately witness to the symbolic unity and harmony which should exist in human affairs. These essays do not exhaust Brownson's analysis of the relationship between socio-economic reform, Christian faith and the Church. However, they provide the basic direction and substance of his thought.

Early Years

Orestes A. Brownson was born on September 16, 1803 in Stockbridge, Vermont. His father, Sylvester, was raised in Connecticut, and his mother, Relief Metcalf, was a native of Keene, New Hampshire. There were six children in the family. Orestes and his twin sister Daphne were the youngest. Orestes' father died a few years after the birth of the twins. At the age of six he was sent to live with an older couple in the nearby town of Royalton, Vermont. The environment in the home was stern and characteristic of the Calvinist Puritan morality which provided the substance of Orestes' early religious training. Although he attended no formal religious services, young Brownson was encouraged to read the Bible daily and he soon developed a keen interest in religious questions. At the age of fourteen he returned to live with his mother in New York State. With very little formal education he accepted employment with a local printer. At this same time his relationship with a Presbyterian minister convinced him that a guide in religious matters would be helpful. He joined the Presbyterian Church in 1822 at the age of nineteen. His sojourn with Presbyterianism was brief. He found the Calvinist belief in predestination too harsh. The bleak outlook of Presbyterianism did not nourish the religious sentiments he had hoped to develop. In 1825 he was teaching in Detroit, Michigan when he moved to the other end of the religious spectrum by embracing Universalism. The Universalists not only denied eternal damnation but promised an eternal reward for all. In 1826 he was ordained a preacher in the Universalist denomination. He subsequently held preaching posts in New England and New York State and became the editor of the *Gospel Advocate,* a journal published by the Universalists. However, his religious quest did not end with the Universalists. Shortly after assuming a position with the Universalists he began to question the divine authority of the Bible. When he concluded that the authority of the Bible could not be proven, he entered into a period of religious skepticism lasting several years. This period of skepticism ended his association with the Universalists.

After abandoning Universalism Brownson satisfied his desire to contribute to the well-being of his fellowman by working with the Workingmen's Party for a period of time. Its members were dedicated to the reconstruction of the economic order and alleviating the deplorable conditions of the poor. Although his association with the Party was not lengthy, it reinforced his conviction about the importance of social reform and the obligation of individuals to contribute to the well-being of society. This sentiment would remain with him throughout his life. At this time Brownson was also attracted to the utopian ideas of Frances Wright and Robert Owen. He shared their vision of a better world. Despite the benefits of this inspiring association Brownson did not find fulfillment in their predominantly secular vision of a new social order. He could not escape his conviction that religious belief had to be the foundation of social reform. He later wrote about this sentiment: "I did not need religion to pull down or destroy society;

4

but the moment I wished to build up, to effect something positive, I found that I could not proceed a single step without it. . . . I need, then, religion of some sort as the agent to induce men to make the sacrifices required in the adoption of my plans."[1]

Acting on his renewed conviction about the need for a religious basis to social reform, Orestes became a member of the Unitarian Church in 1832. He favored the Unitarians because they tolerated considerable latitude of beliefs among their preachers. He felt free to espouse his own religious convictions and explored the relationship between Christian faith and economic reform with a new vigor. Brownson was also attracted to the writings of Saint-Simon and other Frenchmen who espoused a social Christianity which looked upon the Gospel of Jesus Christ as a vehicle for social and economic reform. Here he found the seeds for his own social Gospel beliefs. Orestes was still in search. Neither Catholicism nor Protestantism could provide the foundation for the reforms necessary in society. Catholicism had lost its ability to speak to men at the end of the Middle Ages. Protestantism was little more than the predominant individualistic spirit of the age wrapped in religious garb. In order to advance his own efforts at social and economic reform Brownson founded the Society for Christian Union and Progress in Boston and published his first book *New Views of Christianity, Society and the Church,* in 1836. This book outlined his thoughts about the relationship of Christian faith to economic reform. In many ways it provided the direction which eventually led to his conversion to Catholicism.

During this period Brownson did not restrict his activities to his involvement with the Unitarians nor to his work with the Society for Christian Union and Progress. The time was ripe with a variety of social reform activities. He continued to associate with the Workingmen's Party and he became more involved in political activities. The year 1837 gave birth to a massive depression in America. Thousands of workers were thrown out into the streets without any means of sustaining themselves. Economic conditions which were deplorable before the depression grew worse. Brownson saw the existing economic order as the root cause of the problem. Industrial capitalism had lost all respect for the human person. The year 1837 revealed the destructive social consequences of a ruthless economic liberalism gone mad. Brownson looked to political reforms as a way of salvaging some good from a tragic situation. In hopes that political reforms could alleviate the terrible economic conditions he endorsed the Democratic Party in the 1840 elections. In an effort to bolster the chances of the Democrats he published "The Laboring Class." His criticism of the existing economic order was so harsh that the Democrats disowned him and the Whigs used his essay as a propaganda piece to support their claim that the Democratic Party would bring socialism to America's shores. When the Democratic Party was defeated in the 1840 elections Brownson grew increasingly disillusioned about the ability of the citizenry to control their own destiny. This intensified his conviction that without a vibrant religious foundation economic reforms simply could not be achieved.

Paralleling his involvement with the Workingmen's Party, and his support for political reform at this period, Brownson maintained a close relationship with a group of writers and thinkers who shared his dedication to social reform. During the 1830's and 1840's Transcendentalism attracted the attention of a number of Americans including Ralph Waldo Emerson, George Ripley, William Channing, Theodore Parker and Henry Thoreau. The Transcendentalists rejected the existing socio-economic order. They abhorred its materialism and individualism. However they also rejected the more popular social reform theories of the day, and promoted a back to nature solution to society's problems. The supporters of Transcendentalism were instrumental in establishing several communes which were religious and socialist in nature. The most famous was Brook Farm founded by George Ripley in West Roxbury, Mass. Ripley described the purpose of Brook Farm: " . . . to insure a more natural union between intellectual and manual labor than now exists; to combine the thinker and the worker, as far as possible, in the same individual; to guarantee the highest mental freedom, by providing all with labor adapting to their talents and tastes, and securing to them the fruits of their industry; to do away with the necessity of menial services by opening the benefits of education and the profits of labor to all; and thus to prepare a society of liberal, intelligent, and cultivated persons, whose relations with each other would permit a wholesome and simple life that can be led amidst the pressure of our competitive institutions."[2] Brownson was attracted to Transcendentalism and to Brook Farm because he shared the members' convictions about the need for social and economic reform. However, his need to find an organic religious foundation for economic reform did not allow him to fully embrace the philosophy of the Transcendentalists. He could not call Brook Farm home. His writings between 1836 and 1844 offer a picture of his search for a permanent home which he would eventually find in the Catholic Church.

The Laboring Class

"The Laboring Class" was published in 1840. Some consider it the most insightful critique of industrial capitalism published in the United States in the nineteenth century. In the essay Brownson reviewed Thomas Carlyle's book *Chartism*. The English Chartists were social reformers dedicated to a radical reconstruction of the economic order. Unfortunately, as Carlyle pointed out, the protests of the Chartists were dismissed by the middle-class elite in England who were determined to protect their economic privileges. Brownson applauded the moral outrage of the English author but faulted his work for failing to provide an adequate program enabling working people to advance their economic rights. "He is good as a demolisher, but pitiable as a builder,"[3] said Brownson. He used "The Laboring Class" to launch his own analysis of industrial capitalism and to outline a program for reconstructing the economic order. Brownson pointed out that the social conditions described by Carlyle in England were not unique to England. They were commonplace in other parts of the world where industrial capitalism held sway. In capitalist countries the rich got richer and the poor got poorer. "All over the world this fact stares us in the face, the workingman is poor and depressed, while a larger portion of the non-workingmen, in the sense that we now use the term, are wealthy. It may be laid down as a general rule, with but few exceptions, that men are rewarded in an inverse ratio to the amount of the actual service they perform. Under every government on earth the largest salaries are annexed to those offices, which demand of their incumbents the least amount of actual labor either mental or manual. And this is in perfect harmony with the whole system of repartition of the fruits of industry, which obtains in every part of society. Now here is the system which prevails, and here is the result. The whole class of simple laborers are poor, and in general unable to procure anything beyond the bare necessities of life."[4] For Brownson the system of economic rewards inherent in capitalism was unjust. The worker was systematically robbed of the fruits of his labor.

In "The Laboring Class" Brownson analyzed the difference between slave labor in colonial empires and the so-called "free" labor which was characteristic of industrialized nations. With unabashed frankness Brownson stated that if he had to choose between the two types of labor, he would choose slave labor. "Of the two, the first (slave labor) is in our judgement, except so far as feelings are concerned, decidedly the least oppressive. If the slave has never been a free man, we think, as a general rule, his sufferings are less than those of the free laborer at wages. As to the actual freedom one has just about as much as the other. The laborer at wages has all the disadvantages of freedom and none of its blessings, while the slave, if denied the blessings, is freed from the disadvantages. We are no advocate of slavery, we are as heartily opposed to it as any modern abolitionist can be; but we say frankly that, if there must always be a laboring class distinct from proprietors and employees, we regard the slave system as decidedly preferable to the system at wages."[5] His concern for the plight of the laborer was not limited to the economic deprivation inherent in the wage system. He recognized that capitalism generated a class system in society which frustrated the creation of community and solidarity among people.

Throughout "The Laboring Class" Brownson offered graphic examples of the socio-economic conditions in American society. "The sufferings of a quiet, unassuming but useful class of females in our cities, in general sempstresses, too proud to beg or apply to the almshouse, are not easily told. They are industrious; they do all they can find to do; but yet the little that there is for them to do, and the miserable pittance they receive for it, is hardly sufficient to keep their soul and body together."[6] Brownson anticipated a twentieth century analysis of the consequences of economic exploitation when he said: "The great mass wear out their health, spirits, and morals, without becoming one whit better off then when they commenced labor."[7] And he was quick to point out the hypocrisy of the age. "The owner who is involved in the systematic exploitation of those poor laborers is frequently one of our respectable citizens; perhaps he is praised in the newspapers for his liberal donations to some charitable institution. He passes among us as a pattern of morality, and is honored as a worthy Christian."[8]

The wage system was a particular target of Brownson's attack. "Wages is a cunning device of the devil, for the benefit of tender consciences who would retain all the advantages of the slave system, without the experience, trouble, and odium of being slave-holders."[9] He rejected the ideology of industrial capitalism which claimed that despite the inadequacies of the system it offered the possibility of advancement for all, especially the poor. In truth, he asserted, capitalism had the opposite effect. "The actual condition of the workingman today, viewed in all its bearings, is not so good as it was fifty years ago."[10] The great work of our age was not only to raise up the poor but to realize in economic conditions the equality between people intended by God. An unjust economic order not only violated the rights of those who were exploited, but it generated a fragmented and broken social order which frustrated God's intention for his people.

In approaching the question of how to redress the existing economic conditions he mockingly rejected the "capital theory" which claimed that the creation of the good society did not require a radical transformation of the existing social order but rather an interior transformation within individuals. "They would have all men wise, good, and happy; but in order to make them so, they tell that we want not external changes, but internal; and therefore instead of declaiming society and seeking to disturb existing social arrangements we should confine ourselves to the individual reason and conscience; seek merely to lead the individual to repentance, and to reformation of life; make the individual a practical, truly religious man, and all evils will either disappear, or be sanctified to the spiritual growth of the soul."[11] Brownson considered the "capital theory" a hoax of the worst sort. While recognizing the need for interior transformation he rejected the idea that interior transformation alone could right the wrongs of an economic system which frustrated God's intention for creation. The "capital theory" extolled by the captains of industry was a sham. "This theory, however, is exposed to one slight objection, that of being condemned by something like six thousand years of experience. For six thousand years its beauty has been extolled, its praises sung, and its blessings sought, under every advantage which learning, fashion, wealth and power can secure; and yet under its practical operations we are assured that mankind, though totally deprived at first, has been growing worse and worse ever since."[12]

"The Laboring Class" called for the radical transformation of existing economic conditions as the only adequate way of protecting the rights of the poor. Converting all the members of society to Christianity would not be enough to assure economic justice. "Could we convert all men to Christianity in both theory and practice, as held by the most enlightened sect of Christians among us, the evil of the social state would remain untouched. Continue our present system of trade, and all its present evil consequences will follow, whether it be

9

carried on by your best men or your worst. Put your best men, your wisest, most moral, and most religious men at the head of the paper-money banks and the evils of the present banking system will remain scarcely diminished."[13] The American people must either accept the consequences of the present system—the exploitation of the poor and laborers—or abolish the system. "No man can serve both God and Mammon. If you will serve the devil you must look to the devil for your wages; we know no other way."[14] Brownson saw a fundamental contradiction in the Christian conscience of the American people. On the one hand, people want to embrace the Christian faith with public fervor, yet they want to enjoy the well-being without considering the consequences of their actions. Devilish as well, according to Brownson, was the assertion that God Almighty has decreed that some people in every society shall be poor, wretched and ignorant while others shall be rich and prosperous. This ideology represented a distortion of God's intent for his family. "God has made of one blood all the nations of men to dwell on all the face of the earth, and to dwell there as brothers, as members of one and the same family."[15] According to Brownson, God's design for society required a cooperative commonwealth.

A distortion of God's plan for society was not solely due to secular forces. The fault also lay at the door of the Christian churches, and especially with clergymen who failed to adequately proclaim the social message of the Gospel. Listen to Brownson's words. "Christianity is the sublimest protest against the priesthood ever uttered, and a protest uttered by both God and man; for he who uttered it was God-Man. What was the message of Jesus but a solemn summons of every priest-hood on earth to judgment, and the human race to freedom? He discomforted the learned doctors, and with whips of small cords drove the priests, degenerated into mere money changers, from the temple of God."[16] He concluded "The Laboring Class" with a vision of a new economic order. His program is twofold in nature. First, it contained a plan for the religious transformation of the present social order through the emergence of the Christianity of Christ. Second, it called upon the government to abandon its prejudicial policies in favor of the wealthy and to come to the assistance of the poor who deserved the support of a benevolent public authority.

At this time Brownson believed that historical Christianity had completed its mission. It had advanced social progress as far as possible within its limited means. Neither Catholicism nor Protestantism any longer had the means to participate in the radical transformation of society. "The Christianity of the Church has done its work."[17] In the years that followed Brownson moved beyond this argument and returned to a defense of historical Christianity, and the Catholic Church in particular, as the only viable vehicle for fostering a reconstruction of the social order. Even during this period Brownson's skepticism about the efficacy of the Church did not lead him to conclude that economic reform could be achieved independently of a religious foundation and inspiration. He argued that the Christianity of the Church and the ineffective message it preached had to be replaced by the Christianity of Christ. The Christianity of Christ as envisioned by Brownson would participate in the reconstruction of the social order. "The Christianity of Christ will re-establish the relationship between belief in the Gospel of Jesus Christ and the reform of society. According to the Christianity of Christ no man can enter the kingdom of God, who does not labor with all zeal and diligence to establish the kingdom of God on earth; who does not labor to bring down the high, and bring up the low; to break the fetters of the bound and set the captive free; to destroy all oppression, establish the reign of justice, which is the reign of equality, between man and man; to introduce a new heaven and a new earth, wherein dwelleth righteousness, wherein all shall be as brothers, loving one another, and no one possessing what another lacketh. No man can be a Christian who does not labor to reform society, to mould it according to the will of God and the nature of man; so that free scope shall be given to every man to unfold himself in all beauty and power, and to grow up into the stature of a perfect man in Christ Jesus. No man can be a Christian who does not refrain from all practices by which the rich get richer and the poor get poorer, and who does not do all in his power to elevate the laboring class, so that one man shall not be doomed to toil while another enjoys the fruits; so that each man shall be free and independent, sitting under 'his own vine and fig tree with none to molest or to make afraid.' "[18] Brownson faulted the Christianity of the Church because it had lost the vitality to awaken believers to the inspiring challenge of the Gospel of Jesus Christ. Under the influence of the Christianity of the Church the Gospel has been reduced to a private affair which mirrors the privitization of economic affairs in American society. "Under the influence of the Church, our efforts are not directed to the reorganization of society, to the introduction of equality between man and man, to the removal of the corruptions of the rich, and the wretchedness of the poor. We think only of saving our own souls, as if a man must not put himself so out of the case, as to be willing to be damned before he can be saved."[19] The Christianity of Christ, on the other hand, looks to the salvation of one's soul and the redemption of the social order and the building of the kingdom of God on earth.

Brownson concluded "The Laboring Class" with an admonition to government to participate in the reform of society. He proposed a number of actions. First, government had to remove the obstacles it had placed in the way of working people and the poor so that their economic rights could be protected. Second, government had to curtail the preferential treatment it gave to the rich and the powerful. Third, government had to come to the aid of workingmen and the poor who suffered the scourge of economic exploitation. In a just economic order the laborers would be able to care for themselves. Until that time the government should provide the necessary assistance. In addition to these practical suggestions for government reform, Brownson also suggested that serious consideration be given to abolishing the hereditary descent of property. " . . . we allude to the hereditary descent of property, an anomaly in our American system, which must be removed or the system itself will be destroyed. . . . We only now say that we have abolished hereditary monarchy and hereditary nobility, we must complete the work by abolishing hereditary property."[20]

The Church of the Future

In 1842 Orestes Brownson published "The Church of the Future." It was a summary of the principal themes he outlined in his first book, *New Views of Christianity, Society and the Church* (1836). He was disappointed that he had not received a better reaction to *New Views* and hoped that this essay would provoke a wider response. Of special interest in this essay is Brownson's analysis of how Christ's Incarnation had been misunderstood in the history of Christianity and the consequences of this misunderstanding for the ministry of social and economic reform. Equally fascinating is Brownson's description of the Church of the future and the pivotal role it could play in the transformation of social and economic life in American society.

Brownson began the essay with a reaffirmation of the importance of religious belief and the Church. "Man lives only by virtue of some theory of the universe, which solves for him the problem of his existence and destiny, and prescribes a life-plan which he must endeavor to realize. This theory, whatever it be, or however obtained, is what man names religion. It is always the highest conception of God and of the law of his own being. Religion is then the ideal and man's effort to realize it."[21] The Church is equally important to man's quest to realize the ideal. "The Church is the organization of mankind for the peaceable, orderly, and successful realization of the Christian ideal or the ideal as held by the early followers of Jesus."[22] Although recognizing that the Church has historically aspired to realize Jesus' ideal, Brownson pointed out that the Church has never fully realized the ideal. Earlier in her history the Church approximated the ideal. No longer was this the case. "For a thousand years and more, it was the Church of the ideal. . . . But it now looks no more to the future. It has realized its ideal. It proposes no new labors for civilization, makes no new demands on the race in behalf of progress."[23] If the historical church is no longer the Church of Jesus' ideal, a new church was needed to reaffirm the Gospel ideal. "It therefore loses sight of the end for which it was instituted, and must now turn its face once more to the future, embrace the ideal, or give way to a new church, which shall be an organization of mankind, not to retain the past, but to conquer the future."[24] The failure of the historical church to represent the ideal of Jesus and promote the continuing transformation of society was due to its failure to fully appreciate the meaning of the Incarnation. "The doctrine of the Incarnation of the Word teaches us that for us there is no God, but God 'manifest in the flesh.' There is no God to love and reverence, but the God that lives and moves in, creates and sustains, what we actually see and know of the universe. God is to us distinguishable but not separable from man and nature. . . . God, if we may so speak, is concreted in his works, a living God, instead of that cold, naked abstraction, which metaphysicians call God, satisfying the demands of a frigid logic it may be, but dead to the heart."[25] The Incarnation is the marvel of Christianity. Christ's redemptive entry into human history proclaims the dignity of the human person. God is known, loved and reverenced only in his visible manifestation. Man is this visible manifestation. To know, love and reverence man, then, is to know, love and reverence God, under the only possible form, and in the only possible manner. The effects of the Incarnation as far as it has been understood are visible and evident in civilization. " . . . in the high rank it assigns to the virtues of meekness, gentleness, mercy, charity, modesty, chastity and love; in the high value it places on man as an individual; in its emancipation of the slaves, and general labors to promote liberty and social well-being."[26] The beneficial consequences of the Church's understanding of the Incarnation can be seen; the contemporary problem is that the Church's understanding has not gone far enough. The Church was right in what she asserted, wrong in what she denied.

Because the meaning of the Incarnation has been compromised historically its impact on society has been privitized. The historical Church has properly understood the reverence which is deserving of the individual human person; however it has not properly appreciated the social meaning of God's entry into human history. This will be the work and responsibility of the "new church." "The ideal of the new church will be the redemption and sanctification of the race as the ideal of the old church was the redemption and sanctification of the individual; or the new will add to the old the redemption and sanctification of the race."[27] A misunderstanding of the meaning of the Incarnation has resulted in a tendency in the Church to emphasize the importance of the things of the "spirit" to the detriment of things "material." As a result the historical church has abandoned jurisdiction for matters political, social and economic to the control of others. For a long time this division of responsibility was not detrimental to society because the public domain remained indirectly accountable to the Church. This was no longer the case. The public domain now acts independently of the Church. It is no longer interested in incarnating the ideal of the Gospel of Jesus Christ into the life of society. "Down to the fifteenth century the church was the true church, as true to the ideal as possible in the circumstances in which it was placed. Down to that period she was the church of progress, and continued herself to advance. But in consequence of the hard line she had drawn between spiritual interests and material interests, she placed necessarily a term to her progress. . . . As soon as the state embodied as much wisdom, intelligence, justice and humanity as she herself embodied in her own organization and canons, her mission in regard to civilization ended. . . . She became, then, a mere parallel organization with the state, having no longer in relation to society an ideal to realize. She had nothing to propose. She could no longer take the lead in civilization. From being the superior of the state, she was forced to become, as she has been for three hundred years, its vassal."[28] Here Brownson becomes caught in a dilemma of his own making. On the one hand, he finds within the state some of the ingredients necessary to support and nurture the continuing progress of society. On the other hand, he is skeptical about the ability of the state to promote the ideal of the Gospel in any sustained fashion. He refused to abandon all hope that the historical church could recapture its dedication to the ideal and carry civilization to the next stages. The seeds for a new transformation were present. " . . . the church must show that she has an ideal, some work for civilization to propose, big enough for men's hearts, equal to their aspirations. Men are now uneasy and confined within her enclosures. They see immense evils in the world which they would gladly redress. Rich feelings kindle up within them; great thoughts swell in their hearts; a mighty energy is working in their souls; and they would go forth and act, lay hold of the ages, and shape them to the glory of God and the redemption of man. But they are blind, confused and in a narrow dungeon. They cry, they foam, they pull at their chains, beat their heads against the dungeon walls, fall back wearied, exhausted and die. There is a universal restlessness; men's great souls are seeking some mode of utterance, but find none. They yearn to act, but yet are held back. Nothing is proposed equal to what they feel moving and working in themselves. There is no vent for the activity which has long been accumulating in the soul."[29] If the Church is to recapture the imagination of the people, it must again reassert her claim to proclaim the ideal and seek to embody it. If the Church is to assume this responsibility, she must overcome the false dichotomy which has been erected between the things of the spirit and the things of matter. "Spiritual interests and material interests will be held to be not only inseparable but indistinguishable. There is no act that really promotes the welfare of the soul that is not also for the welfare of the body; there is no act demanded for the well-being of the body not also demanded by the well-being of the soul. What is for man's good in time is for his good in eternity; and the only sure way of gaining a heaven hereafter is to create a heaven on earth."[30] The Church of the future will be based upon two great principles— first, appreciation of the social meaning of the Incarnation of Jesus Christ; second, a new unity between the things of the spirit and the things of matter. When this is achieved the Church will once again become a powerful force for the ongoing transformation of society.

Writing in 1836 and again in 1842 Brownson is uncertain how the Church of the future will emerge and who will hold responsibility for it. At times he appeared to suggest a merger between Church and state which could create a new organic unity to advance the ideal of the Gospel; at other times, he foresaw the emergence of a new church. What was clear to Brownson was that this new church could play a primary role in eradicating the economic injustices which plagued society. And it could foster a new sense of the Christian obligation to care for the poor and the powerless. "Her mission will not be merely that of fitting men to die and to gain a happier world, but fitting them to live and to make the earth itself an abode of plenty of peace and love. She will not enjoin poverty, but justice, so as to direct the industrial activity of the race, and establish such laws for the distribution of the fruits of industry, that all will have a competence, and none any temptation to abuse his powers or to rob another."[31] Again he writes: "The church of the future will place the worship of God solely in the redemption and sanctification of the race, especially the poorest and most numerous class, in loving all men as we now love Jesus, and doing all that is possible to do to raise up every man to his proper estate; in a word, to realize equality between man and man in his material relations that we now recognize in his material relations. But she will not be merely utilitarian. She will not be cold and naked and barren. In accepting material interests she will not become less, but even more spiritual."[32]

The Present State of Society

In "The Present State of Society" written in 1843 Brownson commented on a book written by the English author Thomas Carlyle, *Past and Present*. Here he gave additional evidence that he was moving closer to the Catholic Church as the only viable vehicle capable of promoting the reconstruction of the social order. In developing his thesis Brownson took pains to point out the tremendous contribution which the Church in the Middle Ages had made to society. He challenged the assertion that the post-Reformation years of Christianity have contributed to the betterment of society. On the contrary, he contended that the spirit of Protestantism—individualistic, materialistic and secular—had exacerbated the social problem in the nineteenth century. The fragmentation of the social order resulting from the Protestant ethos had fueled the competitive spirit of the Industrial Age and the dehumanization of the person. The condition of workers described by Carlyle in his book was common throughout the Christian world. "The tendency is throughout all Christendom to bring us to the point where no small portion of the population can obtain the lowest wages for work done, but where they can obtain no work to do."[33] Revolution was in the air. Brownson did not espouse the use of violence to bring about the necessary social and economic reforms. However, he recognized that pressures were building in this direction throughout the industrial world. Listen to this description of Christian Boston. "In this industrious, charitable, wealthy, Christian city of Boston, where we now write, we have come the last winter to our bread and soup societies! Bread and soup societies for the poor already in the blessed land of America, free democratic America, and in the very heart of thrifty, religious New England. So alas! We have managed it."[34] Brownson's portrait of the children was especially moving. "With our own eyes we have seen poor children gliding along the cold streets, thinly clad, with their tin cans to receive their modicum. We have set our own feet in the miserable alleyways of those who have been thus fed, and knelt down in prayers by the poor many dying of a fever brought on by anxiety and insufficient food."[35] With these tragic social conditions in mind Brownson cannot help but ask: "Now, in all soberness, we ask, if a state of things in which such incidents can occur, however rare, is the best that we can have in the nineteenth century, in this blessed land of America, of universal suffrage, universal education, under the blessed light of the Gospel, dotted all over with industrial establishments, school-houses and churches? Is this a God's world, or is it a devil's world."[36] Brownson is not fooled about why these conditions prevailed in a land of plenty. "There must be somewhere," he says, "a fatal vice in our social and industrial arrangements, or there would not, could not, be these evils to complain of. Never, till within the last few centuries, were men, able to work, brought to the starving point in the time of peace, and in the midst of plenty."[37]

For Brownson the source of the present social discontent could not be ascribed exclusively to the emergence of industrial capitalism. An even more fundamental explanation had to be sought. "For the last three hundred years we have lost or have been losing our faith in God, in heaven, in life, in justice, in eternity, and have been acquiring faith only in human philosophy, in mere theories concerning supply and demand, wealth of nations, self-supporting, labor saving governments; needing no virtue, wisdom, love, sacrifice, or heroism on the part of the managers; working out for us a new Eden, converting all the earth into an El Dorado land, and enabling all of us to live in the Eden Regained. We have left behind us the living faith of the earlier ages; we have abandoned all our old notions of heaven and hell; and we have come, as Carlyle well has it, to place our heaven in success in money matters, and to find the infinite terror men call hell, only in not succeeding in making money. We have thus come where we are. Here is a fact worth meditating."[38] He does not deny that the Industrial Age has led to some progress in society; however, this progress has come at an enormous price.

Brownson took no relish in celebrating the end of the Middle Ages. Differing with much of the dominant public opinion, he stated that the Middle Ages represented a period of enormous development for civilization, and it was clearly morally superior to the present age which fostered a disrespect for the individual and a lack of concern for the common good. " . . . the chief thing that we admire in the Middle Ages, is that men did believe in God, they did believe in some kind of justice, and admit that man, in order to reap, must in some way aid the sowing; that man did, whatever his condition, owe some kind of duty to his fellow man; and admit it, not merely in theory, in speeches or in loud windy professions, but seriously in his heart and his practice."[39] During the Middle Ages less class antagonism existed, and even the slaveholder had to admit of some relationship with his slave which is more than can be said about the relationship between the present day laborer and his employer.

In "The Present State of Society" Brownson identified four specific developments which contributed to the moral decline of society in the nineteenth century. These developments were: the new art of war resulting from the discovery of gun powder; the revival of secular literature; the invention of the printing press; and, finally, the discoveries in the East and the West. In sweeping fashion Brownson argued that these developments severed the social order from its moral and ethical moorings. More fundamentally, these developments severed the social order from faith in God. The evidence was obvious enough. "We have here glanced at some of the causes which have operated to destroy the religious faith of the Middle Ages, to abolish the worship of God in Christian lands, and to introduce the worship of Mammon— all triumphant Mammon. Going along through the streets of Boston the other day we remarked that it has become the fashion to convert the basement floors of some churches into retail shops for various kinds of merchandise. How significant! The church is made to rest on TRADE; Christ on Mammon. Was anything ever more typical. The rent of these shops in some cases, we are told, pays the whole expense of the minister's salary. Poor minister!"[40]

Near the conclusion of his essay Brownson asked how to remedy the existing fragmentation and oppressiveness of the existing social order. "Our industrial arrangements, the relations of master-workers and workers, of capital and labor, which has grown up during these last three years, are essentially vicious, and, as we have seen, are beginning throughout Christendom to prove themselves so!"[41] He dismissed the romanticism of those who advocated a simple return to the Middle Ages. It was not possible, he said, to reconstruct the Middle Ages. "We grieve not that we can have these ages no more; that feudalism is gone, and the church of Gregory VII, that napoleon of the ecclesiastical order, is gone, never to return; but we do grieve that in getting rid of them, we have supplied their place by nothing better; by nothing good. In contrasting them with the present, we have asked to show our countrymen that they should not be contented with the present, nor despair of something better; for better once was and may be again; though not in the old form."[42] Brownson was not as much interested in a return to a medieval age as he was in the revitalization of the spirit and values of that time. He hoped for a church with the boldness to proclaim the ideal of the Gospel and become a visible embodiment of that ideal in an imperfect world. He called for a benevolent social order concerned about the needs of all the people and acting with a special generosity toward the poor and the powerless. Finally, Brownson anticipated a reconstructed social order where the division between morality and politics and religion and economics was overcome in favor of a society where cooperation between brothers and sisters in pursuit of a common destiny was reflected in the halls of government and in the work places of America.

Orestes Brownson was unwilling to offer a detailed plan of how the Church of Christ could be restored. But he left his reader with no doubt that this was the pre-eminent challenge confronting society. He increasingly leaned in the direction of asserting that the Catholic Church must assume the responsibility for the social and economic transformation of society which was sorely needed. The Catholic Church must again become the symbolic manifestation of those fundamental moral values and ethical ideals which should be reflected in social life. Within a short time of this assessment Brownson entered the Catholic Church. Here he hoped to find a home which would better enable him to realize his dreams for the creation of a just society.

No Church, No Reform

In April of 1844, a few months before his entry into the Catholic Church, Brownson published "No Church, No Reform." Here he examined the relationship between the Catholic Church and the reconstruction of the social order. During the previous decade he had become increasingly convinced that social reconstruction had to be based on a religious foundation and inspiration. By 1844 he was convinced that only the Catholic Church could provide this necessary foundation. He began the essay with a summary of his commitment to social and economic reform. "It is now over twenty years since my mind was first called to questions of social reform, and I was led to reflect on the discrepancies which everywhere exist between society as it is, and society as all, in their serious moments, feel that it should be."[43] Earlier in his writings Brownson tended to ascribe the social evils in society solely to the existing social arrangements. Economic conditions created an antagonism of interests between various classes. "It is for the interest of the trader to cheat—to buy under value and to sell over value; it is for the interest of the master to oppress the workman, by paying the least possible wages for the least possible amount of labor. This is the interest of one opposed to the interest of the other; and every man in pursuing his own interest must needs, as far as possible, overreach and supplant every other man."[44] Because the nature of the existing social unrest could be explained by a universal antagonism of interests, the remedy must be found in a remodeling of society which would harmonize the interests of each with the interests of all. Brownson admitted that at one time he thought this could be achieved through a secular corporate order which would nurture a cooperative ethos among people in economic life. In 1844 he confessed that he was no longer confident that a secular corporate order could be the basis for reconstructing the economic order. This labor called for a kind of selflessness and sacrifice which a secular ethos could not provide. If a cooperative economic commonwealth was to be created, it had to be built upon a foundation more powerful than a secular reform movement could provide.

In "No Church, No Reform" he admitted that when he first came to the work of social and economic reform he didn't believe that either Protestantism or Catholicism could provide the foundation for economic and social reform. Protestantism could not offer this foundation because its religious ideology had contributed to the fragmentation of society by promoting the spirit of individualism and materialism. Catholicism could not provide the foundation because it had surrendered the public domain of economics and politics to secular forces. In "No Church, No Reform" Brownson gave evidence of a fundamental shift in his analysis of the role of the Catholic Church in the social reconstruction of society. This happened for two reasons. First, he had grown skeptical about the ability of individuals to sustain themselves in the values embodied in the Gospel unless they were part of a community of faith embodying those values. "No scheme of reform, then, is, or can be, practicable, that does not bring along with it the 'wisdom of God and the power of God'; for its own realization it must be an institution embodying the Holy Ghost, and able to communicate the Holy Ghost. We say an institution. If it be a doctrine, it will be inadequate; if it is the truth uninstituted, it is beyond our reach."[45] Second, if the object of social reform was to bring the social order into harmony with God's plan, then any effort which hoped to be successful had to be a part of God's historical intervention into human history; it had to find its life in the life of the Church. "Our blessed Savior did not come merely to teach the truth, for he was it; he did not come to establish a true philosophy, for he was that of which all sound philosophy is the doctrine. The purpose of his mission into the world was to found the Kingdom of God on earth, which should be the Kingdom of kingdoms, and in which he should live and reign as King of kings and Lord of lords."[46] Christ established the Church as a model for the kingdom to be established on earth. Christ is present in the Church, and life and membership in the Church feeds the body and the soul enabling the follower of Christ to participate in building God's kingdom on earth. Without a social vision drawn from life within the Church the believer is without a model of the kingdom which he is obliged to carry into the social order.

Here Brownson overcame his earlier secular vision and argued that without the Church the social reconstruction of society was a labor in vain. And he chided himself and others who proposed that economic reform could be achieved independently of the Church, God's visible manifestation in human history. "Here is the fundamental vice of all modern advocates of reform. All our reformers proceed on the false assumption that man is sufficient for his own redemption, and, therefore, are trying always with man alone to recover the long lost Eden, or to carry us forward to a better Eden. Here is the terrible sin of modern time. We vote God out of the state; we vote him out of our communities; and we concede him only a figurative, a symbolic relation with the churches, denying almost universally the Real Presence, and seeing it as a popish error; we plant ourselves on the all sufficiency of man, and then wonder that we fall, and that, after three hundred years of effort at reform, nothing is gained, and a true state of society seems to be as far off as ever."[47] Efforts at social and economic reform which rejected the need for the Church, Brownson said, were doomed to failure. "Man is, in no sense, sufficient for himself."[48] Particularly unacceptable to Brownson at this point was the idea that men dedicated to the work of social reform could simply create a new church. "Where is the power to form the new church? Can man constitute a church which shall embody Christ? Is Christ unembodied? If so, is there any human power that can give him a body? No! Then, either Christ is embodied, and there is already existing a true Church, through which he carries on his work of redemption, individual and social, or there is no redeemer, and no redemption for us."[49]

Here Brownson reached a point in his thinking where the Catholic Church became essential for the reconstruction of the social order. "Then, if the Church be essential for individual salvation, so it is essential to social salvation. But does the Church of God still exist? Doubt it not. Is it still living, and in a condition to do its work? Yes, if you will return to it, and submit to it. You may have abandoned the Church, but it still exists, and is competent to do its work, and all that reformers have to do is, cease to be "Come-outers", and to return to its bosom and receive its orders."[50] Orestes Brownson was at home at last. The work of social and economic reform will continue; it will be rooted in the life of Christ's presence in the Church. The Church will create a new consciousness of God's intentions for society, and through celebration and worship God's intentions for all his people will be carried into the public domain once again.

The Social Vision of Orestes A. Brownson

Writing in the middle of the nineteenth century Orestes Brownson brought enormous insight to his analysis of the social ills of the day and his vision for the reconstruction of the social order. Few students of American society can fail to be impressed with his ability to anticipate the eventual consequences of an economic order motivated primarily by the desire to accumulate wealth and power. There was a sadness to Brownson's analysis of social life in America. It was the picture of isolated individuals in search of wealth who had no compassion for one another and a picture of countless men, women and children who were denied the basic necessities they needed in order to flourish as human beings. His scathing attack on industrial capitalism in "The Laboring Class" has deservedly led some to regard him as the American Marx. Some have even suggested that Brownson's analysis was more profound because he recognized the need for the creation of a new organic unity—a new experience of solidarity—within the life of contemporary society. If he deserves the title of the American Marx, he likewise has earned the right to be seen as America's Charles Dickens. His descriptions of the plight of those victimized by the ruthlessness of industrialization in the nineteenth century are classics. They not only depict the physical consequences of an economy insensitive to human needs, but show how poverty and economic oppression menace and destroy the human soul and spirit. He invited his readers to share the agony of those who have been cast aside and ignored by those who worship Mammon. It is interesting that Orestes A. Brownson eventually found a home in the Church. However careful reflection reveals the reasonableness of this choice. Brownson was not a nostalgic dreamer. He appreciated the experience of social solidarity which was characteristic of the Middle Ages. At the same time he was a modern man anxious to move ahead and embrace the good that could be found in the nineteenth century. The contributions of Orestes Brownson to the social vision of the Church are not easily summarized. Perhaps this is why they have not been fully appreciated by his fellow Catholics today. However, even a brief summary can give some sense of the energetic mind and the passionate convictions of this Catholic pilgrim of the nineteenth century.

Orestes Brownson had the ability to foresee the inherent contradictions in industrial capitalism in America in the mid-nineteenth century. Even a cursory reading of the recent pastoral letter of the Catholic bishops of the United States, *Economic Justice for All,* reveals that the concerns which were paramount in Brownson's mind a century ago remain significant concerns for those who look closely at the workings of the economy in America today. Central to his analysis was his description of the social fragmentation which resulted when individuals pursued their economic self-interest regardless of the consequences for other members of society. The collapse of community which Brownson saw as synonymous with the growth of industrial capitalism sent millions of men, women and children adrift. The restoration of a shared sense of responsibility for one another in economic affairs was a persistent theme in his work and thought. The rugged individualism and competitiveness which he harshly criticized were characteristic of the spirit of the age and they contributed immensely to the breakdown of solidarity among people. Brownson's vision was broader than that of many of his contemporaries who quickly took note of the "progress" of the age but who were neither able nor willing to recognize the debilitating social consequences of capitalism.

He did not limit his analysis of the social consequences of industrial capitalism to a recital of its detrimental effects on laborers and the poor. He anticipated much of the twentieth century's analysis of capitalism. Brownson foresaw that patterns of economic activity not only influence how people act in the workplace, but they also have a profound effect on how individuals view and understand other aspects of life. Brownson did not restrict the power of capitalism to the marketplace. It entered into the deepest aspirations and the fondest dreams of those who were touched by its influence. Industrial capitalism shaped the parameters of religious faith and belief; it molded the kinds of relationships which were possible in society; and it had a profound effect upon how men and women viewed their responsibility for one another. In his mind the power of industrial capitalism was all-absorbing. The urgency which he brought to the work of reconstructing the social order was tied to his realization that industrial capitalism had an abiding effect on the way men and women understood the meaning of their lives and their purpose as children of God.

In recent years a variety of developments in the life of the Catholic Church in the United States has promoted a new appreciation for the social message of the Gospel. Anyone who reads Brownson's work cannot help but marvel at how his understanding of the social meaning of God's redemptive entry into human history anticipated so much of modern Catholic social thought. The social message of the Gospel involved more than simply an attempt to humanize economic activity. It sought to create an awareness of the need to view social reality in its entirety as an important arena within which the believer achieved his salvation. Brownson pointed to the religious purpose and meaning of economic activity. He wanted to lift up the workplace and reveal its religious import. In doing he spoke to the need to overcome the secularization of economic activity divorced from the deeper aspirations of men and women.

Clearly Orestes Brownson was not a romantic dreamer. Although he had high praise for social life in the Middle Ages, he did not envision a return to the Middle Ages as part of his program for social and economic reform. Nor did he view social developments during the prior four centuries in an entirely bad light. History will move forward and social "progress" will not be halted. However, the ongoing progress of society must be characterized by a renewed respect for the dignity and worth of the individual person. Economic structures must be established which will embody this respect. Here again we find Brownson's aspiration to lift up economic activity into a new realm. Let the progress go forward but only in a way which will be protective of those moral values which are essential for personal and social well-being. It is transformation that he has in mind, not destruction. If he characterized the present economic order as the work of the devil, he looked to the creation of an economic order which would be the work of the Lord, and this would only be possible through the emergence of a new sense of responsibility among people and a new awareness of significance of the task at hand.

His sense of the Church of the future indicated that he did not envision a reconstruction of the Church of the Middle Ages nor did he regard this as advisable. The Church of the future had to be a new Catholic Church in the sense that it was present to a new history, and yet it could not allow itself to become a captive of the present age. We find in Brownson's writings a sense that the Church must be willing to stand against the dominant culture when it threatened the well-being of individuals and the community. On the other hand, the Church could not be out of touch with the realities of the present day and be unable to speak its redemptive message to those who were engaged in the work of creating society. The Catholic Church of the future, instilled with the fundamental moral values of community and solidarity, and deeply sensitive to the intrinsic worth of every person, would play its role in drawing up society to a profound new appreciation of man's destiny and a deeper understanding of the importance of social, political and economic activity in the eventual realization of the kingdom of God.

Although Brownson recognized that the Church had to play a fundamental role in the reconstruction of the socio-economic order, he also saw that the civil government had an important role in fostering the life of the community and protecting the rights, and in particular the economic rights, of the members of society. He did not look upon the government as detached from the economic life of society. Civil government had an important role to play in the creation of community. There was no question of this in his mind. Not only was the civil government obliged to become involved in the process of building and nurturing community, it also had a responsibility to be concerned about the plight of those members of society who were not able to care for themselves. In advocating the necessary separation between Church and state, Brownson did not envision these responsibilities as being mutually exclusive. Both the Church and the state had to look to the well-being of society; both have an important role in fostering the creation of just social order.

In his writings shortly after his formal entry into the Catholic Church Brownson seems to have lost some faith in his earlier belief that involuntary poverty could be completely eradicated from society. However, this did not lessen his conviction about the need for fundamental economic reforms. In response to this new awareness, he began to talk about the need for people to adopt a life-style of voluntary poverty as a sign and a symbol of the need to temper the materialistic spirit of the age, and as a way of providing the believer with some moral fortification for the difficult struggles that lay ahead. Coincident with his advocacy of the need for voluntary poverty, he also spoke about the need for new forms of monasticism which would give concrete and visible expression to the solidarity which was so sorely needed in society. Again Brownson was not a romantic. He did not envision a return to the monasticism of old. But he had an abiding belief in the transformative power of symbols in the life of society. If some small group of believers could gather together and give witness to the fruits which flowed from a social order wherein people were responsible for one another, he believed that this could have a transformative effect on the other members of society. Eventually it might have a significant effect on the social order itself. Earlier I indicated that Orestes Brownson was a man of his time and a man ahead of his time. His advocacy of voluntary poverty and the creation of new forms of monasticism anticipated what Catholics found later in the thought and the work of Dorothy Day and Peter Maurin. In standing against culture Brownson also felt the obligation to offer to culture a vision of a better day—a vision of a social order grounded in a profound respect for the dignity of every one of God's children.

Religious belief is always as much about mystery as it is about reason. It is difficult to say why Orestes Brownson finally came to find a home in the Catholic Church in 1844. His stated reasons are available for study and reflection. But the explanation goes deeper than the eye can see. From his earliest years Orestes was imbued with a sense of the mystery and majesty of life and creation. Throughout his long life he continually struggled to understand God's intentions for himself and for all his children. His life was a pilgrim's in quest of God himself. He never allowed himself to divorce this quest from his love of his fellow man. In his middle years he found a home in the Catholic Church not because the Church had been wholly faithful to the Gospel of Jesus Christ, nor because the Church offered all the answers to his questions. He came to the Church because Christ had come to the Church. It was a place for him to call home, a place which allowed him to continue the work of building the kingdom of God.

Notes

1. Henry F. Brownson, comp., The Convert, *The Works of Orestes A. Brownson* (Detroit, 1883–87), Vol. V, pp. 65–66.
2. Quoted from Lindsay Swift, *Brook Farm, Its Members, Scholars, and Visitors* (New York, 1900), p. 15.
3. "The Laboring Class," *The Boston Quarterly Review,* Vol. III (New York, 1965) p. 358.
4. Ibid., p. 367.
5. Ibid., p. 368.
6. Ibid., p. 369.
7. Ibid.
8. Ibid.
9. Ibid., p. 370.
10. Ibid., p. 372.
11. Ibid., p. 373.
12. Ibid., p. 374.
13. Ibid., p. 375.
14. Ibid., p. 376.
15. Ibid., p. 377.
16. Ibid., p. 384.
17. Ibid., p. 388.
18. Ibid., p. 389.
19. Ibid., p. 390.
20. Ibid., p. 393.
21. "The Church of the Future," *The Works of Orestes A. Brownson,* comp. Henry F. Brownson (Detroit, 1883–87), Vol. IV, p. 60.
22. Ibid.
23. Ibid., p. 61.
24. Ibid.
25. Ibid., p. 62.
26. Ibid., p. 63.
27. Ibid., p. 65.
28. Ibid., p. 68.
29. Ibid., pp. 69–70.
30. Ibid., p. 71.
31. Ibid., p. 71.

32. Ibid., pp. 73–74.
33. "The Present State of Society," *The Works of Orestes A. Brownson,* comp. Henry F. Brownson (Detroit, 1883–87), Vol. IV, p. 430.
34. Ibid., p. 433.
35. Ibid., p. 434.
36. Ibid.
37. Ibid., p. 435.
38. Ibid., p. 438.
39. Ibid., p. 441.
40. Ibid., p. 450.
41. Ibid., p. 452.
42. Ibid., p. 455.
43. "No Church, No Reform," *The Works of Orestes A. Brownson,* comp. Henry F. Brownson (Detroit, 1883–87), Vol. IV, p. 496.
44. Ibid., p. 497.
45. Ibid., p. 505.
46. Ibid., p. 504.
47. Ibid., p. 508.
48. Ibid., p. 509.
49. Ibid., p. 511.
50. Ibid., p. 512.

EDWARD McGLYNN

⌒

The Fatherhood of God and the Brotherhood of Man

In the late nineteenth century the mention of the name Fr. Edward McGlynn evoked a passionate response in the hearts of American Catholics who advocated social and economic reform. McGlynn came to public attention in large part because of the public controversy between himself and Michael A. Corrigan, the archbishop of New York. Their conflict centered around McGlynn's support for Henry George and the economic theories he presented in his book *Progress and Poverty* published in 1880. Because of his dispute with Corrigan he was excommunicated from the Church in 1887. His reinstatement in 1892 by Pope Leo XIII was welcomed by McGlynn's followers as a vindication of his passionate defense of the poor. One commentator summarized McGlynn's contribution in this way: "Dr. McGlynn was one of the first priests in New York City to see the size and the importance of the rapidly developing social problems brought about by industrialization, and to warn against relying on charity alone to cure them. He saw that charity was not a substitute for justice, and that major structural changes were necessary."[1] McGlynn's conflict with Corrigan made him a rallying point for progressive Catholics who took seriously the Church's social message and its implications for life in America. He insisted that the communitarian aspects of Catholicism were solely lacking in the economic life of American society which extolled the rights of the individual at the expense of the common good. McGlynn insisted that the government had to play an important role in fostering the common good by balancing the rights of society and the rights of the individual. "It is the function of civil government," said McGlynn," to maintain equally these two natural rights."[2]

Those who have studied McGlynn's life have often concentrated on his public controversy with Archbishop Corrigan. Although this conflict was an important part of his story, it should not obscure the substance of his analysis of the relationship between Christian faith, economic life and the rights of the poor in America. In the twenty-five years prior to his conflict with Corrigan, McGlynn was a priest and a pastor in New York City. His theological and economic views were not shaped in a vacuum. They were nurtured on the streets of St. Stephan's Parish in lower Manhattan where most of his parishioners lived in poverty. Here he painted vivid pictures of the conditions he encountered. "We find lots of people driven out of the world by actual starvation here in New York City. There is a fearful tragedy going on right under our eyes, ladies and gentlemen, and some of you don't see it and some of you know nothing about it. It has been my lot to touch these tragedies too often as if with my very hand. My ears have been oppressed by them. My heart has been rent by them. And small wonder if I could stand it no longer, and thought it high time to raise my voice and my hand to high heaven and as good as swear that I would do what I could to abolish this iniquity."[3] Throughout his priestly life McGlynn concerned himself with the relationship between Christian faith and the poor. He refused to embrace the conventional social wisdom which emphasized almost exclusively the obligation of Christian charity toward the poor. He knew the importance of charity and his life was a reflection of this awareness. However, he didn't believe that charity alone was sufficient. The practice of Christian charity had to be coupled with a commitment to social justice, and economic justice in particular. "Father McGlynn insisted that charity 'too often is taken as meaning the mere doling of alms. . . . Charity is a noble virtue, but to make the whole world an almshouse is carrying it to the absurd. The noblest charity is to do justice.' "[4] The Church should minister to individual souls in need, but the ministry of social reform was also required. Christ's call to the practice of the virtue of justice was a moral obligation. "Justice is the will of God concerning the relations between men and especially concerning those things that are essential for the maintainence of this life. Justice is the will of God, the natural law reinculcated by revealed religion, concerning the rights of property, concerning the rights of men, women and children who are born into this world with material bodies as well as spiritual souls. We must love justice because of our love of God and men, and enforce it as a religious principle. We should be eager to see justice done to everybody, because it is the holy will of God."[5] No element better accounts for the notoriety which accompanied McGlynn than his efforts to explore the relationship between existing economic conditions and the plight of the poor. This work was necessitated by his vocation as a Christian. His ministry frequently brought him into conflict with those who belonged to the privileged class. He found himself at odds with the political establishment of New York City and the ecclesiastical authorities who were more inclined to promote private virtue than social change. The evolution of McGlynn's thought also brought him into close association with men and women who saw the need for a fundamental reordering of the existing economic order. Unfortunately his association with these social reformers was often interpreted as a sign of bad faith by some of his fellow Catholics.

Fr. Edward McGlynn enjoyed the gift of an enormous personality. Few who encountered him were unaffected by his character and his passionately held convictions. He was a strong person willing to defend his views and beliefs even against seemingly insurmountable odds. At the same time he was not without human limitations and shortcomings. He was a man of considerable temper and he did not always deal gently with those who opposed the ideas he cherished deeply. Fr. Edward McGlynn was not a saint without blemishes. However, his life is a truly refreshing story of a man who embraced the Gospel with a passion. His faith in Jesus enabled him to surmount the many difficulties he faced in both the Church and society. In an age when respectability was the principal aspiration of so many, Edward McGlynn had the courage to resist its charms and dedicate his time, his energy and his life to the plight of those who had no place to lay their heads.

Early Years

Edward McGlynn was born of Irish parents in 1837 in New York City. His father, a contractor of some financial success, died early in Edward's life and his mother was left with the responsibility of raising eleven children alone. His earliest education took place in New York's public schools. At the age of thirteen he was sent to Rome to begin his studies for the priesthood. He spent nine years in the Propaganda and his final year in the North American College. A very bright student, he finished at the top of his class. Ordination to the priesthood came in Rome on March 12, 1860. In the years following his ordination McGlynn was assigned to various parishes in New York City. In December of 1861 he was appointed pastor of St. Ann's where he remained for only one year due to ill health. In 1862 he was assigned as chaplain to the Military Hospital in Central Park where he remained until the end of the Civil War. In June of 1866 he was appointed pastor of St. Stephan's in New York City succeeding his mentor, Fr. Jeremiah Cummings. McGlynn held the pastorship at St. Stephan's for the next twenty years until his suspension from the priesthood by Archbishop Corrigan in 1886. St. Stephan's was one of the largest Catholic parishes in the United States at the time. Its pulpit provided McGlynn the opportunity to address a national audience.

In 1883 McGlynn read the work of the economist and social reformer, Henry George. His book, *Progress and Poverty,* a scathing critique of the human deprivation caused by urban industrialization and the concentration of wealth in America, profoundly influenced McGlynn's thinking until the end of his life. There were other influences as well which contributed to McGlynn's social and economic analysis of late nineteenth century American life including his membership in the Accademia, a group of progressive minded clergymen who had studied with McGlynn in Rome; his association with various Catholic thinkers who were interested in exploring the unique character of American Catholicism; and, finally, his friendship with a group of American social reformers who were dedicated to the proposition that America had failed to live up to her promise of "liberty and justice for all."

The Accademia was composed of socially and theologically progressive priests who were interested in awakening the Church to the values and ideals of the American spirit. The original group included Fr. Thomas Farrell, Fr. Richard Burstell, Fr. Sylvester Malone and Fr. McGlynn. They believed that the Catholic Church in the United States would suffer immensely if it failed to open itself to the American spirit of innovation, change and a greater reliance on the wisdom found among the people. The goals of the Accademia were not shared by conservative members of the hierarchy who felt more comfortable in taking direction from Rome. The members of the Accademia were at times brash in their ways and bold in their actions. This attitude stemmed from their idealism, their love of the Gospel and their strongly held conviction that the Church would suffer if she remained an alien in America. Although never the actual leader of the Accademia, McGlynn was for many years its rallying point. His orations calling for the love of God and the creation of a just society reflected the deepest aspirations of its members. In one fiery address he outlined the vision of the members of the Accademia. "We believe in the Declaration of Independence, we love our American Constitution, we acknowledge no inferiority in our enthusiastic patriotism to any men or set of men; we believe that this country of ours is in the providence of God our Father, freighted with the destinies of the whole human family; and we feel, therefore, how exceedingly important it is that this land of ours shall go on progressing from truth to truth, purging out more and more what is unworthy of the magnificient Gospel and charter of our Declaration of Independence."[6] His years of participation with this group influenced him enormously. The members of the Accademia drew attention to the relationship between the preaching of the Gospel of Jesus Christ and the Church's obligation to challenge social conditions which created havoc in the lives of millions of Americans. "It was not for nothing that He who came to save the souls of men did so much to minister to the relief of their bodily wants. It is a mistaken, false and an exceedingly perverted notion of true religion to suppose that we must exalt the spirit, the things of God and eternity to such an extent as to ignore, to revile, to curse God's handiwork in the material world. A large part of our duties, without respecting and obeying there can be no true religion, is the obligation that men owe to one another in those relations that concern their temporal abode and the necessities, comforts and happiness of their material world."[7] McGlynn carried a strong sense of this responsibility throughout his life.

Another important influence on McGlynn's thinking was a group of Catholic thinkers, led by Fr. Isaac Hecker, the founder of the Paulist Fathers, who emphasized the role of the Holy Spirit in personal life as well as the communal life of the Church. A greater emphasis on the life of the Holy Spirit reinforced McGlynn's desire to encourage the laity to assume more responsibility in the life of the Church. This was a worthy objective and compatible with the American value of participation. Hecker looked for the compatibility between Catholicism and the American spirit. McGlynn supported this direction. He believed that the Catholic Church in America had a right and a responsibility to understand the Gospel in a manner compatible with the American spirit.

Equally important in McGlynn's life was his association with a group of social reformers who contributed to his vision of a just society. Although Henry George was eventually to become the most influential voice, others included Terrence Powderly, the founder of the Knights of Labor; Michael Davitt of the Irish Land League; Henry

Ward Beecher; Samuel Gompers, founder of the American Federation of Labor; the socialist Daniel DeLeon; Rabbi Stephan Wise; and a host of other leaders who sensed an urgent need to combat the economic injustices they found in New York City and elsewhere. McGlynn's openness to the social reform views of these men enabled him to develop his own analysis of the ills plaguing society. It gave him an opportunity to overcome a narrow parochialism which others tried to impose on his understanding of Christian faith and ministry. These influences also convinced him of the basic goodness of the American spirit. McGlynn's dedication to social and economic reform also had a transformative power in the lives of those who listened to him. The great Baptist social gospel advocate Walter Rauschenbush remembered "how Father McGlynn, speaking at Cooper Union in New York in the first Single-Tax campaign in 1886, recited the words, 'Thy Kingdom come! They will be done on earth,' and as the audiences realized for the first time the significance of the holy words, it lifted them off their seats with a shout of joy."[8]

McGlynn's relationship with members of the Accademia, his sensitivity to the thought of Hecker and others, and his close association with a band of vibrant social reformers had an enormous impact on his life and thought. However, the most powerful influence on his social vision came from the social conditions he encountered daily in New York City in the 1860's, 1870's and 1880's as he went about his pastoral duties. St. Stephan's parish included approximately 25,000 families. Many of his parishioners were recent immigrants to the United States and most were poor. McGlynn's duties led him into frequent encounters with his parishioners and the conditions they had to endure. They were crowded into dangerous tenements, unemployment was very high, and parents often did not have adequate food to feed their children. "Who are the poor?" McGlynn asked. "Not merely the disinherited ones, the wanderers, the tramps, the beggars, but the tired and struggling masses of mankind who are at best only a few degrees above pauperism; those to whom a somewhat protracted period without employment or a serious domestic affliction might reduce to absolute poverty. The poor are the great masses of men everywhere. The rich are few, the poor are the many."[9] The pastor experienced these conditions as an enormous contradiction in a land promising justice for all. He saw it as a violation of the rights of God's children. One of his most ambitious projects was to build an orphanage to care for hundreds of homeless children. When it was completed McGlynn vowed to embark upon a work which would change economic conditions dramatically so that orphanages would no longer be needed in the future.

Earlier I indicated that a basic tension was present throughout McGlynn's life in his struggle to understand the proper relationship between Christian charity and justice. His pastoral activities were evidence enough of his dedication to Christian charity. However, the more time he spent with his parishioners, and the more he reflected on the social conditions which characterized their lives, the more he became convinced that charity alone was insufficient. The Church had failed to adequately emphasize the Christian virtue of justice. He was drawn to this conclusion by the poverty in his midst and the indifference of those who lived in luxury. "I began to feel life made a burden by the never-ending procession coming to my door of men and women and children, begging not so much for alms as for employment, and felt that no matter how much I might give them, even though I reserved nothing for myself, even though I hopelessly involved myself in debt, I could accomplish little or nothing. It would be but a drop in a bucket, and I began to ask myself, 'Is there no remedy? Why are things thus? Is this God's order that the poor shall be constantly becoming poorer in all our large cities all the world over, the rich richer and the poor poorer'."[10] The growing gulf between the rich and the poor in New York was scandal. It called for a concerted effort to transform the existing economic conditions. By the time he arrived at St. Stephan's McGlynn was already reading in economics and political economy in his search for a way to conceptualize his convictions about the need for a fundamental change in existing economic conditions. He had reached the conclusion that the affluence of the rich was often gained at the expense of the poor. There would be no end to the number of people needing alms unless economic reform measures were implemented immediately. Not until 1883 did McGlynn begin to study the ideas of Henry George. When he did he became convinced that George offered a viable program for economic reform.

Fr. McGlynn and Henry George

Henry George had a greater impact on McGlynn's economic thought than any other person. Today George is best remembered for his book *Progress and Poverty* published in 1880. A self-taught man,

George dedicated his entire life to the work of social and economic reform. *Progress and Poverty* was both a scathing attack on the social consequences of industrialization in the late nineteenth century and a proposal for economic reform designed to remedy the most glaring social ills. George believed that his plan for economic recovery would deliver the poor out of their misery and deprivation.

George's impact on the economic reform movement in the United States was due in large part to his popularity among Irish immigrants, especially among those who supported the Irish Land League which advocated sweeping economic reforms in Ireland. At the time of the publication of *Progress and Poverty* the majority of the people in Ireland were experiencing terrible economic conditions. Many identified the root cause of this misery with the economic exploitation resulting from the practices of absentee land owners. George agreed with this assessment. He argued that the wealth realized from the possession of private property should be more equitably shared with all the members of the community. Although individuals had a right to own private property, the wealth realized simply from the increase in the value of the land should be used to meet the needs of the entire society. Private property owners had a right to the wealth which was created by their productive activity on the land. However, they did not have an exclusive right to wealth which was realized simply through the increase in the value of the land. George believed that the increase in the value of the land was in reality a function of the general development of society to which all citizens contributed. The wealth realized simply through land ownership, as distinguished from productive activity on the land, should be recaptured in the form of a Single-Tax and used to satisfy the social needs of the entire community.

In *Progress and Poverty* George defended the principle of private ownership and the right of land owners to enjoy the economic fruits of their labor. However, he considered the land itself as a common bounty. When private property owners alone were allowed to enjoy the wealth resulting from the simple increase in the value of the land they robbed from the other members of the community. Underlying George's thesis was an understanding of land as essentially social in nature. Individuals have a right to a stewardship of the common treasury but their exercise of this right can never be absolute in nature.

Throughout his book George brought a balance to the historical tension in economic affairs between the rights of the individual and the rights of the community, between the individual good and the common good. Contrary to the charges of some of his critics, George did not advocate the socialization of all economic activity nor did he reject the traditional right of private ownership. However, he argued passionately that the economic advantages enjoyed by some individuals could not be morally justified when they were realized at the expense of the common good. Individuals had a right to a measure of freedom in economic affairs. The exercise of this freedom by a few could not be tolerated if it became a vehicle for the domination of the many. When individual economic rights were exaggerated leading to the monopolization of the land wealth in the hands of a few the well-being of the entire community was jeopardized.

Progress and Poverty was music to Fr. McGlynn's ears. "I found an excellent exposition of the industrial and social conditions of man in Henry George's book, a poem of philosophy, a prophecy and prayer. In language rare and unequalled the author presents a picture of perishing lives, and in glowing poetic language tells of God's bounties to His children, but that somehow with the increase of the use of wealth there is an increase of poverty, and where there is a congregation of the greatest wealth, by its side is the greatest poverty and misery. I had never found so clear an exposition of the cause of the trouble, involuntary poverty, and its remedy, as I found in that monumental work. I became all aglow with a new and clearer light that had come to my mind in such full consonance with all my thoughts and aspirations from earliest childhood, and I did, as best I could, what I could to justify the teachings of that great work based upon the essence of all religion—the Fatherhood of God and the Brotherhood of Man. The concluding chapter of *Progress and Poverty* is more like the utterance of an inspired seer of Israel, or of some ecstatic contemplating the great processes of eternity, than the utterance of a mere political economist."[11] Before reading George's book McGlynn had already reached the conclusion that the monopolization of wealth through the absolute privitization of land ownership was the greatest social ill of the day. The uneven distribution of economic power caused by the monopolization of land ownership enabled a small group of people to dictate the economic conditions of the majority. McGlynn believed that the economic conditions of the Irish peasants, as described by George, were the same conditions he found in his parish and throughout the industrialized areas of the United States. The cause of the misery and exploitation was the same. He endorsed George's analysis of the root cause of the economic injustices and he found in George's

Single-Tax theory a simple yet effective remedy to the problem. "We are not opposed to property. We are of all the people on earth the people who are making the most desperate fight for the right of property. We believe in its sacredness. But land is not property. It is an opportunity for the production of property. There is a distinction between what God through nature has given equally to all His children because He is the equal, impartial and loving Father of them all, and the private property which by God's own law is the proper reward of man's individual industry. We must distinguish between the gifts of nature and the product of human industry. God never designed that one of His children should be excluded or any other from the bounties He provided for all. 'The earth He hath given to the children of men'. It is a goodly habitation in which he has placed His family. And it is a monstrous usurpation of God's property to permit any man to call himself the absolute owner of any portion of it. Not the property even of the whole human family. God alone is the owner, and He has simply given, as Jefferson tells us, the usufruct of these bounties to each succeeding generation of living men. Free the earth from the curse of landlordism by taking the entire rental value of land in taxation, leaving to private holders possession of the land they choose to use, and leaving to them also all that they produce by their labor of hand and brain."[12] In advocating George's Single-Tax theory McGlynn had found a way to promote the social and economic development of the poor. "We must have the people acknowledged as the supreme owners of the land, and those who are permitted to hold choicer portions of our common estate must pay to the people in the shape of a tax a perfect equivalent for the privilege that they enjoy, so that men shall not have to pay to their brethren for the enjoyment of a value that is a product of the whole community and not of an individual brother."[13] Equally attractive to McGlynn was George's understanding of the need to balance the rights of the individual and the rights of the community in economic affairs. He had long sought a pathway out of the economic deprivation he found wherever he looked. However, while he recognized the economic abuses which resulted when power was held in the hands of a few, he did not believe that the socialization of all economic activity in the hands of the state could provide the economic remedy which was so sorely needed. McGlynn's sentiments as an American, imbued with the spirit of individual initiative and creativity, obliged him to reject a narrower socialist response to the economic injustices he encountered. The theory and program for economic reform outlined by George impressed McGlynn as an appropriate middle road between the excesses which result when the individual is given absolutely free reign in economic affairs and when economic activity is placed exclusively in the hands of the state.

Fr. Edward McGlynn was more of an orator and organizer than a theoretician of economic reform. When he read *Progress and Poverty* he immediately became a convert to George's thought and his program for economic recovery. His support for George throughout the rest of his life took on the form of a religious crusade. In George he had found a plan for sweeping economic reforms which was both simple and straightforward. It would capture the imagination of the masses who were so eager for a vision of a better day. From the very beginning McGlynn saw George as much more than an economist with a moral vision. He believed that in order to preach the Gospel of Jesus Christ he had to be involved in the development of society. He regarded George's plan as much more than simply a secular vision for a better life; it represented God's intentions for society. He likened George to a new Moses and repeatedly referred to him as "one sent by God" to eradicate the evils of industrial society. This conviction was best expressed in his eulogy at George's funeral. "We stand upon ground that is made sacred by what remains of a man who was raised by a peculiar providence of the Father in Heaven to deliver a message to men of righteousness and justice and of truth. He died in the struggle upon which he had enthusiastically entered to deal blows and willing to take blows in a conflict for the rights of men for universal justice. To fight for a cause that would make the magnificent intentions of the preamble of the Declaration of Independence no longer 'glittering generalities.' The chair of the President of the United States is all too small for such a man. This man was not merely a philosopher and a sage, but he was a seer, a prophet, a preacher and a forerunner sent by God, and we can say of him as the Scriptures say, 'There was man sent of God whose name was John', and I believe that I am not guilty of any profanation of the Christian Scripture when I say there was man sent of God whose name was Henry George."[14]

McGlynn and Corrigan

McGlynn's enthusiastic support for Henry George and his economic theories would alone have been enough to warrant an interesting story. However, when he clashed publicly with the conservative archbishop of New York, Michael A. Corrigan, all the ingredients were present for a heated controversy. McGlynn's support for George and his Single-Tax theory had resulted in an earlier conflict between himself and Corrigan's predecessor, Archbishop McCloskey. Conservative Catholics in New York looked upon George's economic reform program as nothing less than socialist propaganda. They complained to McCloskey about McGlynn's support for George, arguing that the Single-Tax theory violated the Church's teaching on private property. McGlynn met with McCloskey to discuss these criticisms and in a spirit of compromise agreed to curtail his public support for George. However, when McCloskey died in 1885 McGlynn no longer felt obliged to refrain from supporting George publicly. A more cautious person might have decided otherwise.

In 1886 Henry George was at the peak of his popularity. With the support of McGlynn and others he entered the race for mayor of the City of New York. George ran under the banner of the United Labor Party, a new political party representing a coalition of moderate socialists, the Central Labor Union and various reform groups. The candidate numbered among his supporters Samuel Gompers, the founder of the American Federation of Labor, and Robert Ingersoll, a well-known social reformer. No one supported George's candidacy more enthusiastically than Fr. McGlynn. When Archbishop Corrigan who had already expressed public criticism of the Single-Tax theory learned that McGlynn intended to support George publicly he forbade him from doing so. McGlynn accepted Corrigan's order but indicated that he intended to honor a prior commitment to the candidate and speak on his behalf at Chickering Hall in New York City on October 1, 1886. McGlynn began his speech with a passion characteristic of his public orations. "Our Father Who art in Heaven, hallowed by Thy name. Thy kingdom come, Thy will be done on earth, as it is in heaven. That is why I, a frocked priest, stand tonight upon a political platform to urge the election of Henry George as Mayor of New York, because the triumph of his ideas means the bringing about of conditions under which it will be possible to do God's will on earth as it is done in heaven."[15] McGlynn proceeded to introduce George as "the most unselfish man of this century, formed by Providence to preach the new Gospel." He called George's campaign "the beginning of a pacific revolution which is destined to have upon the whole world a more beneficial effect than our first revolution and the great Declaration which give it its justification and battle cry." McGlynn bestowed on George the mantle of a leader who would help the nation realize God's plan for America in the creation of a more just society. When Archbishop Corrigan heard about McGlynn's speech on behalf of George he suspended him from the priesthood for two months. This was the beginning of a controversy which was to last until late in 1892.

The differences between Corrigan and McGlynn might not have developed into a major controversy were it not for the fact that both men were strong-willed. Archbishop Corrigan regarded McGlynn as a disobedient priest who refused to obey his legitimate ecclesiastical authorities. McGlynn regarded Corrigan as an obstacle to social reform. He felt that Corrigan's order had unjustly intruded into his legitimate prerogatives as both a priest and an American citizen. If a personality clash was an important element in the conflict between priest and archbishop, it was not the only element. The other elements were more substantive in nature and reveal different attitudes about the relationship between Church and society. These differences reflected a larger debate with the American Catholic Church at the time pertaining to the role the Church should play in the creation of a more just society.

In March of 1887 Fr. McGlynn received formal notification from Rome that he had been excommunicated from the Church. During the next six years Church authorities insisted that McGlynn's excommunication was primarily a result of his refusal to obey a Vatican directive to come to Rome and discuss his theories on economic reform with the Pope. From the very outset of the affair McGlynn considered his suspension and excommunication unjust—an arbitrary action on the part of Corrigan without justification in Canon Law. In his heart McGlynn was convinced he had become the target of conservative forces in the Church, including members of the hierarchy, who disagreed with his program for economic reform and his criticisms of the economic conditions in New York. McGlynn believed he had been done in by a small group of wealthy Catholics and their supporters in the hierarchy who were more interested in preserving the status quo than in advancing any meaningful economic reforms in society. There is no question that McGlynn's refusal to go to Rome contributed significantly to his troubles, but only a naive mind would reduce his troubles to this one act of disobedience. From the time Corrigan became the archbishop of New York McGlynn had been a thorn in his side. The archbishop not only disagreed sharply with McGlynn's economic philosophy and his support for Henry George, but he was equally anxious about the support McGlynn received from members of the clergy, the working class and the poor in New York City. McGlynn's suspension and excommunication had discredited a worthy opponent. It enabled Corrigan to reassert his authority as the archbishop of New York.

The Anti-Poverty Society and
The Cross of the New Crusade

On March 29, 1887, shortly after his excommunication from the Church, Fr. McGlynn appeared at the Academy of Music in Brooklyn and delivered his most famous speech, "The Cross of the New Crusade." The address summarized both his reasons for supporting George's economic theories and the relationship between the Gospel of Jesus Christ and the Church's obligation to participate in the transformation of the existing economic order. By all accounts this was McGlynn's most inspiring speech and he repeated it countless times during the next six years to audiences all across the United States. "The Cross of the New Crusade" gave McGlynn an opportunity to launch the Anti-Poverty Society to bring their economic reform program to the public. The constitution of the Anti-Poverty Society was adopted on July 7, 1887. It read: "The time having come for an active warfare against the conditions that, in spite of the advance in the powers production, condemn so many to degrading poverty, and foster vice, crime and greed, the Anti-Poverty Society has been formed. The object of the Society is to spread, by such peaceable and lawful means as may be found most desirable and efficient, a knowledge that God has made ample provision for the needs of all men during their residence upon the earth, and that involuntary poverty is the result of human laws that allow individuals to claim as private property that which the Creator has provided for the use of all."[16] With the organizational resources available to him through the Anti-Poverty Society McGlynn was hopeful that he could build a national movement dedicated to the work of economic reform.

"The Cross of the New Crusade" became the religious foundation for the work of the Anti-Poverty Society. It served as the Society's rallying cry inviting all Americans of good will to participate in the creation of a more just society. Its principal themes touched on the relationship between economic activity and Christian faith. McGlynn was convinced that the evil social consequences of industrialization, especially the monopolization of land, were so pervasive in American society that only a concerted effort could correct these injustices. He had no illusions about the extent of the problems in the existing economic order and he talked about "unjust social arrangements in society by which so large a portion of the people either cannot get work at all or have to work at starvation wages."[17] "The Cross of the New Crusade" provided McGlynn with an opportunity to reaffirm his Christian faith and to indicate that despite his difficulties with his ecclesiastical authorities he did not intend to relinquish his responsibility to preach the Gospel of Jesus Christ.

The new crusade for economic reform was essentially religious in nature. "This new crusade then, while, to use a modern phrase, there is nothing sectarian about it, is necessarily a religious movement. And permit me to say, and I am not at all singular in saying it, if it were not a religious movement you might at the very outset count me out of it; for I think that any cause, any movement, any object that enlists the thought of men and the affections of the heart of men must have a religious inspiration, a religious justification and a religious consummation, or the cause is not worth wasting our breath, our time and our strength upon. It were useless to prate about truth and beauty and goodness and justice and humanity, and the brotherhood of man, if this truth and justice and goodness and beauty, and this universal brotherhood, found not their resource and their centre, their type, their ideal, their justification, in God himself."[18] The struggle for economic justice had faltered because Christians had not assumed their responsibility in economic affairs. Christians hid their light under a bushel basket. The light of the Gospel, and especially Jesus' proclamation of the Fatherhood of God and the Brotherhood of man had, to be brought into the light of day. "It is my opinion—of course that does not add any great weight to it—but the secret is that in my opinion that the Christian church would speedily gather in the whole world into the flock of Christ if she would preach more generously and more self-sacrificingly to men and women and children wherever they will listen to her, and would carry out with all her wondrously potent influences the blessed lesson of the Fatherhood of God and the Brotherhood of Man."[19] Early in "The Cross" McGlynn pointed out that the new crusade was an effort to reaffirm the best of the Church's commitment to economic reform which found its origins in the early years of the Church. Many Christians had forgotten that Jesus calls the believer both to the salvation of his immortal soul and to participate in the salvation of all God's children.

Paramount to McGlynn's thought and clearly stated in "The Cross of the New Crusade" was his clarification of the distinction between the realm of the spiritual and the realm of the material. For McGlynn material well-being, including the presence of just social and economic institutions, foreshadowed the spiritual well-being of the people. When people were subjected to unjust material deprivation their openness to the love of God was undermined. McGlynn pointed to Jesus' ministry in the Gospel. Jesus fed the hungry, clothed the naked and cared for the sick as a pre-condition to his proclamation of God's love for every person. Jesus' example obliged all Christians to respond to those in need. Unless the Church is actively involved in the work of economic reform her profession of love for the poor would fall on deaf ears and the power of the Gospel would be muted.

McGlynn believed passionately that God's creation should be shared by all his children. The earth is a sacred trust given by God to all his creation. "God is the Father of all His children, all are equally brothers and therefore He has given to all of them equally His natural bounties. He has placed us here as if in one goodly household, and He is abundantly able, as He is most willing to make the table long enough and broad enough to accommodate all of his children and with elbow room to spare."[20] When some members of the community are denied access to the land and its fruits God's will is frustrated and the poor are denied their proper inheritance from the Lord. A share of God's good creation belongs to every person as a matter of right. "All men are created by Almighty God with certain inalienable rights; these inalienable rights are rights to life, liberty and the pursuit of happiness; life cannot be had without proper access to the materials of which this earth is made; and therefore, God has given an equal and indefeasible right to each and every one of His children who deserves access to these materials; no prescription, no vested right, no law, can deprive the child of a beggar that may be born in a barn tonight of the same right as the child that is born to inherit an imperial throne, to equal common proprietorship, or tenacy, if you will, of the natural bounties of God."[21]

No economic injustice was more apparent to McGlynn than the monopolization of land in the hands of a few who used their wealth and power to oppress their brothers and sisters. Land monopolization was a direct affront to God's design for His people. "The monopoly that is the parent monopoly, the great monopoly, that overshadows all other monopolies, is the monopoly of the natural bounties, and the reason why this monopoly exists at all is because there comes to these natural bounties a great value from the growth and the very needs of the community and from the increased capacity of the community to produce good things, since it is only on the land and by the land and out of the land that anything can be produced by human labor. Therefore those who have the exclusive control of the land enjoy the faculty, the power, of placing practically what conditions they please upon the use of that land, and where mere selfishness is the rule they will naturally place upon it the highest price that they can extort from the necessities of mankind. Hence the evils and horrors of landlordism, of land monopoly, of land grabbing here and elsewhere. Hence the fact that in spite of increase of wealth, of civilization, of labor-saving machinery, the masses of men are not benefitted, that poverty is actually increased with the increase of wealth, and there comes to those communities that are the wealthiest a new, more degrading and more soul-killing poverty than exists in the free and simple conditions of barbarism."[22] McGlynn realized that in an industrial society land could not easily be distributed equally to all the people, nor did he reject in principle the right of private ownership. However, he argued persuasively that although individuals had a right to own property, they did not have an absolute right to the profits which flowed from that ownership. Throughout the nineteenth century in America the increase in the value of land was more a result of the general development of society than the result of the efforts of private land owners. Therefore a portion of this increased value should be recaptured annually and used for purposes which serve the entire community, for example, education, housing, health care, etc. The owner of the land could continue to enjoy the profits which were derived from his productive activity on the land, but the increased value of the land itself should be used primarily to serve the needs of the community.

McGlynn was convinced that the implementation of George's Single-Tax program would end many of the economic abuses resulting from land monopolization. Because the profits flowing from the simple possession of land would be used to meet the needs of the entire community, private land owners would be encouraged to use their land more productively resulting in the creation of more jobs. When more jobs were created the exploitation of the worker would lessen. "Capital will then find nothing to invest in except human labor and its products. Don't you see the general demand for labor that will result? In every society there is capital, and it is the interest of men not to keep capital lying idle if they can use it, and the only means in which they can use it is by producing something, so that there will be a steady demand for labor."[23] The creation of more jobs would respond to a right which every person had and a responsibility he would assume if given an opportunity. "The average man is not going to lie down and die of hunger if he can get any kind of a fair chance to dig in the soil for food; the average man is not going to perish by the winter's cold if he can get a chance to make a shelter; nor to freeze if he can get a chance to make clothes for himself."[24] McGlynn had no interest in creating a permanent welfare state. He believed that workers would assume responsibility for their own self-development if given an opportunity to work and receive a just wage for their labors.

At the heart of "The Cross of the New Crusade" was McGlynn's conviction that the Church should support economic reform as part of her responsibility to advance the creation of a just society. In the past the Church had too often compromised efforts at social reform by emphasizing the obligation to practice Christian charity at the expense of promoting the virtue of justice. By advancing the work of justice the Church participates in bringing about the kingdom of God. "And when men's bodily necessities have been satisfied, when their minds shall begin to be cultivated, and they shall have begun to take on as a common thing the graces and refinements of culture and science and art, then you will have by the doing of natural justice, the following of God's economic laws, a way prepared for the coming of the kingdom of heaven. Then will blasphemy cease upon lips of children of men, and men will recognize the handiwork of the Creator; shall we not make some attempt to prepare the way for the coming of that better day foretold by the master of old, who, as he gathered around him the faithful few, foretold that the little flock should grow and spread until it shall take in all the kingdoms of the earth? Shall we not do our share toward hastening the time that was foretold by the Master when he taught us to look up and say, 'Our Father who art in heaven,' and then to say, 'Thy kingdom come; Thy will be done on earth as it is in heaven.' "[25]

Reconciliation

In the years between 1887 and 1892 several efforts were initiated to reconcile the differences between Fr. McGlynn and Rome. Many people had grown weary of the controversy and few believed its continuation benefited either the Church or the prospects for economic reform. The record indicates that Archbishop Corrigan may have been more anxious to end the affair than McGlynn. Even Cardinal Gibbons of Baltimore became involved in the resolution of the affair. His role was not made easier by the fact that he did not enjoy a close personal relationship with Corrigan. Gibbons wanted an end to the affair because it generated needless tension in the life of the American Church. In 1892, shortly after the publication of *Rerum Novarum* by Pope Leo XIII, the Pope appointed the first Papal Ablegate to the United States, Msgr. Francis Satolli. One of his first responsibilities was to seek a speedy resolution to the McGlynn-Corrigan affair. He hoped to achieve a resolution which would enable all the parties involved, most especially Corrigan and McGlynn, to maintain their integrity. In the end the resolution came quickly and with relative ease.

After a meeting with Msgr. Satolli McGlynn was asked to submit a written statement to the Papal Ablegate in which he outlined his views on economic reform in the United States, and especially his thoughts on private property. McGlynn prepared his "Doctrinal Statement" and submitted it to Msgr. Satolli in December of 1892. The Statement was then presented by Msgr. Satolli to four professors at the Catholic University of America in Washington, D.C., and they were asked to judge whether McGlynn's teachings were in accord with the teachings of the Church. Their reading of the "Doctrinal Statement" led them to conclude that McGlynn's teachings, and in particular his position on private property, were in accord with the mind of the Church. Based upon this evaluation, and acting with the authority given to him by the Pope, Msgr. Satolli lifted the excommunication of Fr. McGlynn immediately. Subsequently, McGlynn traveled to Rome and met with the Holy Father. When Leo XIII asked him if he embraced the Church's teachings on private property McGlynn responded affirmatively and the affair was ended.

McGlynn's "Doctrinal Statement" was a carefully prepared exposition of his views. It focused on the economic principles which were central to his thought for several years. He affirmed that individuals have a right to own property; however, at the same time he insisted that no economic system was just when some individuals were denied the opportunity to exercise this right. When the Church proclaims the right of private ownership she proclaims that all persons have this right. No economic system which accords the exercise of this right to a powerful few who act ruthlessly in the marketplace deserves the support of the Church. McGlynn was also quick to point out that the right of private ownership was never absolute in nature. At times the right of the individual to own property may conflict with the common good of society. When the common good is jeopardized by the individual right of ownership, the good of the community must take precedence. Economic activity may only be pursued in a way which protects both the rights of the individual and the rights of society.

Although it is the responsibility of every Christian and every citizen to participate in the creation of a just economic order which balances the good of society and the good of the individual, civil government has a special responsibility to see that a proper balance is maintained. "It is the chief function of civil government to maintain equally sacred these two natural rights."[26] Actually McGlynn went even further than simply asserting that civil government should nurture a proper balance between these two rights. He argued that the civil government was ultimately responsible for holding all of God's natural bounties in trust for the community. The distribution of these bounties to individuals is proper only in the form of stewardship. The bounty can be reclaimed if its private use frustrates the good of the community.

In his "Doctrinal Statement" Fr. McGlynn did not draw back from either his stated position on the nature of private property or his call for fundamental economic reforms. In American society fundamental and inalienable rights had to be respected and protected. McGlynn considered it foolish to talk about the joys of a political democracy when countless millions of people were denied access to economic resources essential to meet their material needs. Democracy was imperiled and the dream of the Founding Fathers was placed in jeopardy as long as so many Americans were denied their just inheritance in the land of "liberty and justice for all."

The Vision of Fr. Edward McGlynn

It is not an easy task to summarize the contributions of Fr. Edward McGlynn's life to the history of the American Church's struggle to participate in the creation of a just economic order. However, his contributions were substantial and they continue to offer insights to those who remain committed to the quest for economic justice. Unhappily McGlynn's conflict with Archbishop Corrigan has proved to be a stumbling block to developing a better appreciation of the significance of his thought. When his thought is dismissed for trivial reasons, his substantial criticism of industrial capitalism in the late nineteenth century is ignored. No summary of his contributions can do justice to the good he accomplished. However, some of the most important contributions should be identified.

At the heart of Fr. McGlynn's ministry was his commitment to the poor as a fundamental Christian moral obligation. This commitment to the poor flowed from his reading of the Gospel. Jesus was his model of compassionate concern for the poor. As a Christian he sought to model his life after Jesus' own ministry. His experiences with the poor in St. Stephan's Parish profoundly influenced his vision. His close identification with the misery and the suffering of those who were ill-fed, ill-clothed and ill-housed aroused his righteous anger and provided him with the moral strength to confront those forces which obstructed economic reform. The poor were not an "issue" for Fr. McGlynn; they were his people. As he identified with their lives he understood the link between their oppression and existing economic institutions. This awareness inspired him to build a movement designed to restore these men, women and children to the dignity deserving of God's children. If McGlynn had not identified closely with those who suffered in his midst, his life's story might have been very different indeed.

"The highest form of charity is to do the work of justice." These words of Edward McGlynn are enough to distinguish him from the dominant Christian social mentality of his day which frequently ignored the Christian obligation to do justice in social and economic life. McGlynn recognized the ideological forces which encouraged individuals to talk about charity and remain silent about justice. He knew that the ministry of justice often obliged a ministry of confrontation with those social and economic forces in society which benefited from a protection of the status quo. However, he never drew back from the challenges he saw before him. Justice, for Edward McGlynn, meant justice for all. He was intolerant of those who preached that justice for some in society entailed a full share of God's bounty while justice for others obliged a patient waiting for a better life to come in the hereafter. Again he drew his inspiration from Jesus' ministry in the

Gospel. Although Jesus preached the coming of the kingdom of God, he did not ignore the plight of the beggar, the agony of the sick or the plight of the leper. In Jesus' ministry doing justice involved actions to restore men, women and children to the dignity deserving of God's children. It would not be different for McGlynn. He questioned the motives of those who spoke about justice and yet were unwilling to confront existing economic conditions which contributed to the oppression of the poor.

The dedication of individual Christians to economic justice was alone not sufficient for McGlynn. The Church as a visible institution had to demonstrate her solidarity with the poor and be actively involved in the struggle for economic justice. To do less was a scandal in his eyes. Unless the Church was actively involved in promoting economic reform she provided legitimation to existing economic conditions which robbed the poor of their dignity. The Church as an institution had to continually struggle to resist the temptation of choosing acceptance by the powerful and the wealthy at the cost of advancing the vision of the kingdom of God proclaimed by Jesus in the Gospel. The task would not be easy. The mission of the Church was to preach the Fatherhood of God and the Brotherhood of Man.

Throughout Edward McGlynn's thought we find a sharp criticism of the social consequences of industrial capitalism and the destructive power it exercised in the lives of so many members of society. Although he repeatedly rejected the charge that he was a socialist, McGlynn was clearly no defender of an economic system which promoted self-interest in economic affairs and tolerated the economic deprivation of millions of men, women and children. In addition to the selfishness which rendered men insensitive to the needs of one another, McGlynn rejected capitalism's spirit of harsh competitiveness which fragmented the life of the community. Capitalism's self-interested individualism and competitiveness fostered materialism reducing the highest aspirations of men to acquiring material possessions. His criticism of industrial capitalism was harsh and sharp. This was not an economic system which promoted or respected the values flowing from Jesus' ministry in the Gospels.

One of the most significant factors motivating McGlynn was his desire to foster the growth of a new communitarian economic spirit in American society. He best summarized this aspiration in his proclamation of the Fatherhood of God and the Brotherhood of Man which he considered the fundamental moral principle of all the great religious traditions. Without the nurturing support of a community individuals are forced to live in fear and isolation from one another. Often the less powerful members of society are subjected to the whims of the powerful. The communitarian spirit McGlynn called for did not preclude the importance of individual responsibility in social life. However, it did provide a supportive framework offering security to those who were not able to care for themselves. The creation of a communitarian spirit in society foreshadowed the eventual coming of the kingdom of God.

McGlynn differed from many of his more conservative colleagues in the Church in his vigorous defense of the American spirit and character. He refused to listen to those who talked about a fundamental incompatibility between Catholicism and the American ethos. Catholicism and the American spirit could be mutually supportive of one another. The Church could learn a great deal from the American spirit of change and innovation. In particular, she could learn much from the democratic traditions within American culture. Catholicism, on the other hand, could contribute a great deal to a better appreciation of the importance of community life in America and the importance of creating cooperative bonds between people. McGlynn had little sympathy for those who viewed the American character with suspicion. Although he was always ready to point out the glaring injustices in American society, he never ceased believing that America was indeed a land of promise. He never lost hope in America's promise of "liberty and justice for all."

Finally, Edward McGlynn contributed his enormous personality to the life of the American Catholic Church at a crucial time in the life of the nation. He advocated economic justice with a passion and dedicated his life to those who were unable to care for themselves. Although his story reveals considerable tensions between himself and his ecclesiastical authorities, he never abandoned his love for the Church or his belief that the Church could play a vibrant role in the transformation of the existing economic order. His temperament was not easily given to compromise. Nor did he always deal gently with those who opposed his ideas. However, there was no maliciousness about this man who was absorbed with the dream of creating a social order foreshadowing the coming of the kingdom of God. His passionate crusade to proclaim the Fatherhood of God and the Brotherhood of Man here and now was refreshing in an age when many others advocated compromising America's promise. Father Edward

McGlynn's life story has never received the respect it deserves in the history of the American Catholic Church. What is most important about his life, and most informative for us today, is that he never gave up the struggle. In an age when skepticism and cynicism paralyze so many, the life of Edward McGlynn continues to serve as a model of dedication grounded in the Christian faith and love of Christ Jesus. Father Edward McGlynn tells us about the good life that awaits those who believe in Jesus enough to dedicate their lives to building the kingdom of God no matter how difficult and long the labor.

Notes

1. Florence D. Cohalan, *A Popular History of the Archdiocese of New York* (New York, 1983), p. 125.
2. "Doctrinal Statement," in Sylvester Malone, *Dr. Edward McGlynn* (New York, 1978), p. 47.
3. Ibid., p. 65.
4. Quoted from Robert Cross, *Emergence of Liberal Catholicism in America* (Cambridge, Mass., 1958), p. 112.
5. Malone, p. 94.
6. Ibid., p. 80.
7. Ibid., p. 76.
8. Quoted from James Hennesey, S.J., *American Catholics* (New York, 1981), p. 189.
9. Malone, p. 64.
10. Ibid., p. 70.
11. Quoted from Stephen Bell, *Rebel, Priest and Prophet* (New York, 1937), pp. 23–24.
12. Ibid., p. 104.
13. Malone, p. 58.
14. Bell, p. 268.
15. Ibid., p. 38.
16. Ibid., p. 130.
17. "The Cross of the New Crusade," Malone, p. 41.
18. Ibid., p. 21.
19. Ibid., p. 24.
20. Ibid., p. 55.
21. Ibid.
22. Ibid., p. 57.
23. Ibid., p. 37.
24. Ibid.
25. Ibid., p. 43.
26. "Doctrinal Statement," p. 47.

PETER E. DIETZ

Christ-Consciousness in the Economy

Peter E. Dietz's commitment to economic justice in the early years of the twentieth century established his reputation as a leader in the Church and the American labor movement. Although his life was marked by turmoil and disappointment, he remained faithful to the struggle for social justice throughout his life. Two stories of Peter Dietz are available for study. One tells us about his public life and the contributions he made to the American labor movement and the social conscience of the Catholic Church in the United States. The other reveals the humanity of a Christian who knew both victory and defeat. It is the story of a priest and a patriot who frequently found himself caught in tensions of every sort. The second story of Peter Dietz is the tale of a man who remained steadfast in his commitment to economic justice long before many others awakened to the task.

The tensions Dietz experienced in his public and personal life reveal much about the journey he traveled. He professed an abiding love for the Church, and yet he continually challenged bishops, priests, religious and lay Catholics to embrace the social message of the Gospel with greater vigor. He dedicated his life to fostering the Church's support for organized labor while consistently opposing the creation of independent Catholic labor unions. He accepted much of the Church's criticism of socialism, and yet he gave little comfort to capitalists who exploited the rights of workers. He was a staunch advocate of the American Federation of Labor, although he criticized the leadership of the A.F.L. when it buckled under pressures from extremists. He championed the right of every Catholic to experience full American citizenship, and publicly opposed those in the Church who looked upon vibrant patriotism with suspicion.

Peter Dietz's dedication to economic justice exposed him to anguish and turmoil. He labored long into the night to realize his enormous dreams, and yet many of his most ardent supporters failed to give him the assistance he needed. Because much of his work was seminal in nature, he never saw his goals fully realized. He set out to organize a Church in the struggle for economic justice, and yet his temperament and personality frequently undermined his fondest intentions. His labors were always directed to fostering the well-being of the community. However, Peter Dietz often found himself alone in the toil to realize his dreams.

The tale of Peter Dietz is not a biography of a saint free of human limitations. Throughout his life he was conscious of his inadequacies. However, he refused to give up. He embraced the frailty of his own human nature and remained steadfast in the work. His social vision outdistanced that of most of his peers. While he relished his own German-American heritage he realized that the future of the Church in the United States belonged to those who could forge a new American Catholic synthesis. Although he endorsed much of the Church's criticism of socialism, he felt no hesitation in scolding his fellow Catholics who were unwilling to support economic reforms designed to alleviate obvious economic injustices. He repeatedly fought the battle against isolationism in American Catholic consciousness. Peter Dietz made a contribution to economic justice which is worthy of continuing respect, admiration and understanding today. One commentator has identified Dietz as "the major labor priest of the progressive period."[1]

Early Years

Peter E. Dietz was born of German immigrant parents on the lower east side of Manhattan on July 10, 1878. His eventual involvement in the American labor movement was keenly influenced by the experiences of his early years. He knew the experience of poverty in his own family. He witnessed the plight of men and women who had to struggle to realize even a meager existence. Dietz's father was a varnisher by trade, although he frequently experienced the deprivations caused by unemployment. Young Peter often accompanied his father to meetings in the union hall where he listened to his neighbors describing the hardships they confronted and their hopes for securing more stable economic conditions. During those early years Peter was caught up in the hopes and dreams of his neighbors. Once he tasted the excitement of the struggle for economic justice it never left him. He sensed very early in his life that he had an important mission to accomplish.

Young Peter did not wonder long about the reasons which accounted for the plight of his neighbors and friends. As a young man he realized the relationship between the poverty of the masses and the power of an economic elite who cared little about other Americans in need. His compassion for those who suffered the indignity of poverty was enforced by his desire to identify the social forces which contributed to the economic injustices of his day. He also realized the need to organize other men and women who would be willing to contribute to a program of social and economic reform. The compassion he felt for the victims of economic injustice was the basis of his commitment. His willingness to analyze the causes of the social ills in society and combat those conditions became the instrument through which he hoped to realize his lofty ambitions.

As a young man Peter expressed a desire to enter the priesthood. He looked upon Church ministry as a means of advancing the cause of social and economic reform. The Dietz family belonged to Holy Redeemer Church in Manhattan. The Redemptorist priests who served the parish encouraged his vocation and welcomed the relationship he saw between social reform and ministry in the Church. In 1894 Peter went off to study at St. Mary's College in North East, Pa. He still wanted to enter the priesthood but his father was convinced that he was too young. During his stay at St. Mary's he became involved in the normal course of school activities. However, in 1895 he fell ill and was afflicted with a serious bout of depression. He discontinued his studies and returned to his family in New York. In the fall of 1896 he was well enough to enroll in St. Francis Xavier College in New York City. Once again he engaged in a full range of activities. Of special importance in Peter's life at this time was his involvement with the St. Vincent DePaul Society. He was a leader in the various activities of the society. This work deepened his convictions about the social ministry of the Church.

In 1899 Peter pursued his call to the priesthood with a new seriousness. He applied to St. Joseph's Seminary, the seminary of the Archdiocese of New York. Because he hadn't taken the necessary Latin courses at St. Francis, Peter was not accepted. Instead, he went off to spend a year at St. Bonaventure College in Allegheny, N.Y. When he applied to St. Joseph's the following year he was again found unacceptable because he hadn't acquired the necessary philosophy courses at St. Bonaventure's. Frustrated by this new roadblock, and influenced by some friends in the Society of the Divine Word, Peter left for Europe in 1900 and entered St. Gabriel's Seminary in Moelding, Germany. Again his life was troubled. The bouts of depression which afflicted him earlier returned. Throughout this trial he remained confident that he had an important mission to accomplish in the Church. The uncertainties he experienced related to his doubts about whether he was worthy enough to enter the priesthood. He even wondered about the possibility of establishing a new religious community in the United States dedicated solely to the ministry of economic reform. His stay in Germany, however, had convinced him that American democratic traditions could provide a very important vehicle for realizing the economic reforms which were so necessary. "I must master the English language, literature, theology and character of the people. I want to penetrate the nature and the spirit of the developing America in order to be able to understand it correctly from the very beginning."[2] The time he spent in Germany awakened him anew to the rich possibilities of his American heritage.

In the fall of 1902 Dietz left the novitiate of the Society of the Divine Word and returned to the United States. After spending a short period of time at Catholic University in Washington, D.C., he was formally received into the diocese of Cleveland and was sent by Bishop Ignatius Hustman to Baltimore to complete his studies for the priesthood. At the age of twenty-six Peter Dietz was ordained to the priesthood by Cardinal Gibbons of Baltimore. Although Dietz was troubled at times during his seminary days, he remained optimistic. America provided a fertile field to advance the cause of social and economic reform. Peter Dietz sensed that it was his mission to awaken others to this goal, and to develop the practical tools necessary for the task.

The Militia of Christ for Social Service

The role Peter Dietz played in the creation of the Militia of Christ for Social Service in 1910 was his first foray into the public arena. It was the first of many efforts which would place him at the heart of the Catholic Church's support of the labor movement in America. "John Ryan and Peter Dietz emerged as the most influential Catholic spokesmen on the labor issue."[3] In his efforts he hoped to build a new bridge between the Catholic Church in the United States and the American labor movement. His efforts in this endeavor were seminal and visionary. In 1909 Dietz attended the national convention of the American Federation of Labor in Toronto. He learned two important lessons. First, the leading Protestant Churches in the United States had already established a quasi-official relationship with the A.F.L. through the Federal Council of Churches of Christ in America. Second, at the meeting a number of Catholic members of the American Federation of Labor expressed dismay that the Catholic Church had failed to take an official position with respect to the work and goals of the Federation. In 1910 Dietz attended the next national convention of the Federation in Toledo, Ohio as a fraternal delegate representing the American Federation of Catholic Societies. During the course of the convention he addressed the Catholic delegates and assured them of the Church's support for trade unionism. During the course of the convention he brought Catholic trade union officials together for the first time into a new organization, the Militia of Christ for Social Service. When it reached full strength the Militia counted more than seven hundred union officials among its membership.

During the life of the Militia Dietz functioned as both the heart and the head of the organization. He had three primary goals for the Militia. First, it would provide a forum for the education of Catholic trade unionists in the principles of Catholic social teaching. Second, the Militia would establish the Church's support for trade unionism. And, finally, it would temper the influence of socialists in the American Federation of Labor. In addition to these three strategic goals, Dietz also hoped that the Militia would help Catholic trade unionists to better appreciate the connections between their Catholic faith and the goals of the labor movement. Dietz spelled out his hopes for the Militia in a letter to Cardinal O'Connell of Boston: "There is no bridge between the Church in America and the labor movement. The pulpit and the press speak to the individual only and existing Catholic societies are an imperfect medium. It is not possible to take hold of the labor movement in these ways. At a critical moment it would be very difficult for the Church to influence a given situation. The Militia of Christ would have a disciplined group of responsible Catholic trade unionists prepared to act in concert at a moment's notice."[4] The Militia would serve as a bridge between the Catholic Church and the labor movement and present the social message of the Christian Gospel. "Upon the battlefield and amid plagues the priest is a familiar sight—why should he not be equally familiar amid the spiritual death dealers and social plagues that have nailed suffering humanity to the cross of wealth and organized industrial injustice?"[5]

In order to enhance the Militia's influence Dietz needed some strong official support from leaders in the Church and the American Federation of Labor. From the A.F.L. he received help from several Federation vice-presidents including Dennis Hayes, president of the International Association of Glass Bottle Blowers; James O'Connell, president of the International Association of Machinists; John Alpire, president of the International Association of Plumbers and Steam Fitters; John Mitchell, former president of the United Mine Workers; T.V. O'Connor, International President of the Longshoremen; and John Golden, International President of the Textile Workers. On November 21, 1910 this impressive group of labor leaders met with John J. Glennon, archbishop of St. Louis, to solicit his official support for the Militia. Shortly after their meeting Dietz received a letter from the archbishop. "I have before me the programme yourself and the men of the committee handed me yesterday. I cordially give my approval to the same. I regard the time opportune for its inauguration and I pledge you my continuous interest and cordial support."[6] With the archbishop's support for the Militia Dietz's dream began to unfold.

According to its Constitution the object of the new organization was "the defense of Christian order of society and its progressive development." Its platform was based upon "the economic, ethical, sociological and political doctrine of Christian philosophy as developed in the course of history—the legacy of tradition—as interpreted to modern times in the letters of Pope Leo XIII and Pope Pius X." In his role as Executive Secretary of the Militia Dietz hoped to realize these goals through "the promotion of social education" and "the development of social action programs." He realized that it would not be easy to fulfill the goals of the Militia. "The work of the Militia of Christ is more difficult than many other Catholic works, because it makes a trade union appeal for which many people have no sympathy or proper understanding."[7] In order to advance the ideals of Catholic social teaching about trade unionism, and further the goals of the Militia, Dietz soon founded and edited its official publication, the *Social Service Journal*. This enabled him to reach out to a growing audience.

Dietz's aspirations in the arena of economic and social reform usually outdistanced the realm of practical possibility. Certainly this was the case with the Militia of Christ. However, this did not dampen his spirits. Throughout the life of the Militia Dietz frequently turned to John Mitchell, former president of the United Mine Workers, for support. He respected Mitchell and depended on him for candid advice. In June of 1911 Mitchell wrote to Dietz: "I have no hesitancy—not even a mental reservation—in saying that you have presented a program of constructive social service that is sound and progressive; a program that is calculated to meet the requirements of our people and our time, and while I do not desire to urge you to make great sacrifices in carrying forward the movement which you have so well inaugurated, yet it must be done by someone."[8] Mitchell went on to say: "I believe that the Catholic people should be in the vanguard in the movement for constructive social change and industrial reform, and whether there be any justification for the change, there is a widespread impression that our Church is just a little too conservative in matters of this kind; therefore it seems to me that our people should adopt and pursue a systematic program for social betterment; that we should identify ourselves with movements to promote legislation for the protection of that great part of the people in our country who are least able to protect themselves."[9] With the encouragement of Mitchell and Father John A. Ryan, Dietz obtained permission from his local bishop in 1911 to resign his pastorate in order to dedicate his full energies to the Militia.

When he became the full-time director of the Militia Dietz was confident that this would enable him to establish chapters of the Militia throughout the country. Although this ambition was never realized, he was instrumental in establishing chapters in several cities including New Orleans, St. Louis, Chicago, Milwaukee, Cincinnati and Knoxville. The shortage of money and personnel presented a roadblock to establishing more chapters. While proceeding with a plan for developing chapters of the Militia across the United States Dietz proposed to John Mitchell that the new organization establish a school modeled after the socialist Rand School of Social Service in New York. The school would advance the goals of the Militia. When Dietz approached officials at the Catholic University of America in Washington, D.C. to sponsor such a venture he was rebuffed. From the outset of the Militia Dietz maintained a close relationship with the American Federation of Catholic Societies. When the Federation decided to establish a permanent Social Service Commission in 1912 to advance the cause of social and economic reform in accordance with Catholic principles Dietz was a logical choice to serve as Secretary. He was hopeful that the broader level of support accorded the Commission both financial and otherwise would enable him to better realize the goals he had outlined for the Militia.

In an article which appeared in *Central Blatt and Social Justice* Dietz spelled out the hopes for the labor movement and society-at-large. "In all of our efforts for social and economic reform we need to rid ourselves of class-consciousness which divides the life of the nation into warring factions and replace class-consciousness with Christ-consciousness."[10] This religious motivation was the core of all Dietz's work. Christ-consciousness would instill in workers and employers a sense of the dignity of each individual and the importance of a vibrant community life. While still a student at St. Bonaventure College Dietz had studied the social evils inherent in the evolving industrial age. Rapid industrialization had fragmented the community life and promoted the false idols of materialism and secularism. The creation of a new Christ-consciousness in economic life would counteract these trends and assure the primacy of the human person in economic affairs. The work of the Militia would not be adequate to realize all his lofty ambitions but Dietz's hopes were never dimmed.

Social Service Commission, American Federation of Catholic Societies

Peter Dietz's role in the creation of the Social Service Commission of the American Federation of Catholic Societies was perhaps his most significant contribution to the goal of economic reform. In 1911 he attended the Federation convention in Columbus, Ohio to report on the work of the Militia. During the course of the convention he proposed that the Federation establish a Committee on Social Reform which could unite the various social and economic reform activities already underway in various parts of the country. The Federation agreed to Dietz's proposal and appointed him Executive Secretary. The first meeting of the Social Service Commission was held on February 8, 1912, at Notre Dame University. In addition to Dietz the other members present included Peter J. Muldoon, bishop of Rockford, Illinois, Chair; Rev. John W. Kavanaugh, president of Notre Dame University; James Hagerty, professor of economics, Ohio State University; and Charles Denechaud of New Orleans. Dietz's proposal to merge the Militia of Christ with the Commission was not approved; however, the members agreed that the *Social Service Journal* of the Militia should be made a part of the *Bulletin* of the Federation. Dietz assumed responsibility for the *Bulletin* content specifically relating to social and economic reform issues.

Dietz's hopes for the Commission were similar to those he had for the Militia. Under the auspices of the Federation he hoped to build a unified economic reform movement based upon the principles of Catholic social philosophy. He was confident that as Executive Secretary of the Commission he could develop "a national program and a great national campaign from which all Catholic social activities would be directed." At the Commission's meeting in 1912 the members agreed to send a questionnaire to every Catholic diocese and organization in the United States to ascertain their concerns about "the social question." The members of the Commission agreed that the Church had a leadership responsibility in the arena of economic reform. Central to this commitment was a recognition of the Church's obligation to support working men and women by advocating trade unionism and social legislation that would improve the economic condition of workers. Equally high on the agenda of the Commission was the desire to develop programs for seminarians so that they could better understand the social mission of the Church in society.

The agenda for the first official meeting of the Commission was developed in large part by Dietz. It focused on the need to support trade unionists and those interested in forming labor organizations. Dietz never tried to hide his belief that the path to economic justice in the United States lay in the advancement of trade unionism. This would give workers economic justice and a share in the economic power of the nation. A major accomplishment of the 1912 convention was the decision to publish a weekly newsletter about the Commission's concerns and activities. It would be distributed across the United States in cooperation with the newly established Catholic Press Association. Dietz understood the power of the written word. He was convinced that if he could bring his concerns before the Catholic people the reasonableness of his cause would receive a fair hearing. " . . . the Catholic press has a very large share of the burden of preparing the Catholic workers of America for their mission in the secular labor movement of America, which is in these days working up to a crisis."[11] The *Newsletter* was published between 1912 and 1918. With Dietz in charge its emphasis was decidedly pro-labor.

Throughout his life the Church remained Dietz's first love. He believed that the Church had to be at the forefront of economic reform in American society. However, Dietz also never lost sight of the fact that the American political system offered unique opportunities for advancing social and economic reforms. He did not harbor a romantic understanding of the protections provided by the Constitution. In 1915 he wrote: "The Constitution is not unalterably fixed and inviolably sacred. It is not proof against the ravages of time. Popular opinion, current thought and new movements poke around the foundations, and if they crumble, the crime is chargeable to those who, in negligent leisures, lounge under the protecting roof of the American liberties."[12] Dietz saw a number of threats to both American democratic principles and the cause of economic reform. They included bigotry, capitalism, socialism and secularism. In order to combat these evils he proposed the creation of the Center Party in the United States to give adequate voice to Catholic concerns about social and economic reform. While the idea received little support, and Dietz exerted little energy in actually promoting it, he did see the necessity for establishing a distinctly Catholic political program which could promote economic reforms. Dietz's economic reform program included social welfare, trade unionism, agriculture syndicates and just taxation. The *Newsletter* presented the specifics of the program. The Commission also published a series of pamphlets on a wide range of social reform issues.[13] They were distributed across the United States.

Mindful of the natural association between the goals of the Federation of Catholic Societies and the American Federation of Labor, Dietz eventually proposed a formal alliance between the two bodies. Although some in the Church opposed such a step, Dietz's inability to establish a formal alliance was primarily due to the fact that the leadership of the A.F.L. didn't support his proposal. Samuel Gompers took the lead in opposing Dietz's plan. Although he agreed that the Church and the American Federation of Labor had much in common, Gompers felt it would be inappropriate to formally link one organization whose mission was primarily religious with one whose mission was primarily directed to organizing working people through trade unionism. Dietz's inability to bring the A.F.L. into a closer organizational allegiance with the Federation of Catholic Societies mirrored his inability several years earlier to bring the Central Verein under the umbrella of the Federation.

The outbreak of World War I set in motion forces which eventually spelled the end of the Commission on Social Service and the Federation of Catholic Societies. The war galvanized the energies of the Church and the nation. The attention which had been focused on the need for economic reforms at home was now directed to supporting the war effort overseas. This development prompted changes in the way the American hierarchy understood its responsibilities in the public arena. As a result of the General Convention of Catholics of the United States in 1917, the National Catholic War Council was established. In September 1917 a Federation meeting was held in Chicago and the decision was made to discontinue the Social Service Commission and to terminate the employment of Peter Dietz as Executive Secretary. Dietz did not attend the meeting and received his dismissal notice by mail. The Federation leaders cited financial limitations as the reason for their action. Dietz never fully accepted this explanation. He understood that the Catholic hierarchy was anxious to exert its own will in the formation of Catholic social and economic policy in the United States. Two years later in 1919 the *Bishops' Program for Social Reconstruction* was published by the bishops. Dietz had been removed from his public position in the Church, and yet many of his own seminal ideas formed the basis of the bishops' own program for social reconstruction.

American Academy of Christian Democracy

In addition to his work with the Militia of Christ for Social Service and the Social Service Commission of the Federation of Catholic Societies, Dietz's efforts to advance economic reforms were reflected in his work with the American Academy of Christian Democracy in 1915 and the National Labor College in 1922. Although neither institution endured beyond Dietz's public career, they both reflected his desire to formalize the Church's involvement in economic reform activities in the United States. Both efforts were seminal in nature. Although neither flourished in the form Dietz initially intended, they were to become models for similar efforts in the future. "In the eight years of its existence the institution provided its hundreds of graduates with a most satisfactory social education which enabled them to assume positions of leadership in almost every major Catholic community."[14]

The American Academy of Christian Democracy opened in Hot Springs, North Carolina in the fall of 1915. The facility was made available to Dietz by a wealthy convert to the Church who shared his commitment to economic reform. The Academy fulfilled Dietz's earlier ambition in 1911 to establish a training school for members of the Militia of Christ similar to the Rand School of Social Service in New York City. Before opening the Academy Dietz tried to enlist the support of the Federation of Catholic Societies in his ambitious plan.

When this support was not forthcoming he struck out on his own. Fortunately for Dietz the Right Rev. Leo Hand, O.S.B., vicar apostolic of North Carolina, supported Dietz's plan and gave him important encouragement. The primary goal of the Academy was to train a cadre of Christian women and men who would dedicate their lives to a variety of projects of social and economic reform activities.[15] Courses taught at the Academy included political science, history, sociology, economics, philosophy and the history of the trade union movement. Dietz planned to organize the Academy and offered a majority of the teaching responsibility to Rev. John A. Ryan. When Ryan was unable to accept his offer, Dietz assumed most of the teaching responsibilities. The Academy was more than an academic program. He wanted to create an atmosphere where spiritual renewal would fortify the students for the work they would eventually assume in the field of social and economic reform. Dietz hoped to attract both men and women to the Academy but only seven women enrolled in the first course offered in September of 1915. They were trained in both the principles of Catholic social philosophy and the tenets of the American democratic tradition. Dietz hoped that the students would learn to carry the values of these traditions into meaningful social and economic reform activities.

After operating the Academy in Hot Springs for two years Dietz moved it to a new location. The move was necessitated by a variety of factors. He encountered some opposition from some of his ecclesiastical supporters; he had a difficult time finding qualified teachers in this rural setting; Hot Springs did not offer adequate opportunities for field education; and he continually faced problems raising the financial resources needed to run the school. Dietz also encountered opposition from some of his earlier supporters who thought the work of the Academy could be better carried out in Catholic colleges. Early in 1917 Dietz proposed affiliating the Academy with the Catholic University of America. Nothing came of the proposal because University officials claimed that they were already over-burdened. In 1917 Dietz moved the Academy to Cincinnati, Ohio where it was located at Good Samaritan Hospital. The number of students grew and Dietz became interested in the use of social science surveys for identifying the social and economic needs in society. In late 1917 Dietz again moved the Academy, to Ault Park, Ohio where he had access to a more qualified faculty. Despite all his efforts at encouraging their support, the members of the Federation of Catholic Societies never adequately supported

Dietz's plans for the Academy. This placed the Academy in continual financial difficulty. In 1918 the Federation's meager support for the Academy ended, and again Dietz found himself alone in his work. Despite these setbacks he was dedicated to carrying on the work of the Academy.

The National Labor College

After 1918 the goals of the Academy evolved from a program designed primarily to develop social service skills to a program geared almost exclusively to training men and women in the principles of trade unionism from the Christian perspective. The evolution of the Academy in this direction was never far from Dietz's mind. Although he recognized the need to develop professional social service programs in the Church, fostering trade unionism was always his primary concern. The evolution of the Academy was complete in 1922 when Dietz announced the establishment of the National Labor College under the sponsorship of the American Federation of Labor. It was the first of its kind in the nation. The life of the College was short-lived. Other than the formal courses offered in the spring of 1922, the National Labor College as a viable entity failed to materialize. Dietz encountered two major problems in establishing the College. The first had to do with the difficulty of raising adequate funds. The second had to do with the difficulties which developed between himself and Archbishop Moeller of Cincinnati. In May of 1922 the archbishop ordered Dietz to leave the archdiocese of Cincinnati and to take the Academy and the National Labor College with him. The record indicates that Dietz's difficulties with the archbishop stemmed from the fact that his critics in the archdiocese who represented some large business interest had gained the ear of the archbishop. Apparently they believed Dietz's continuing success could be detrimental to their own economic interests. A direct appeal to Moeller to reverse his decision by some leaders of the American Federation of Labor proved futile.

Dietz's twin dreams of establishing an Academy to train men and women in the principles of Catholic social service programming and his desire to create a national center to train men and women in the principles of trade unionism as outlined by Pope Leo XIII never developed as fully as he had hoped. Despite all of his labors between 1915 and 1922, Dietz came to realize that his mission was primarily one of planting seeds which would eventually be brought to fruition by others. History has indeed vindicated Dietz's vision. One can only wonder if the history of the labor movement in the United States, and the general state of economic conditions today would be different if Dietz's contemporaries in the Church had been more sympathetic to his vision and supportive of his efforts.

Dietz's Contributions

Peter E. Dietz's views on the economic conditions in the United States in the early years of the twentieth century were shaped by a variety of factors. He believed that the existing structure of industrial capitalism was in need of urgent and comprehensive reform. Without significant reforms the existing economic conditions would continue to deteriorate and greater injustices would plague future generations. Dietz was convinced that present-day economic conditions held the key to the larger social question. Unless changes were realized here there was no real hope of improving social conditions in other areas. Throughout his long years of service as a social reformer Dietz remained optimistic about the future. He felt that people of good will would come together and resolve the existing economic and social problems. Even when the odds seemed insurmountable Dietz recognized the power rooted in the solidarity of working people.

Those who have carefully studied Dietz's life have pointed out that he placed primary emphasis on the importance of trade unionism as a means of achieving a more just economic order. This is an accurate assessment of Dietz's thought. However, he did not advocate a narrow philosophy for economic reform. He was clear about the need for comprehensive changes in existing economic conditions. The trade union movement could provide the instrumental means to achieve these reforms. Trade unionism provided workers with an avenue enabling them to reassert the traditional rights which had been lost in the process of industrialization. The trade union movement could also temper the abuses which resulted when the economic power of society fell into the hands of a small minority. Trade unionism not only benefited the individual workers involved, but society-at-large.

Central to his support for the American labor movement was Dietz's conviction that the rights of workers were compromised by the existing economic conditions. He saw this early in his own life as he watched workers suffer because they lacked any effective control over the economic forces which enveloped their lives. Economic conditions were key to the larger social question. And the dignity of the worker was the key to the economic question. Until working people were protected in their natural right to form associations, the exploitation of workers would continue unabated. Dietz criticized industrial capitalism because it treated workers as expendable commodities deserving no special consideration. This understanding violated every tenet of Catholic social philosophy. The worker was the most important element of economic life.

Because he dismissed the proposals of some radical union activists, Dietz was sometimes looked upon as a conservative. Likewise, because he opposed the policies of the socialists, Dietz was at times seen as an uncritical defender of capitalism. These perceptions were erroneous. Although Dietz favored the reform of industrial capitalism rather than any socialist alternative, this choice should not be interpreted as representing a defense of the existing economic order. Dietz was a progressive when compared to many of his contemporaries. Certainly he held economic views far more progressive than most of his fellow Catholics. Although he opposed the economic alternatives proposed by the socialists of his day, his critique of capitalism demonstrated that he held a good deal in common with moderate socialists. Indeed, he held more in common with a number of socialists than he did with some of his fellow priests and members of the Catholic hierarchy who failed to recognize either the evils of the existing economic order or the need to commit the energies of the Church to the work of advancing economic justice. "If Socialism succeeds in America it will be because labor unionism failed . . . therefore, the Catholic has a most important and responsible share in the industrial readjustment of society. By his intelligent, Christian membership he will be the only solid guarantee that the labor unions will not become socialistic but the keystone of a social reform that will remove the most distressing features of the social problem as they confront us today."[16] In 1915 he spoke even more sharply: "There is no point to sending lecturers to fight Socialism by mere word of mouth and then fall down in the application of Christian principles to the actual conditions of the industrial struggle."[17]

Dietz repeatedly pointed out that one of the major failures of industrial capitalism was the social fragmentation it generated in society. Trade unionists who were committed to the plight of working people recognized the transformative power of worker solidarity. Dietz believed that worker solidarity could serve as the foundation for a new communal economic ethic. This ethic would be embraced by those willing to place the good of society above the absolute pursuit of self-interest. The human person, Dietz argued, was best nourished in the midst of a community of concern. Trade unionism could provide this sense of solidarity for workers. Union solidarity would in turn serve as a model for economic relationships in other areas of the economy.

No Catholic in the early years of the twentieth century deserves more credit for introducing the thought of Pope Leo XIII into the practical life of the American Catholic Church than Peter E. Dietz. One commentator has said that "he made the word of Leo XIII's *Rerum Novarum* come alive."[18] Throughout his public career Dietz considered the thought of Pope Leo pivotal to his own efforts. Leo's thought not only shaped Dietz's practical program of action, but it also established the appropriateness of the Church's involvement in the labor movement. From Leo's writings Dietz developed a sensitivity to Christ's redemptive action in human history as both personal and social. Dietz talked repeatedly about the need for social redemption in American society and urged the Church to assume a major responsibility in this work. He also shared Leo's conviction that the transformation of existing economic conditions was essential if other social injustices were to be adequately addressed.

Even prior to his ordination in 1904 Dietz understood that the Church had a moral obligation to better economic conditions in American society. This obligation was not as well understood by many of Dietz's colleagues in the Church. Throughout his public career he exerted an enormous amount of energy presenting the thought of Pope Leo XIII and its application to American society. In all of these efforts he continually opposed forms of religious individualism and parochialism which placed a concern about social issues outside of the legitimate responsibility of the Church. At the American Federation of Labor Convention in 1912 Dietz talked about the social dimension of Christian faith. "The first point I want to make is this: that mere economic strength is not a determining factor in industrial progress . . . it must be built upon the foundation of justice to God . . . to yourselves . . . to your fellow man. . . . God has planted that seed (justice) in every soul and he has established religion to foster that seed. The (second) part is this: religion is not a private matter . . . it is necessary that religion penetrate into the union and into the factory, into the marketplace and into the parliaments of the nation."[19] At times Dietz specifically attributed the Church's inability to influence social life more effectively to her failure to adequately understand the importance of Leo's thought. Because many members of the clergy had failed to study Leo's encyclical letter *Rerum Novarum,* appropriate responses to the existing economic conditions in America had not been adequately developed. In addition to these acts of omission, Dietz realized that some influential and wealthy Catholics had a vested interest in maintaining the existing economic order. The people often tended to monopolize the attention of Church leaders. Finally, the reform movements supported by Dietz were considered disruptive by many bishops in the Church. Because of these fears, many bishops underestimated that social havoc which resulted from the existing economic injustices in American society. Dietz heralded the role of labor unions as an appropriate vehicle for creating a sense of solidarity among workers who suffered at the hands of those who ignored their rights. Likewise, the Church could help to create a new communal consciousness in society. If the Church had the courage to join forces with the labor movement, society-at-large would be the beneficiary. Dietz did not believe any other institutions in American society could play such a vital role in economic reform.

Dietz frequently spoke about the need to replace class-consciousness in American society with Christ-consciousness. The class-consciousness he deplored was generated by the existing conditions of industrial capitalism; it was a by-product of the present economic order and not the figment of a socialist imagination. The socialists had simply named the consequences of the existing order. Christ-consciousness, reaffirmed through the active involvement of the Church in the arena of economic life, could promote the establishment of economic conditions rooted in human solidarity and respect for the rights of workers. The Christ-consciousness promoted by Dietz was a source for realizing the transformation of economic life so urgently needed. Christ-consciousness could re-establish the priority of labor in economic life and activity.

The Legacy

Despite the numerous difficulties he confronted in his work, Peter Dietz never wavered in his belief that American society was rich in the moral resources necessary for social and economic reform. He focused particularly on four resources for achieving a more just economic order. If individuals and communities were willing to take advantage of these resources, significant improvements could be achieved. The unifying element of these resources was Dietz's belief in the inherent dignity of the human person and the role of a cooperative economic ethic in fostering a just society. Dietz believed that existing economic conditions reflected a failure of industrial capitalism to respect and nurture the mutual rights of individuals and communities.

Dietz considered the Catholic Church as potentially the most powerful force for achieving economic reform. The Church had a moral vision of economic life to share with the larger society and the membership capable of carrying that vision into the marketplace. No other institution could rival the Church in this regard. "The true Catholic citizen shall stand for no law contrary to the divine law, provide cooperation but not union of church and state, defend the necessity of religion for the well-being of the state as a public policy, champion a progressive conservativism and open up to the American commonwealth the fountains of true Catholic humanity."[20] The network of small communities and parishes and working people throughout the United States represented a strategic asset for achieving social and economic reforms. The national hierarchy was capable of providing the nationwide leadership for the effort. Although he was frequently disappointed because the Church was unwilling or unable to carry forward the programs he proposed, he never ceased believing that significant economic reforms could be achieved if the Church had the will to act boldly and decisively.

The American democratic political ethos offered another tremendous resource for achieving economic reform in the nation. Economic reforms were more likely in the United States because existing democratic institutions could temper the power of a wealthy elite who had already assumed far too much power in economic affairs. The American political tradition was rooted in a defense of the dignity of the individual and the obligation of every citizen to contribute to the common good of society. "Social service is not only a religious duty, but is also a duty of national and patriotic importance. Peace is the foundation of prosperity in the nation; therefore to promote, to create and to extend industrial peace is a work of national and patriotic importance."[21] Dietz believed that a renewed patriotic consciousness had the ability to call industrial capitalism to a greater accountability when it violated the rights of individuals simply for the sake of economic gain. The shared experience of national solidarity and the willingness of the American people to come together in pursuit of a more just economic order was also an important resource. The advent of industrial capitalism had resulted in a fragmentation of the social body. This trend could be reversed if working people were willing to come together and assume mutual responsibility for one another. A new communal ethic in America could overcome the forces of a rugged individualism in economic life which fragmented the life of the community.

Finally, Peter Dietz believed in the ability of traditional values to provide a defense against the continuing onslaught of a competitive and materialistic ethos. Dietz was neither a romantic nor a nostalgic dreamer. The early twentieth century represented a turning-point in American life. He refused to accept the premise that traditional values did not have a place in a new age. Peter Dietz was ever the optimist. The necessary economic reforms could be achieved if people were willing to commit the energies necessary for the task. If the Catholic Church in the United States accepted the challenge offered by Pope Leo XIII, enormous gains could be achieved. The American political ethos was on the side of reform, if citizens were willing to lay claim to their national heritage. The creation of a new shared solidarity among workers and a renewed reliance on traditional moral values could again serve as a significant force for moral transformation and the creation of a more just economic order.

In 1922 Fr. Peter E. Dietz's public career both in the Catholic Church and in the American labor movement came to an end. For the next twenty-five years he observed from the sidelines the development of programs and the growth of a Catholic social conscience which he had vigorously supported in his early years. From 1923 until his death in 1947 he served as pastor of St. Monica's Parish in Whitefish Bay, Wisconsin. Although removed from the national limelight in the Church and the labor movement, Dietz did not abandon his commitment to social justice and economic reform. In 1928 he organized the first parish credit union in the state of Wisconsin which became a model for similar efforts around the country. Parish work also gave him the opportunity to educate a small Catholic community in the tenets of Catholic social teaching. He considered his parish a laboratory which if duplicated could provide the basis for the emergence of a network of Catholic parishes dedicated to economic and social reform. He did not limit his interests to his own parish community. He assumed responsibility for a variety of social projects in the city of Milwaukee

and worked closely with the St. Vincent de Paul Society. He also saw
the need to expand the moral vision of his parishioners by establishing
a partnership between St. Monica's and the efforts of the Church in
other countries. His brother Fred was working in China as a Maryknoll
missionary. He became the beneficiary of the social vision of the people
of St. Monica's.

The publication of *Quadragesimo Anno* in 1931 by Pope Pius XI
provided an occasion for rejoicing by Dietz. Pius XI's encyclical explicitly affirmed the legitimacy and importance of the vision which
Dietz had promoted in his early years. Pius XI challenged the members
of the Church to more fully embrace the ministry of social and economic reform as a work central to the mission of the Church. Dietz
welcomed the encyclical's explicit criticism of those forms of capitalism
which placed a quest for profit and economic self-interest above the
needs of the poor and the good of the community. Here Dietz found
a confirmation of his earlier call for the creation of a new Christ-
consciousness among all those involved in economic affairs.

After the publication of *Quadragesimo Anno* a number of individuals rediscovered the Peter Dietz who had ended his public career
in the Church and the labor movement a decade earlier. They found
in Pope Pius XI's encyclical a vindication of Dietz's earlier vision and
turned to him for advice and counsel in the formation of organizations
and programs which could foster the goals outlined by *Quadragesimo
Anno*. For the most part Dietz overcame the temptation to be drawn
back into the national limelight. After almost a decade at St. Monica's
he was comfortable with his pastoral duties. From time to time, however, he did respond to invitations to speak to Catholic groups about
the social teaching of the Church. In 1936 he accepted an invitation
to address representatives of the Holy Name Society during Catholic
Social Action Week. He repeated a theme he had expressed a decade
earlier when fewer ears were interested in listening. "Is the Catholic
Church merely an institution for the protection of capitalist interests
or has she a right to ask that their temporalities be put into the service
of God and the Commonwealth?"[21]

The contribution of Fr. Peter E. Dietz to the formation of the
social conscience of the American Catholic Church and the ministry
of economic and social reform was both seminal and visionary. He
came to the labor of awakening Catholics to the social message of
the Gospel long before most of his contemporaries. In 1912 he joined
with a group of labor leaders who called upon Cardinal Gibbons to

embrace and articulate a comprehensive program of social and economic reform. In 1919 the *Bishops' Program for Social Reconstruction* was published. His work with the Social Service Commission of the American Federation of Catholic Societies demonstrated the need for a coherent movement for social and economic reform among Catholics in the United States. Later this vision was vindicated by the establishment of the Social Action Department of National Catholic Welfare Conference. His Militia of Christ for Social Service was organized in 1910. More than twenty-five years later the Association of Catholic Trade Unionists embraced his idea and built an organization which dramatically influenced the labor movement and the nation. Dietz's efforts in establishing the National Labor College in the early 1920's were vindicated in the late 1930's and 1940's as a network of labor institutes were developed at Catholic institutions across the United States.

On October 11, 1947 Fr. Peter E. Dietz died in Whitefish Bay at the age of sixty-nine. His dedication to the goals of economic and social reform characterized his life to the end. His love for Christ and his Church was the hallmark of his life's efforts. He continually explored new ways to instill his brothers and sisters with an awareness of the need for Christ-consciousness which would awaken each person to the needs of others. Christ-consciousness could provide the basis for the creation of a cooperative commonwealth. Peter Dietz died before his dream could be realized. However, his dream is no less valid today. Those who continue the work of social and economic reform which he so boldly began can learn a great deal from the vision and the work of this Christian man who labored all his years to make Christ's love come alive in the marketplace of America.

Notes

1. Neil Betten, *Catholic Activism and the Industrial Worker* (Gainsville, Florida, 1976), p. 9.

2. Mary Harrita Fox, *Peter E. Dietz, Labor Priest* (Notre Dame, 1953), p. 229, note 15.

3. Betten, p. 13.

4. Fox, p. 47.

5. Ibid., p. 22.

6. Ibid., p. 45.

7. Ibid., p. 64.

8. Ibid., p. 51.

9. Ibid., pp. 51–52.

10. Ibid., 71.

11. Ibid., p. 105.

12. Peter E. Dietz, *Newsletter,* Social Service Commission, January 26, 1915.

13. Fox, p. 109.

14. Aaron I. Abell, *American Catholicism and Social Action* (New York, 1960), p. 183.

15. Fox, p. 154.

16. Ibid., p. 30.

17. Ibid., p. 65.

18. Henry J. Browne, "Peter E. Dietz, Pioneer Planner of Catholic Social Action," *The Catholic Historical Review,* January 1948, p. 448.

19. Dietz, *Bulletin,* VI, December 1912, p. 8.

20. Dietz, *Newsletter,* Social Service Commission, January 26, 1915.

21. Fox, p. 58.

VIRGIL MICHEL, O.S.B.

〜

Eucharistic Economics

Benedictine monk Virgil Michel, O.S.B., was a man of many gifts. Summarizing his contributions to the Catholic Church and the nation in the decades of the 1920's and 1930's is difficult. In an essay written shortly before his death Michel described the moral challenges confronting American Catholics. " . . . so while many Catholic Christians mind their own business, the injustices suffered by share-croppers, the gross discrimination against negroes (even at times within the walls of Catholic churches), economic oppression of all sorts, crying court injustices, violent vigilante antics based on the principle that might is right, etc., go on, with hardly a prominent Catholic voice raised in protest. How the Church Fathers of old would have made the welkin ring with the righteous indignation of the Lord and with the incessant denunciation on the one hand and guiding exhortations on the other. They knew of no compromise between Christ and the world. Why hesitate today when we all know that the support of Church and school comes not from the coffers of the wealthy but from the mites of the poor?"[1] In his activities as monk, liturgist, educator, philosopher and social reformer Virgil Michel gave witness to his faith in Jesus Christ and his love for all God's people. At the time of his death in 1938 at the age of forty-eight his friends and colleagues in the United States and Europe marveled at how much he had accomplished. Throughout his life Virgil Michel remained ever hopeful about building a socio-economic order in the United States embodying the values of the Christian Gospel.

First and foremost Virgil Michel was a monk. His life at St. John's Abbey in Collegeville, Minnesota provided the foundation for his work. However, Michel did not enter the abbey in order to escape the world. He looked upon monastic life as a resource to strengthen his soul and mind enabling him to participate more fully in the transformation of American society. Few other monks in the history of the Catholic Church in the United States have so dramatically bridged the gap between the cloister and the public arena. The need to build cooperative bonds in all aspects of social life in America was the central theme of his work. From an early age Virgil participated in a vibrant Christian community at St. John's. He hoped to carry this experience into the life of American society. As a monk he labored to balance the needs of each monk at the abbey with the common good of the community. In his work Virgil Michel called upon his fellow Catholics to participate in building an economic order which balanced the rights of each individual with the rights of the community.

Michel's contribution to the liturgical reform movement in the United States is certainly his most lasting legacy. The work which continues today at St. John's is a testimony to his labors. In the mid 1920's Virgil was sent to Europe by his abbot, the Rt. Rev. Alquin Deutch, O.S.B., to study philosophy. This experience had an enormous impact on young Virgil. Although he found his philosophical studies in Rome less than challenging, he was deeply inspired by the liturgical reform movement already underway in France, Belgium, Spain and Germany. He came to regard liturgical reform in the American Catholic Church as a means of promoting Christian renewal and the reconstruction of the social order in harmony with Christian principles. Shortly after his return to the United States Michel became the founding editor of *Orate Fratres*. It became a leading journal promoting both liturgical and social reform. St. John's Abbey became the center of the liturgical movement in the United States attracting the support and interest of Catholics throughout North America and Europe. Once begun Virgil never abandoned his apostolate of liturgical reform. This work became the foundation for all his other labors.

Throughout his life Virgil Michel was an avid student of St. Thomas Aquinas. His interest in Thomas was the impetus for his philosophical studies in Europe after earning a doctorate at the Catholic University of America in 1926. Although Michel found his philosophical studies in Europe something less than intellectually stimulating, this did not lessen his interest in Thomas. He regretted that many contemporary Catholic philosophers had silenced Thomas' social vision which had provided the philosophical foundation for Christian society in the Middle Ages. He longed for a program of Thomistic studies which could grapple with the social problems of the twentieth century. While in Europe Michel also studied the work of Emmanuel Mounier and other advocates of Christian personalism. He was deeply influenced by their thought and its relationship to his own interests. Encouraged by the understanding of St. Thomas as presented by Mounier and others, Michel found a home within contemporary Catholic philosophical thought. After his return to St. John's he continued in his philosophical interests and built upon his European studies to develop a socio-economic analysis of contemporary American society. His studies of Thomas' understanding of "social justice," "common good," "property rights" and the "human person" remain meaningful instructions in the area of Catholic social and economic ethics today.

Virgil Michel is probably least appreciated for his work as a social and economic reformer in the 1920's and 1930's. This is regrettable because many of his contributions here have become even more relevant today. Michel was an avid student of Pope Leo XIII and Pope Pius XI. Pius' *Quadragesimo Anno* (1931) shaped the direction of Michel's social thought throughout the 1930's. He was not content, however, to simply parrot the teachings of *Quadragesimo Anno*. He asked probing questions about the application of the Christian social and economic principles promoted by Pius XI to American society. He did not simply advocate superficial changes in American economic institutions. He spoke about the need for fundamental changes in the socio-economic order. The bourgeois spirit born of economic liberalism was leading American society toward moral bankruptcy. Only a reconstruction of the economic order could avoid imminent moral disaster. Michel viewed the present crisis in the economic order as the result of centuries of moral decline. "The march of history has for centuries been progressively under the inspiration of a denial of the Church of Christ, then of Christ, and finally of God."[2] Viewed from the perspective of the late twentieth century Michel's analysis was prophetic. Many of the social evils that Michel predicted would worsen if capitalism was not checked are even more evident in America today. The Catholic bishops of the United States drew attention to this fact in *Economic Justice for All,* a pastoral letter which owes much of its inspiration to Benedictine monk, now Archbishop Rembert Weakland, of Milwaukee. Some of his fellow Catholics were critical of Michel's economic views in the 1930's. At times he was harshly criticized. However, viewed from the vantage point of the present hour, Virgil Michel was at the forefront of a small group of Catholic men and women who dared to criticize the structure of capitalism in America in the mid-1930's.

At the time of his death in 1938 Virgil Michel was dean of St. John's College, Collegeville, Minnesota. In addition to his other activities he was a teacher and an educator throughout his life. Here again Michel did not fall into a traditional mold. He considered education essentially moral and social in nature. Education's primary purpose was to awaken students to an abiding sense of their moral responsibility to participate in the creation of a just society. Education was by nature value-oriented. He repudiated educational methods which were designed primarily to fill the minds of students with facts. All education should promote critical consciousness enabling students to question the moral quality of society in all its aspects. Shortly before his death Virgil was engaged in discussions with Robert Hutchinson about the possibility of initiating a Great Books program at St. John's. He envisioned a program focusing on the history of Catholic social, political and economic thought and its application to contemporary socio-economic conditions in American society. In a memorial edition of *Orate Fratres* published after Virgil's death, Mortimer Adler described him as one of the most important educators in America in the 1930's.

If Virgil Michel had limited his contributions to the Church and the nation to his work as educator, philosopher, liturgist and social reformer no one could help but admire his endeavors. But he did not stop here. He had the special ability to maintain a balance between his academic pursuits and his support for a variety of social and economic reform efforts underway in the United States and elsewhere. He never tired of offering his support to those in the streets and in the fields who were struggling to implement elements of his own vision of a Christian social order. From the very beginning of the Catholic Worker Movement he was a friend and supporter of Dorothy Day and Peter Maurin. He vigorously supported the cooperative agrarian reform movement. He praised the value of rural life and was an early supporter of the National Catholic Rural Life Conference. He championed the rights of workers and supported their efforts to establish independent labor unions.

People like Virgil Michel do not come along very often. Throughout his life he relished the wisdom he found in the Middle Ages, especially the spirit of community and solidarity reflected in its social and economic life. He dedicated his talents to incorporating the best of the social vision of the Middle Ages into the social fabric of American society. Virgil Michel was as comfortable supporting the cause of migrant workers suffering economic exploitation as he was in his philosophical and theological pursuits. His life gave witness to the dynamic relationship between the Eucharist and the creation of a just society. There is little doubt that Virgil Michel was a dreamer. However, he never allowed himself to become overwhelmed by his dreams. He accepted the role of seed-planter. Unless others joined in the work he knew that no meaningful social reform could be achieved. While he admired the Middle Ages, and especially the social wisdom he found in medieval society, he was no reactionary seeking to turn back the clock to another age. Virgil Michel was born at the dawn of the twentieth century and he remained a twentieth century man. His wisdom and insight still have much to offer to those of us who stand at the edge of the twenty-first century.

The American Bourgeois Spirit

Virgil Michel's work as a liturgist and social reformer was co-extensive. It is difficult to develop a proper appreciation for the vigor he brought to his liturgical activities without understanding his analysis of contemporary American society and culture. Michel believed that a proper celebration of the Church's liturgy required the participants to be keen students of the socio-economic realities in American society. Otherwise liturgical worship can unhappily become a means of legitimating the social and economic injustices in society. Virgil understood Christian liturgy, especially the Eucharist, in terms of personal and social transformation. As Christians come together to celebrate the Eucharist they are called to become more conscious of the Christian values which should be incorporated in American social and economic life. Celebration of the Eucharist should awaken the faithful to the moral inadequacies of the present social order. A dialectical tension should always be present between the liturgical life of the Church and the transformation of society. According to Michel the Christian should never lose sight of this dynamic.

Virgil's analysis of the social and economic conditions in the United States in the 1920's and 1930's was never superficial. He labored to understand the root causes of the social conditions which consigned so many millions of Americans to lives of impoverishment and despair. Because much of his socio-economic critique of American society was developed during the Depression era of the 1930's, some critics have charged that Michel exaggerated the social inequities in capitalism. He rejected this assertion. He considered the Depression a logical consequence of capitalism and not an aberration from an otherwise acceptable economic system. The Depression of the 1930's would be repeated in decades to come unless fundamental changes were achieved in the existing economic order. Capitalism was morally flawed. No amount of tinkering with it could correct the inequities that were inherent in an economic philosophy which promoted the priority of capital and profit over labor and human dignity. The governmental programs proposed by the New Deal were, according to Michel, additional evidence of the inequities of the existing economic order. Capitalism generated economic dependency among millions of people. No government, however benevolent, could adequately compensate for the social dependency caused by capitalism. Only the creation of a new economic order founded on the primacy of the human person in economic affairs could achieve this end.

Michel's criticism of the socio-economic conditions he encountered in the 1920's and 1930's was anchored in both his assessment of the social inequities inherent in capitalism and the bourgeois spirit in American society. These factors were interdependent. His words describing the consequences of bourgeois capitalism are sharp and to the point. "In dethroning God and turning to the worship of self man has without knowing it signed his own death warrant."[3] Any meaningful effort to achieve social and economic reform required a twofold analysis of society. Simply trying to alter the structural inadequacies within capitalism would meet with failure unless accompanied by an analysis of the bourgeois imagination generated by capitalism. This imagination profoundly shaped the thought of those who were caught up in the capitalist milieu. Likewise, any effort to change the bourgeois imagination of the times without a parallel effort to change existing economic conditions would meet with failure. A twofold effort was required. Michel had a keen appreciation for the thought of Karl Marx. He accepted Marx's analysis of the power of socio-economic conditions to deeply influence human consciousness. Unless Christian social reformers were willing to accept this truth much of their labor would be in vain. Here we have a sense of the dialectical process which Michel saw between socio-economic life and the creation of human consciousness. Unless Christian values permeated society in its economic, social, political and cultural institutions individuals would easily fall prey to a false understanding of the meaning of social and economic life. This was the tragic state of affairs he found in American society. Only a concerted effort could alter existing conditions.

In 1940, two years after his death, a two-part article appeared in *Orate Fratres* entitled "The Bourgeois Spirit and Christian Renewal."

In this article Michel analyzed the nature of the present-day bourgeois spirit and its consequences for living the Christian life. "The supreme guiding motive of the bourgeois mind is precisely the personal gain and profit which the medieval idealist rejected as a final goal. The principle of gain for its own sake, of an endlessly increasing profit, is now set up as the one sensible goal of all human life and endeavor. All the aspects of human life are with logical thoroughness rationalized into this one end. Where the Gospel had told Christians not to be solicitous about the morrow, the new ideal held forth a constant solicitude for the future, not merely in regard to the necessities of life, for it was not satisfied with such a moderate goal, but in regard to the ever greater accumulation of material goods."[4] Although the bourgeois spirit was part of the economic conditions fostered by the rise of capitalism in the fifteenth and sixteenth centuries, today it had to be understood as an even more powerful reality deeply affecting the minds of people in the twentieth century. The bourgeois spirit of the twentieth century embodied a set of personal and social values that was hostile to the moral values which permeated social life in the Middle Ages. They presented an obstacle to Christian life and ideals. "To what extent the spirit of the modern man, the typical bourgeois spirit, is the very antithesis of the ideals of the Christian tradition and of the civilization of the Christian centuries is self-evident. Without any intention at present of passing judgment, we may point out that the old Christian ideal, for instance, was one of working for a livelihood. The man of today does not merely work for a livelihood, he wants a maximum of profit. He in fact lives for work, i.e. for accumulation far beyond the needs of decent living; he lives for profit."[5] The bourgeois spirit was reflected in the present-day socio-cultural reality of the United States through its emphasis on individualism, hedonism, materialism and secularism. The bourgeois spirit of individualism encouraged men and women to place their own private self-interest above the needs of the community. Its spirit of materialism heralded the pursuit of material well-being as the highest value in life. "Wealth alone counts. The highest criterion of rank or position among one's fellowmen has in our day been decided almost entirely by the amount of money a person was able to accumulate."[6] Hedonism divorced human life from any appreciation for the importance of self-discipline and sacrifice. Finally, the secularism of the bourgeois spirit divorced human life from any relationship with God. "The bourgeois soul is by temperament narrow and self-contained; it is willing to take everything to itself, but it knows nothing of the joy of giving, least of all of the joy of giving unto God."[7] The bourgeois spirit generated by capitalism preaches a gospel of this-worldliness and divorces both individuals and the community from the transcendent meaning of human life. "The bourgeois spirit knows nothing of denying oneself the comforts and goods of this world for the sake of growth in spiritual things or for the sake of another world. All his ideals and his life are directed in terms of his existence here on earth. His position and his rank are judged by his possession of material wealth; he has apotheosized physical well-being and esteems it above all to be well thought of by his fellowman who professes his own bourgeois ideals."[8]

As a liturgist Michel was keenly aware of the power of religious myths and symbols and their impact on human consciousness and social life. Religious beliefs anchor human life and accord the believer with a vision and understanding of life's meaning. Religion is powerful because it has a world-creating ability when believers take the tenets of their faith seriously. But it is not religion alone which has the power to create human consciousness. In the 1920's and 1930's the bourgeois spirit emanating from modern capitalism had a similar kind of power. The bourgeois spirit of capitalism creates a false consciousness which reduces human life to a set of values and a social vision which are basically hostile to the Christian spirit. "It is no wonder then that the culture of our day is characterized as being the very opposite pole of any genuine Catholic culture. Its general aim is material prosperity through the amassing of national wealth. Only that is good which furthers this aim, all is bad that hinders it, and ethics has no say in the matter. The bold glorification of material progress has been accompanied by a denial of the spiritual, so that all joys and pleasures were sought on the level of the material. The denial of the supernatural was accompanied by the reduction of religion to a man-made myth. The supremacy of the irrational, of impulse, emotion, passion replaced that of reason and all permanent truths; eternal principles were laughed out of existence together with spiritual values of every kind. Hence the social conditions of human life which result from this, the open fostering of injustice, of selfishness and oppression, even the exaltation of ignorance, vulgarity and venality. Instead of the Christian virtues of love, fellowship, compassion, and sympathy, it has engendered fear, cruelty, hatred, etc."[9] Differing dramatically from the Middle Ages when a compatibility existed between the spirit of the age and Christian ideals, the twentieth century reflected a battle between a Christian understanding of human life and the dominant socio-economic ideology. This split between socio-economic life and the values of Christian faith was a tragic consequence of the power of capitalism. Even more tragic was the fact that many Christians fully endorsed the bourgeois spirit and structured their lives accordingly, without understanding that it represented a vision of human life which was diametrically opposed to the Gospel of Jesus Christ. The bourgeois spirit of capitalism in American society had the power to reach into the very sanctuaries of Christian churches and influence the preaching of the Gospel and the celebration of the Eucharist.

Virgil Michel saw the difficulties involved in awakening Christian men and women to the need for social and economic reform. Because so many Catholics were deeply affected by the bourgeois spirit of the times, it would be difficult to awaken them to a new critical religious consciousness. "Even most Catholics of our day have no definite conception of their true Christian cultural heritage. They have indeed imbibed the principles of it, but at the same time they have been living for generations in the atmosphere of the prevalent unchristian naturalism and materialism, they have been inhabiting the world wrought by this unchristian thing, and in many ways they have not remained entirely uncontaminated."[10] Nonetheless this was the work which was required. Michel never lost faith in the possibility of socio-economic reform. This was one of the reasons why he placed so much emphasis on the importance of the liturgical movement. If the Church's celebration of the liturgy, especially the Eucharist, could awaken men and women to their responsibility to participate in the transformation of society, tremendous advances could be made even in a short period of time. If, on the other hand, liturgical reforms were frustrated, the Church would continue to fall prey to those forces in society which benefited from the bourgeois spirit of capitalism and the economic philosophy which gave it life.

The Nature of Capitalism

Virgil Michel's analysis of the bourgeois spirit in American society and his analysis of capitalism were inseparable. However, for the purpose of this presentation they can be viewed independently of one another. Michel was unequivocal in his condemnation of industrial capitalism. In the 1930's his was one of the clearest Catholic voices calling for a fundamental restructuring of the economy as the only viable way of eradicating the evils of capitalism. "Everyone is aware today of the momentous turning-point in human history that is upon us. Christians in particular are keenly aware of the gigantic forces tending to crush out all Christianity, but they are also conscious of the many beginnings of a new life in Christ that is germinating among non-Catholic Christians as well as among Catholics. But are there not many Catholics among us today who would balk at the statement that the whole capitalistic system is doomed, and that it must go if there is to be anything like a Catholic revival? Capitalism is finished. Can any intelligent person doubt it is? But whether the sequel to capitalism will be Christian or unchristian is not so evident. This depends greatly on Christians themselves."[11] Capitalism could not be modified adequately enough to allow for its reformation. It had to be replaced. It was inherently unjust in the way it understood the nature of economic activity, and the primacy it gave to economics in an overall understanding of human life. At the most fundamental level capitalism demonstrated the consequences which result when the economic dimensions of human life are divorced from any foundation in God's plan for creation. Paul Marx, O.S.B., Michel's principal biographer, offers this description of Michel's critique of capitalism: " . . . the capitalism which Michel condemned was the oppressive, mismanaged system which grew out of the unchristian philosophy of individualistic liberalism with its false concept of man, of society, of economic life, of the purpose of material goods, and of human life, of the universe itself. This liberal capitalism proclaimed the ethical autonomy of man and the autonomy of economic life. It also regarded enlightened self-interest as the promoter of the common good, the inevitable natural laws of economics and unlimited competition as the ruling principles of economic life."[12] Michel's writings pointed in the direction of the need to expose the fundamental inequities of "atheistic capitalism," an economic system which sensed no obligation to be responsive to God's intentions for material creation.

In his critique of capitalism Michel was deeply influenced by Pope Pius XI's *Quadragesimo Anno* and the thought of Pope Leo XIII. He always viewed his condemnation of capitalism to be in keeping with the principles of Catholic social and economic thought. And certainly he considered his position defensible in light of the teachings of St. Thomas Aquinas. Michel's book, *Christian Social Reconstruction,* carefully examines the application of Catholic economic thought, especially the thought of Pius XI, to the American scene. In 1938 he wrote: "In a recent issue of the *Catholic World* a writer goes so far as to call Christ 'the first preacher of capitalism and the most workable thesis for society'. What unconscious blasphemy. As if there were anything really Christian about our modern capitalism."[13] He was alarmed that the American Catholic Church was so preoccupied with promoting Leo's and Pius' condemnation of socialism and communism that it was indifferent to their harsh criticism of capitalism. He found hypocrisy in this attitude. Too much energy was expended in condemning socialism and communism while far too little energy was spent in exposing the social evils inherent in capitalism. "If I mention the blindness of spiritual leaders to this immensely important trend of events, I am not referring to a disregard of the menace of communism, to human civilization . . . but rather to the more insidious menace that modern capitalism or bourgeois civilization has constituted for all spiritual values."[14] Michel explained this shortcoming by the fact that many American Catholics, including members of the hierarchy, had become imbued with the bourgeois spirit of capitalism. As a result they had lost their ability to be critical in their assessment of the socio-economic conditions in American society.

What were some of the other factors which contributed to Michel's condemnation of capitalism? The most glaring deficiency was the fact that capitalism was built on an inverted set of priorities which emphasized the priority of capital over labor. In an article published in *Commonweal* entitled "What Is Capitalism?" Michel offered a poignant outline of his condemnation of capitalism.[15] Capitalism looks upon human rights and human needs as subservient to the creation of wealth. This distorts God's intention for material creation. By placing a priority on capital over labor, capitalism as an economic system is unable to embody God's plan for the human family.

The ruthless competitive spirit of capitalism was another reason which warranted its condemnation by Christians. Michel recognized that individuals have an obligation to assume responsibility for their self-development. At times a spirit of fraternal competition may even be fruitful. However, the spirit of competition within capitalism went beyond the acceptable limits of fraternal competition. Capitalism promoted levels of competition which pitted people against one another regardless of the personal or social consequences. This created a hostile environment which frequently undermined any sense of human solidarity. Capitalism championed a level of competitiveness which rendered individuals and human needs subservient to the realization of increased profit and productivity. The materialism inherent in capitalism was an additional sign of its moral bankruptcy. Michel saw the material world as the creative gift of God intended to be used by man in order to fulfill his deepest vocation in service of God and human solidarity. The material goods of creation were a means to an end and not ends in themselves. Capitalism corrupted this understanding by promoting the acquisition of material goods as the primary goal of human life. In emphasizing the value of materiality at the expense of other values, capitalism undermined the development of man's spirituality resulting in a distorted understanding of the meaning of human life.

Capitalism was a moral failure because its operation fractured the life of the community. By advocating a rugged individualism based upon the ideology of economic self-interest, the bonds of fellowship and solidarity between peoples were fractured and communal life were undermined. "The progress of rugged individualism, or laissez-faire economics, we have seen, is one of competition or economic warfare of each against all; and it makes material riches, profits for their own sake of power and domination, the supreme end of life."[16] As a result of the bourgeois spirit of capitalism, individuals no longer assumed responsibility for one another. Relationships were expedient and based solely on the need for some level of cooperation in order to advance one's own economic self-interest. Capitalism introduced a sense of insecurity into the lives of people in society. Capitalism inevitably created a class of people who were unable to compete in a capitalist economy, and it failed to provide meaningful social supports for those unable to care for themselves. This class of people was looked upon as disposable. By placing the highest priority on the creation of wealth, capitalism created a permanent class of dependent citizens. This dependent class, created by capitalism, became the responsibility of the state. However, the state never adequately met its responsibility to care for the poor and the powerless. Furthermore, the creation of a large government bureaucracy to meet the needs of the permanent poor introduced another element into society which fractures the social. It left those who have achieved some level of economic success with the sense that they have no obligation toward the poor.

Capitalism distorted the proper meaning of property leading the members of society to regard the right of the private ownership of property as absolute in nature. When the ownership of property is seen as absolute, individuals sense no obligation to share their bounty with those in need. Consequently as the rich become richer, the poor are abandoned to fend for themselves. Capitalism negated the notion of stewardship which is fundamental to the Christian understanding of the material universe. In Virgil Michel's mind no aspect of capitalism was more hostile to the Christian spirit than the secularism which characterized its operation. Capitalism operated independently of God's plan for humankind. As a consequence, it was incapable of responding to any social code above the pursuit of profit. Michel rejected the possibility of reforming capitalism. Reformation was impossible because capitalism was built on a set of inherently immoral premises. Within capitalism the pursuit of wealth became an end in itself, and it was not accountable to any higher law, let alone the law of God. The moral principles which ground Christian faith ultimately had no place in a capitalistic economy, despite the fact that these values might be given lip service by the captains of industry in America.

When studied in its entirety Virgil Michel's critique of capitalism in the 1930's was harsh and relentless. He leaves no room for the weak at heart. "The first requisite is the consciousness that capitalism as we have had it is dying and should die."[17] What about the benefits which have come as a result of capitalism? Does he simply dismiss these? Obviously not. He recognized that some personal and social benefits have resulted from capitalism. However, he rejected the claim that more benefits have been realized than the harm which has been created. Even were this not the case, Michel would have still insisted on a condemnation of capitalism because of the false premises on which it was founded. Despite the harshness of his criticism, Michel remained hopeful about the future. This hopefulness was grounded in his belief that capitalism would eventually collapse because it was inherently evil. Furthermore, he believed the human spirit harbored a need for community and solidarity which was more powerful than the desire for material goods in abundance. Eventually society would reject capitalism because it was unable to fulfill the deepest longings of the human spirit. When the oppressiveness of the bourgeois spirit became too much to bear, even for those who were the beneficiaries of the economics of self-interest, a new economics rooted in Christian values would emerge out of the ashes and ruins of capitalism.

Liturgical Reform and Social Reconstruction

Virgil Michel's studies in Europe in the mid-1920's had an enormous impact on his contributions to Catholic liturgical reform in the United States. Although he found his formal philosophical studies less than challenging, his encounter with the liturgical movement in Europe provided the foundation for his vision of Church reform in the United States.

It is difficult to categorize Michel's liturgical thought. Although he deserves credit for promoting the liturgical movement in all its aspects, his interest in liturgical reform is best understood in the context of his commitment to social and economic reform. In one issue of *Orate Fratres* he wrote: " . . . no person has really entered into the heart of the liturgical spirit if he has not been seized also with a veritable passion for the re-establishment of social justice in all its wide ramifications."[18] Michel's liturgical thought and his socio-economic thought were dimensions of a common vision. If his liturgical writings are studied in isolation from his socio-economic thought, the former are neither sufficiently appreciated nor properly understood. Conversely, the significance of his economic thought is diminished when isolated from his liturgical thought and his dedication to liturgical reform.

As a liturgist Michel was not an original thinker. His most significant contribution was as a bridge-builder between the liturgical thought of European Catholics and the Church in the United States. In its early years this was the principal contribution of *Orate Fratres*. However, in 1933 *Orate Fratres* took a decidedly significant turn in the articles it published. It began to emphasize more consistently the relationship between liturgical reform and the social reconstruction of society. This is where Michel's work as an innovator is most apparent. Some liturgists have commented that Michel's contribution surpassed that of many of his European colleagues, because he had the vision to see the connection between the liturgy and social life in a dramatic fashion. "A Christian, to be such, must be united with Christ spiritually and supernaturally; and he cannot be united with Christ by himself alone, or in total isolation from his fellowman. By his intimate spiritual union with Christ he is also most intimately united with other Christians. The two, union with Christ or with God through Christ, and union with all the brethren in Christ stand or fall together. That is why Christ said long ago that it does not avail anyone to bring an offering to God's altar as long as his neighbor has something against him. We cannot be united with God if we are isolated from or stand against our fellowman. This fellowship-status of the Christian must also express itself in his daily actions, first and foremost, in his worship of God in the sacrificial offering. All of these must be collective or cooperative. To try to perform them in the spirit of pure individualism is to mock God."[19] After Michel's death in 1938 the social emphasis found in *Orate Fratres* began to lessen. Since his death, few Catholic liturgists in the United States have focused as much attention on the relationship between the liturgy and social reform.

Although Virgil Michel dedicated a great deal of time and energy to exploring the relationship between the liturgy and the reconstruction of society, he was not unconcerned about the liturgy in itself. "The liturgy is the ordinary school of the development of the true Christian, and the very qualities and outlook it develops in him are also those that make for the best realization of a genuine Christian culture."[20] He considered the liturgy, especially the celebration of the Eucharist, as central to the life of the Church; the liturgy is the source of God's continuing activity in human history calling believers to participate in the redemptive activity of Jesus Christ. Michel disagreed sharply with those who tended to look upon the liturgy as merely external acts pertaining to the Church's worship. On the contrary, in the midst of the liturgy the message of the Gospel of Jesus Christ is proclaimed and awakened in human consciousness, and the believer experiences personal transformation enabling him to participate in the transformation of society. "What the early Christians thus did at the altar of God, in the central act of Christian worship, they also lived out in their daily lives. They understood fully that the common action of worship was to be the inspiration of all their actions. They knew well that their common giving of themselves to God and to the brethren of Christ was in fact a solemn promise made to God that they would live their lives in this same love of God and of God's children, their brethren in Christ, throughout all the day. Unless they did that, their action before God's altar would be at best lip-service, a lie before God."[21] Through participation in the liturgical life of the Church the believer becomes mindful, both cognitively and affectively, of the meaning of Christian life. By the mid-1920's Michel was convinced that unless liturgical reform was realized neither personal transformation nor the social transformation of society could be achieved. In the following I want to briefly highlight some additional elements which were central to Michel's understanding of the liturgy and its relationship to social reconstruction.

Prior to the 1930's few Catholics in the United States focused much attention on understanding the Church as the mystical body of Christ. Catholics tended to think of the Church almost exclusively as a hierarchical structure. In reaction to the Protestant Reformation's emphasis on the common priesthood of all believers, the Catholic Church tended to move in the opposite extreme by placing almost exclusive emphasis on the hierarchical nature of the Church. As a result, lay Catholics were less able to see themselves as full partners in the redemptive work of the Church in the world. Many Catholics tended to think of themselves as mere spectators. Michel believed that a renewed emphasis on the Church as the mystical body of Christ could awaken Catholics to a deeper appreciation of their Christian vocations. A renewed emphasis on the Church as the mystical body of Christ could give birth to a new communal consciousness in the Church which would carry over to the larger society. "The liturgy, in the mystical body, furnishes man with the divine model of a social fellowship made up of individually responsible persons; it gives to each member the inspiration of a personal growth in this life from within through the grace of God, and it is itself the very source of all supernatural grace and help, by which alone man can achieve his highest development as a person and as a member of the fellowship."[22] A new communal ethic born of Catholic liturgical renewal could be an important element in the transformation of American society.

Consistent with Michel's emphasis on the Church as the mystical body of Christ was his commitment to enriching the role of the laity in the life of the Church. He saw liturgical reform and a renewed emphasis on the mystical body of Christ as critical to involving the laity more fully in the life of the Church. The individualism which was characteristic of the bourgeois spirit of contemporary culture had infected the life of the Church. Many Catholics tended to think about salvation solely in terms of self. By emphasizing the role of the laity in liturgical reform, Michel hoped that Catholic men and women would reawaken to their baptismal responsibilities to participate more dramatically in the transformation of society. By articulating the relationship between the lay apostolate and Church renewal, Michel hoped to create a broad basis of support for the Church's social role in society. He was convinced that a renewed laity could carry the message of the Gospel more effectively into the public arena. "In the Christian renewal of our day, every member of Christ has his active part to play, a part that derives directly from his position in the organic fellowship of souls in Christ that is the Church. It goes without saying that the spirit of the work must be the spirit of unity expressed in the two great commandments of love of God and of neighbor, neither of which is complete without the other, while both together give the whole spirit of Christ. If in past centuries men of the Church failed in this charity, as did all the world of the time, it was a temporal manifestation of what is human in the Church. Now the time seems to have come for a greater manifestation of that which is eternal in her. And it is the role of each member of the Church, not only to let the grace in him develop unto greater growth, but to cooperate more directly with and more consciously in the great work of the renewal of all things in Christ our King."[23]

If Michel believed that liturgical reform would lead to a renewed emphasis on the lay apostolate, he also hoped that a revitalized laity would give birth to new forms of social action countering the dominant trends in American society which threatened both personal and social well-being. As a student of the Middle Ages Michel admired the compatibility which existed between the values preached by the Church and the values incorporated in the socio-economic life of society. Church and society reinforced each other, and the individual experienced a sense of well-being and wholeness. "The life of the Middle Ages was rich in its economic organization, but the latter was part and parcel of the general organization of life that went far beyond the narrow scope of purely economic activity."[24] This was not the case in the early decades of the twentieth century in the United States. Michel considered many aspects of American society and culture hostile to the values of the Christian Gospel, especially its economic institutions. He predicted that social conditions would only worsen unless new forms of Catholic action in society, flowing from the liturgical life of the Church, were developed. "The nature of Catholic Christianity is expressible in one word, it is liturgical. In the liturgy the dogmas of the faith are embodied but not buried. There they live and enter vitally into the action of worship, forging also an inspiration for continued activity outside the structured liturgical worship itself."[25] Catholic action had the ability to promote the presence of a radically new way of understanding social life countering the materialism, secularism, individualism and hedonism so prevalent in American society.

No theme was more central to Michel's life and work than community. The greatest evil in American society was the rugged individualism which fragmented the bonds between people and undermined their experience of solidarity. " . . . the original model of prayer, the *Our Father* given to us by Christ, naturally divides into two parts of which the first is a giving unto God for His own sake, while only the second requests favors of God: and the whole of it is a *we* and *our* prayer and not all an *I* and *me* prayer. It starts with 'Our Father' and not 'My Father,' and asks later 'give us our daily bread' and not 'give me mine'."[26] Few in society seemed to adequately sense their responsibility to be concerned about the needs of others. The pursuit of self-interest was extolled and countless millions of people were abandoned to despair. They had no one to turn to for help in their hour of desperation. A new communal consciousness among Catholics, born out of liturgical reform, could provide a corrective to the social imagination generated by bourgeois capitalism and contribute to building new forms of social solidarity among people. Central to his understanding of the Eucharist was its celebration of the common fellowship of all peoples in the life of Jesus Christ. But for Michel this common fellowship was not limited to a mystical or spiritual experience. A Christian awareness of the common fellowship of all peoples was sterile and meaningless unless it was carried into the very life of society. "Christian life is the life of a supernatural fellowship in which all the members pray and live in mutual spiritual cooperation. For a right living of the supernatural life, all the members of the fellowship need a sufficiency of material goods as instrumental means; and they need to obtain these with relative ease in order to give time and effort to their moral and spiritual development. For the acquiring of the necessary material goods by all with relative ease, the mutual cooperation of the members of the fellowship is necessary. Hence the members of the Christian fellowship must give one another mutual or cooperative aid also in the economic field."[27] Christian faith is essentially incarnational. Unless the values of the Gospel were embodied in the social, economic, cultural and political fabric of society the labors of the Church were in vain.

In summarizing Michel's understanding of the role of the Christian liturgy in relationship to social and economic life, it is not an exaggeration to speak of his understanding as counter-cultural, at least in the context of American society in the 1930's. Through the celebration of the Church's liturgy Michel hoped that Catholics would experience the grace to stand against the dominant elements in society which threatened to undermine the values of the Gospel. The liturgy provided a refuge so that Catholics could participate in bringing about the kingdom of God. In this regard Michel talked about the need for the Church to be watchful, lest her celebration of the liturgy contributed to reinforcing those values in society which threatened the dignity of the person and the well-being of the community. The early Christians clearly recognized the relationship between liturgy and social life; they saw the need to draw strength from the liturgy in order to stand against a hostile culture which refused to accept the Gospel. Michel saw the need for the same kind of Christian social awareness in the 1930's. He rejected the notion that Catholics should simply withdraw from society and seek salvation in isolation from the world. The vocation of the Christian was to be in the world struggling to realize the kingdom of God. Liturgical reform could provide the basis for such a movement in the American society.

Building a New Society

By the early 1930's Virgil Michel had reached the conclusion that capitalism had already demonstrated its moral bankruptcy and its inability to foster meaningful economic and social well-being within American society. He based this judgment on both moral and pragmatic grounds. The foundations of capitalism were at odds with Catholic moral principles. Its promotion of materialism, individualism, hedonism, secularism and a destructive competitiveness were at odds with the Church's call for an economic order which placed material well-being in a proper relationship to fostering human dignity and protecting the common good. In addition to his condemnation of capitalism on moral grounds, Michel argued that capitalism had failed to produce the economic well-being its proponents had promised. The gospel of wealth was true, but only for a small powerful elite who built their fortunes on the exploitation of others. Michel refused to see the economic Depression of the 1930's as an aberration to an otherwise viable economic system. The Depression was the logical consequence of an economic system incapable of protecting the common good. "The present depression has brought home to many the fact that we are definitely at the end of an era in the history of the world. We are witnessing the inadequacy and the breakdown of a culture that is thoroughly individualistic, materialistic, and naturalistic. And in parts of the earth's surface we are now witnessing the attempted rise of a culture that is collectivistic but otherwise at least as materialistic and naturalistic as its moribund predecessor. Both of these cultures are anti-Christian and un-Christian for Christianity is always spiritual and supernatural and stresses a middle course between the extreme of anti-social individualism and anti-individual socialism."[28] The government's New Deal was warranted because of the need to provide immediate relief for millions of Americans who were suffering. However, the state could not provide a long-term remedy to the evils of capitalism. Fundamental changes were necessary. Unless they were forthcoming the obvious social ills present in the Depression would become permanent dimensions of social life in America.

Michel insisted that the pillars of capitalism were already under attack. The Depression and the need for massive government intervention in the economy were two indications. The continuing expansion of a class of permanently poor Americans was another. Increasing protests from the masses of poor Americans were a further sign of serious social discontent. American culture provided evidence of the inadequacies of capitalism as a morally defensible economic system for those willing to look below the glitter. It could be seen in the growing problem of class conflict, the alienation of workers, the deterioration of family life and a lack of concern for the common good in public policy. Eventually these and other social injustices would reach a point where capitalism could no longer survive. "The masses are determined that there be a new social order—and so is the Holy Father, and he bids us vibrate with the same unflinching determination. The change is coming, that is all there is to that point. But whether it will come through the masses without the guidance of Christian leadership and encouragement in the right direction, or not, depends on us Catholics. It no longer depends on the Pope, for he has done all that he can do in the matter. Only one thing is certain: the masses have so far been wonderfully patient with the obtusiveness of those in a position to lead. But if once their rising resistance reaches rebellion, many innocents, too, will reap the reward of the blindness of those Christians who should be seeing with the very light of Christ himself."[29]

One of the questions still unanswered for Michel in the 1930's was whether the collapse of capitalism would come through violent or non-violent means. He hoped violence could be avoided. However, there was growing evidence that fundamental economic changes would not be achieved without a struggle. The potential for violence lay with those who wanted to protect their privileged positions, and with the masses of Americans who wanted their fair share of economic well-being. Although Michel was reluctant to predict how the struggle would be resolved, he was adamant about the obligation of Catholics to participate in and support social movements which were anxious to foster non-violent change. If Catholics were willing to support these efforts, they would have to bear some of the responsibility for the social disorder which would eventually develop. Despite his critical assessment of existing conditions, Virgil Michel remained hopeful about the future. He identified and aligned himself with a variety of social reform efforts which he hoped would play an important role in the social and economic transformation of society. A brief description of some of these efforts and Michel's role with them is instructive in demonstrating that he was far more than a philosophical theorist. Throughout his lifetime he was actively engaged in efforts to achieve a reconstruction of the social order.

Virgil Michel was an eager supporter of the labor movement in the United States. He insisted on the right of workers to organize on their own behalf in order to advance and protect their rights and legitimate interests in economic affairs. These rights were defended by Catholic social teaching and reflected in the writings of Pope Leo XIII and Pope Pius XI. Quite often Michel was ahead of actual trade union leaders in his defense of the rights of workers. He was one of the first to argue that a worker's job becomes a form of ownership which cannot be arbitrarily taken from him simply to advance the economic interests of capitalists. Although he was a staunch advocate of the labor movement, Michel did not simply parrot the philosophy of others. He was frequently critical of labor unions and workers when they failed to live up to their obligation and potential to contribute to the common good. Michel looked upon the union movement as a social consequence of the class consciousness generated by capitalism. He spoke of "labor's belated answer to the unspoken but most definite challenge of capitalism. As this challenge arose out of the class struggle inherent in modern capitalism, so the answer is as distinctly in terms of struggle of class against class."[30] Labor unions were a reaction to the greed of capitalism. This accorded workers the opportunity to come together in their own defense. The inherent danger in the labor movement was the possibility that trade unionists would fail to move beyond an adversarial relationship with the capitalists and thereby fail to contribute more substantively to the creation of a just economic order. If labor union members could not embrace a broader vision of social and economic reform, their ability to contribute to a fundamental reconstruction of the social order would be muted.

The labor movement faced an important choice. On the one hand, labor unions could simply remain focused on the concerns of their own members, seek to advance their own economic advantage and refuse to assume responsibility for a more comprehensive reform of economic life in American society. If they followed this course, labor unions would simply reflect the self-interested individualism characteristic of modern capitalism. A different course of action was possible. If the labor union movement found the strength to act in a manner broader than its own limited self-interest, it could contribute to a deeper level of social reform in American society. "The labor movement is possibly the most vital and important movement of the day in our century. Beyond the movement as such, however, lies the still more important question of whether it will continue to operate with the heart of the present capitalistic set-up and go down with the latter, or whether it will turn its attention to the creation of a better social order in which not one class only but all men will be the beneficiaries of the modern culture and civilization."[31] The important values promoting the labor union movement were solidarity, community, concern for the common good and social justice. These were the same values which had to be incorporated into the fabric of economic life in American society. If labor unions could develop a program to foster this effort, its impact would be felt far beyond its limited membership.

Michel remained uncertain about how the choices confronting organized labor would be resolved. If Catholics exerted their influence in the labor movement, others might come to see a broader social role for the labor movement in American society contributing to the reconstruction of the socio-economic order. Time alone would provide the answer. Michel remained hopeful. The values which grounded the labor movement, including solidarity, community, economic justice and concern about the common good, were the same values which could provide the basis for a new economic order in American society. The labor union movement had an opportunity to provide an enormous service for the entire community if it had the will and the courage to act for the sake of the common good.

As Michel reflected on the relationship between the liturgy of the Church and socio-economic reform in American society, his interest increased in the cooperative movement in the United States and Canada. Here he found a fertile field of economic activity in which to promote the values fundamental to Catholic economic thought. He visited St. Francis Xavier University, Antagonish, Nova Scotia and he met with Father James Tompkins in Reserve Mines, Nova Scotia where he studied the principles and the philosophy of the cooperative movement and its relationship to economic and social reform. He came away from these meetings with a new hopefulness about the future. In the cooperative movement he found a philosophy and program for social and economic reform which advanced the vision he advocated. Here was a practical economic program which had the support of Pius XI. In emphasizing the values of social justice, community, solidarity and concern for the common good, the cooperative movement demonstrated that economic activity could be productive while still being respectful of those moral values which were essential for personal and social well-being.

Shortly before his death he wrote an article entitled "Liturgical Reform and the Cooperative Movement" in which he outlined in greater detail the relationship between economic reform and the liturgical life of the Church. In this article he said: "For the Catholic then, the liturgical movement, and for every Christian, the spiritual movement toward greater Christian fellowship, must be both the inspiration and the model of the cooperative movement in economic life."[32] At the time of his death Michel was developing a series of courses at St. John's College which examined the significance of the cooperative movement and its relationship to the liturgical reform movement in the Church. He felt that the students at St. John's should be exposed to this important model of economic activity. Perhaps it would enable them to counter the destructive social tendencies within capitalism. Unfortunately, his early death frustrated this plan, and the course of studies he envisioned was never developed.

Closely associated with his support for the cooperative movement was Michel's respect for the rural life movement in the United States. He was an early and active supporter of the National Catholic Rural Life Conference. It represented an effort on the part of the Church to reaffirm the social and moral values found in America's rural and farming heartland. Although Michel did not completely reject modern industrialization and the urbanization it spurned, he found many aspects of urban life at odds with the economic and social values he hoped to promote. Rural life, on the other hand, was more conducive to fostering a sense of community and solidarity among people. When the values of rural life came under attack he considered this a threat to a more comprehensive program for social reconstruction in America. He frequently gave his time in the promotion of rural life interests. Recalling Michel's support for the rural life movement and the co-operative movement, Bishop Aloisius J. Muench of Fargo, North Dakota praised Michel after his death: "The cooperative movement was for Father Virgil but another manifestation of the workings of the mystical body of Christ among men."[33]

Michel was also an avid supporter of the Central Verein, an association of German-American Catholics. With other members of the Central Verein he established the Institute for Social Study at St. John's in Collegeville. Although the Institute did not survive his death, throughout the 1930's it offered valuable resources to Catholics in the United States who sensed the need for fundamental reforms in the economy. Perhaps the Institute's most noteworthy accomplishment was the publication of a series of pamphlets which examined various aspects of Michel's program for socio-economic reform. This work was significant because it created a theological and philosophical framework for economic reform, and it helped to organize Catholics in the pursuit of some common social and economic goals.

No summary of Virgil Michel's activities in support of social and economic reform would be complete without mentioning the support he gave to Dorothy Day, Peter Maurin and other members of the Catholic Worker movement. Whenever he could he visited Day and Maurin in New York City and at the Worker Farm in Easton, Pennsylvania. Although Michel expressed some differences with respect to the Worker's approach to social and economic reform, and especially with some of the vision expressed by Maurin, he was a staunch defender of their critique of capitalism and praised them as models for other Catholics to follow. Dorothy Day frequently talked about Michel as one who stood by the side of the Catholic Worker movement when others, including members of the Church, ridiculed them for their efforts. Not long before his death Michel wrote: "Catholic Workers and apostles! You have your faults and your shortcomings. But who among us on earth is not burdened with them? If people slander and calumniate you, so did they Christ. You are indeed an eyesore and a scandal even to Catholics, but usually only to such as revel in their self-complacency, whose religion is one of asking from God and knows not the blessedness of giving. If you are a scandal to the self-righteous, so was Christ. And he told us that it was not the Pharisee but the

Publican who went away justified. Blessed are you if you are among those who suffer persecution for justice's sake, since 'theirs is the kingdom of heaven.' "[34]

The Legacy

A thoughtful reading of "the signs of the times" suggests that Virgil Michel's concerns about social and economic justice in American society are as justified today as they were fifty years ago when he died. Throughout his lifetime Michel endeavored to bring the social vision of St. Thomas to bear on an analysis of the moral fabric of American society. Today we are challenged to bring Michel's social vision to bear on an analysis of the socio-economic structures of American society. More than fifty years before the publication of *Economic Justice for All* Virgil Michel was engaged in the work of applying the values of the Christian Gospel and the moral principles of Catholic socio-economic thought to conditions in America. During his life Michel's vision was prophetic. So too were his activities directed at the reconstruction of the social order. A half century after his death Virgil Michel's thought and life remain a prophetic challenge to those engaged in the transformation of society.

Decades before the emergence of "liberation theology" in South America Virgil Michel was talking about the need for a "liberation theology" in the United States. Although he never considered himself an advocate for the thought of Karl Marx, Michel was able to discern both the wisdom and the moral implications of Marx's analysis of the relationship between the structures of socio-economic life and the creation of human consciousness. He rejected Marx's assessment of religion as "the opiate of the people," and yet he realized that a narrow presentation of the meaning of the Christian Gospel can obscure the relationship between Christian faith and the transformation of society. When Christian faith becomes asocial it can contribute to the legitimation of unjust social and economic structures. Michel repeatedly urged his listeners to be attentive to the socio-economic implications of Christian faith.

Michel's most enduring legacy was the relationship he explored between the Church's liturgical life, especially the Eucharist, and the transformation of society. Few American liturgists since Michel have continued to develop and expand on this aspect of his work. Although the bishops at the Second Vatican Council recognized the relationship between the liturgy and the creation of culture and society, few Catholics in the American Church have adequately explored this relationship in the context of American socio-economic life. When the relationship between the liturgy and social life is not properly understood, a privatization of religious belief and worship results which renders Christian faith asocial and apolitical. A privatized understanding of the Church's liturgy mutes its power to participation in the transformation of society in accordance with Christian values.

Throughout his life Virgil Michel was both monk and social activist. His Christian faith nourished his social vision, and his activities with a variety of social reform groups enriched his moral imagination and enabled him to better understand his own Christian spirituality. In this respect Virgil's life modeled that of the prophets in the Old Testament. He understood that Christian spirituality and faith were for the sake of the community and human solidarity. Although he lived a monastic life, he did not consider his religious vocation an end in itself. Religious life was for service. Here he anticipated many of the reforms in religious life which were born at Vatican II. Today more needs to be done in order to further develop Virgil's understanding of religious life. Religious men and women bear a special responsibility in the Church for evaluating the moral fabric of socio-economic life in American society.

Virgil Michel was not a grand planner, nor did he offer a comprehensive blueprint for the social reconstruction of society. This explains why he was always willing to give his time and energy to people active in the cooperative movement, to those promoting labor unions, to rural life advocates and to Catholic workers. He accepted the fact that a transformation of the socio-economic structures of American life would not be realized overnight. Furthermore, participation in the transformation of society was the responsibility of all Christians, and it could not be left to a few people in the Church. Virgil's trust in the Holy Spirit nourished him. He found the Holy Spirit present in the various social reform groups active in society. Labor union members, Catholic workers, members of economic cooperatives and farmers were already engaged in a work which contributed to the gradual transformation of society. These movements and activities were of profound significance. They were building up the kingdom of God. Throughout his life Virgil Michel maintained a quiet confidence that eventually all people of good will would come together in a spirit of human solidarity in the work of building up the kingdom of God.

In the summer of 1988 a symposium was held at St. John's Abbey in Collegeville, Minnesota to commemorate the one hundredth anniversary of the birth, and the fiftieth anniversary of the death, of Virgil Michel, O.S.B. The theme of the symposium was "The Legacy of Virgil Michel and the Future of the Catholic Church in America." Participants from across the United States and Europe came together to reflect anew on the significance of Virgil's life and work and the challenge he continues to extend to Catholics in the United States. The topics discussed were the same topics that absorbed Michel's attention during his lifetime. The simple truth which emerged from the symposium was that Virgil Michel was a visionary far ahead of his times. His legacy stands as a testimony to the social vision of the Christian Gospel and a compelling challenge to all people of good will to do justice day in and day out.

Notes

1. Virgil Michel, "Timely Tracts: Social Injustices," *Orate Fratres,* vol. XI, December 1937, p. 79.

2. Virgil Michel, *St. Thomas and Today* (Collegeville, 1936), p. 9.

3. Virgil Michel, "The Bourgeois Spirit and Christian Renewal," Part II, *Orate Fratres,* vol. XIV, May 1940, pp. 304–05.

4. Virgil Michel, "The Bourgeois Spirit and Christian Renewal," Part I, *Orate Fratres,* vol. XIV, April 1940, p. 257.

5. Ibid., p. 260.

6. Ibid., p. 258.

7. Michel, "The Bourgeois Spirit and Christian Renewal," Part II, p. 306.

8. Michel, "The Bourgeois Spirit and Christian Renewal," Part I, p. 259.

9. Virgil Michel, "Christian Culture," *Orate Fratres,* vol. XIII, May 1939, p. 299.

10. Ibid., pp. 298–99.

11. Virgil Michel, "What Is Capitalism?" *Commonweal,* XXVIII, April 23, 1938.

12. Paul Marx, *Virgil Michel* (Collegeville, 1957), p. 302.

13. Michel, "What Is Capitalism?" p. 6.

14. Ibid., p. 7.

15. Michel, "What Is Capitalism?" pp. 6–9.

16. Virgil Michel, "The Cooperative Movement and the Liturgical Movement," *Orate Fratres,* vol. XIV, February 1940, p. 156.

17. Virgil Michel, "The Labor Movement," *Commonweal,* XXVIII, January 3, 1938, p. 146.

18. Virgil Michel, "Timely Tracts: Social Justice," *Orate Fratres,* vol. XII, January 1938, pp. 131–32.

19. Michel, "The Cooperative Movement and the Liturgical Movement," p. 154.

20. Michel, "Christian Culture," p. 303.

21. Michel, "The Cooperative Movement and the Liturgical Movement."

22. Virgil Michel, "Personality and Liturgy," *Orate Fratres,* vol. XIII, February 1939, p. 159.

23. Virgil Michel, "The Layman in the Church," *Commonweal,* XX, June 4, 1930, p. 125.

24. Michel, "The Bourgeois Spirit and Christian Renewal," Part I, p. 254.

25. Virgil Michel, "The Liturgy and Modern Thought," *Orate Fratres,* vol. XIII, May 1939, p. 207.

26. Michel, "The Cooperative Movement and the Liturgical Movement," p. 153.

27. Ibid., p. 160.

28. Virgil Michel, "The Liturgical Movement and the Future," *America,* LIV, October 12, 1935, p. 6.

29. Michel, "Timely Tracts: Social Justice," p. 131.

30. Michel, "The Labor Movement," p. 147.

31. Ibid.

32. Michel, "The Cooperative Movement and the Liturgical Movement," p. 158.

33. *Orate Fratres,* Memorial Edition, vol. XIV, February 1940.

34. Virgil Michel, "Timely Tracts: Catholic Workers and Apostles," *Orate Fratres,* vol. XIII, November 1938, p. 30.

PETER MAURIN

∿

Apostle of Christian Personalism

Peter Maurin was born on May 9, 1877 to a peasant family in the mountains of southern France. In the seventy-two years of his life Peter never moved far from the values and traditions which nurtured him in his early years. He remained proud of his peasant heritage, remarking frequently: "I have roots. I am a peasant."[1] His early education with the Christian Brothers at St. Privat's in Mende awakened in him a spirit of inquiry and reverence for life which characterized all his future endeavors. Peter's schooling with the Brothers provided the foundation for the Christian Personalism which became the cornerstone of his philosophy life in later years.

In the fall of 1893 Peter's life took on a new direction when he entered the novitiate of the Christian Brothers in Paris. From all accounts Peter found happiness and fulfillment in religious life and he took an active role in the affairs of his community. Peter saw his religious vocation as a way of promoting his concern for building a Christian social order in France. He was especially concerned about the poor and the need to better understand the causes of their poverty. During his years as a Christian Brother Peter held several assignments but none more fulfilling than when he was given the opportunity to work closely with poor orphan boys. From his earliest years he experienced an affinity for the poor. A Christian responsibility for the poor in society was at the heart of his understanding of the Gospel of Jesus Christ.

> In the first centuries
> of Christianity
> the hungry were fed
> at a personal sacrifice,
> the naked were clothed
> at a personal sacrifice,
> the homeless were sheltered
> at a personal sacrifice.

And because the poor
were fed, clothed and sheltered
at a personal sacrifice,
the pagans used to say
about the Christians
"See how they love each other."[2]

After several years with the Christian Brothers Peter's spirit of inquiry turned his life in a new direction. He left religious life on January 1, 1903. Prior to his formal departure from the Christian Brothers he had become attracted to the work of the Le Sillon in France. He was inspired by the tenets of this Christian social movement and its dedication to building a new democratic Christian social order. Le Sillon, founded by Marc Sangnier, distinguished itself in France by its support for the principles of a Christian democratic order. The Sillonists advocated a central role for the laity in achieving both ecclesiastical and social reforms. The members often found themselves at odds with more conservative Catholics who longed for the return of the monarchy and a France defined by traditional class lines. In the years immediately after he left religious life Peter threw himself into the work of the Le Sillon movement. He carefully studied the writings of Sangnier and others who advocated a new Christian personalism. He defined Christian personalism in his usual simple terms.

To be our brother's keeper
is what God wants us to do.
To feed the hungry
at a personal sacrifice
is what God wants us to do.
To clothe the naked
at a personal sacrifice
is what God wants us to do.
To shelter the homeless
at a personal sacrifice
is what God wants us to do.
To instruct the ignorant
at a personal sacrifice
is what God wants us to do.
To serve man for God's sake
is what God wants us to do.[3]

Much of Peter's own thought about the meaning of Christian personalism and the relationship between the Christian Gospel and the socio-economic order was nurtured during this period. In 1906 Peter separated himself from Le Sillon but not from the Christian personalism which inspired it. Sangnier's decision to politicize the movement in hopes of advancing some pragmatic political ambitions apparently soured Peter. In 1909 Peter's life changed dramatically again when he joined thousands of other French citizens and emigrated to Canada. Initially he joined forces with a fellow Frenchman and took advantage of a homesteading offer in the Alberta Province of western Canada. He worked the land for a few years until the death of his partner in a hunting accident. Between this point in his life and his first encounter with Dorothy Day in New York City in late 1932 little is known of Peter's life.[4] For the next two decades he wandered about Canada and the United States. He held a variety of menial jobs while continuing the more important task of working out a clarification of his own Christian social philosophy. In 1925 he worked in Chicago as a French teacher. Sometime during this period he experienced a new religious awakening which deepened his own religious sentiments. Shortly afterward he moved to the New York City area where he found work as a caretaker for a New York City pastor who operated a summer camp for poor children in upstate New York. He traveled to New York City whenever possible to use the available library resources. By the early 1930's Peter was sharing his writings with some Catholic publishers in the hopes of gaining a wider audience for his thoughts about the need for a Christian personalist revolution in the United States. He met George Schuster, editor of *Commonweal,* who encouraged him to share his work with Dorothy Day, a recent convert to Catholicism who was deeply interested in Christian social reform in American society. The first meeting between Peter and Dorothy took place in December of 1932. This chance encounter between a peasant wanderer from southern France and a socialist turned Catholic set the foundation stone for the birth of a new radical social movement within American Catholicism.

At the time of their first meeting Dorothy was already searching for a plan to promote her vision of Catholic social reform in the United States. Just five years earlier she had converted to Catholicism. She brought into the Church a burning desire to reform the economic life of American society and a passionate concern for the poor whom she saw as victims of an oppressive economic system. Her conversion to Catholicism was both satisfying and unsettling. On the one hand, she knew that the Church had to become her home; and yet, it caused her to sever many relationships with her socialist, communist and radical friends with whom she had worked in earlier years. Dorothy was able to leave her friends and colleagues, but she could not abandon the social ideals which she held so deeply.

The first meeting between Peter and Dorothy was not as successful as many imagine.[5] Peter, although gentle of personality and manner, could be very demanding when it came to convincing others to share his vision of Christian social reform. At first Dorothy found Peter overwhelming, and she was not sure that she could be the willing student he hoped for. Nonetheless the relationship endured beyond its rocky start. Years later Dorothy wrote: "He was my master and I was his disciple."[6] Between the fateful day of their first meeting in December of 1932 and Peter's death in 1949 the two were almost inseparable, although the record of the *Catholic Worker* indicates their close bond allowed for significantly different approaches to Christian social reform from time to time.

Peter was convinced that the western world, and the United States in particular, stood in urgent need of fundamental social and economic reforms. He spoke about reform in this way.

> To foster a society
> based on creed
> instead of greed,
> on systematic unselfishness
> instead of systematic selfishness,
> on gentle personalism
> instead of rugged individualism,
> is to create a new society
> within the shell of the old.
> Modern society
> is in a state of chaos.[7]

Only Catholic social philosophy could provide the basis for a genuine reform movement in the economic life of American society. As his first task he set about the process of indoctrinating Dorothy with Catholic social philosophy so that they would be of one mind in the work which lay ahead. Because she was a recent convert to Catholicism, and not well read in the tradition of Catholic social thought, she welcomed Peter's instruction. He introduced her to the classical Christian writers, the work of the modern Catholic personalists like Léon Bloy and Jacques Maritain, and the social thought of the modern Popes.

Although Peter has frequently been characterized as a dreamer, he recognized the need for a practical plan to advance his program for a Christian personalist revolution. He saw the passion in Dorothy's commitment to the Church and to social reform, and he knew that she would serve as a better vehicle than he would in translating his ideas into a meaningful program of economic reform. He frequently referred to himself as the "idea man" and looked to Dorothy to translate his ideas into the fabric of American society.

On May 1, 1933 the budding radical alliance between Dorothy and Peter took shape in the publication of the first issue of the *Catholic Worker*. It marked the birth of a new movement in American Catholicism which has become the training ground for thousands of Catholic social activists for more than half a century. One author has described the Catholic Worker movement in this way. "The Catholic Worker was a radical movement. To define its radicalism, however, is like trying to bottle the morning fog. Day and Maurin were not systematic thinkers. They enunciated principles, lived according to them, and expected others to do the same. The Catholic Worker put no hope in the modern state; it put hope in the community of the sacred; the spiritual was more critical to life than the material; peace was better than war; love in action was superior to love in dreams; the ideals of Christian perfection far surpassed the minimalism of the natural law tradition; personalism outranked pragmatism; and in the end, the primacy of love would redeem history."[8] The publication of the first edition of the *Catholic Worker* was not achieved without some conflict. Peter wanted the new paper to be titled the *Catholic Radical* and he objected strenuously to the pro-labor tone of the first edition. He felt that the tone of the first issue played into the hands of those who advocated socio-economic reform through class conflict. Peter believed that the *Catholic Worker* had to embrace a broader and more encompassing vision, a more radical vision which would give credibility to the need to transform the existing economic order into a new order founded on Catholic social and economic principles. Peter was so annoyed with the first edition of the paper that he absented himself from New York for several weeks. Eventually reconciliation was achieved between himself and Dorothy but not before he insisted that his name be removed from the list of editors. Henceforth he would sign all of his contributions to the *Worker*. This would enable readers to distinguish his Catholic social philosophy from those views in the *Worker* which he did not personally embrace.

Peter's criticism of industrial capitalism in the 1930's and 1940's remains one of the most comprehensive repudiations of capitalism which can be found in the history of American Catholic thought. Few Catholic writers have even approached Maurin's assessment of the absolute incompatibility between the Christian Gospel and industrial capitalism. Simplicity was always a hallmark of his analysis of the socio-economic order. Capitalism embodied a set of values which rendered the individual subservient to the production of wealth. No economic system which placed greater value on the accumulation of wealth than on the dignity of the human person deserved the support of those who claimed to be followers of Jesus Christ. Catholic historian David O'Brien has offered this assessment: "Implicit in Peter Maurin's indictment of industrial capitalism was a perception of many of the problems that disturb contemporary social critics: alienation, loss of a sense of personal participation in community life, the inability to locate and define responsibility amid the complexities of economic and social organization, the cultural inertia produced by the loss of meaning in work."[9] Because his condemnation of capitalism was unequivocal, it received mixed reactions. On the one hand, it was ridiculed by those bold enough to defend capitalism as the embodiment of Catholic economic philosophy. On the other hand, Maurin's thought was applauded by those who shared his belief that the basic tenets of industrial capitalism were incompatible with Catholic economic principles. This peasant wanderer from southern France remains a thorn in the side of American Catholic economic thought, and today many believe that his ideas may deserve more attention than ever before.

Announcer, Not a Denouncer

Peter Maurin saw his Christian vocation as a call to articulate a vision of Catholic socio-economic reform in the midst of American society. Although he was neither unwilling nor unable to point out the gross moral inadequacies of industrial capitalism in light of the message of the Christian Gospel, he felt more comfortable in announcing the social order which should be created out of the shell of the present order. He hoped to outline a plan for economic reform which would capture the attention of others eager to build a new society based upon the Christian Gospel. He believed that other social critics who exerted their energy in condemning the status quo frequently failed to adequately present a positive program for social reconstruction. This would not be a failing of Peter Maurin.

Peter did not believe that Catholics had to scurry about looking for a formula to cure the ills of the socio-economic order. The formula was already present within the Catholic tradition if Catholics were only willing to live out the principles they professed in faith.

> The central act of devotional life
> in the Catholic Church
> is the holy Sacrifice of the Mass.
> The Sacrifice of the Mass
> is the unbloody repetition
> of the Sacrifice of the Cross.
> On the Cross of Calvary
> Christ gave His life to redeem the world.
> The life of Christ was a life of sacrifice.
> The life of a Christian must be
> a life of sacrifice.
> We cannot imitate the sacrifice of Christ
> on Calvary
> by trying to get all we can.
> We can only imitate the sacrifice of Christ
> on Calvary
> by trying to give all we can.[10]

Peter took the simplicity of the Gospels as his starting point. Jesus was more than sufficient as a model for Christian life and the reform of society. Jesus epitomized Christian personalism. His concern for the poor, the outcasts, the oppressed and the weak was the model for Christian living. However, Jesus' life was not the only source for inspiring a Christian social imagination. The faithful Christian tradition spoke of a communitarian Christian personalism which proclaimed the dignity of the human person as the highest value in society. Peter was an avid student of the thought of St. Thomas Aquinas. Here was a vibrant resource for Catholic economic reform. Thomas' writings on property and the relationship between the individual and the common good were ignored in the highly competitive and individualistic ethos of industrial capitalism. The Popes of the modern era, especially Leo XIII and Pius XI, offered a vision for Catholic social and economic reform which was frequently dismissed. And a host of other Catholic writers including Léon Bloy, Jacques Maritain and Charles Péguy provided direction to Catholics who wished to participate in building a new economic order. In a special way Peter believed that St. Francis of Assisi provided a model for Catholic social life. Francis' life demonstrated the Christian liberation which comes from the practice of voluntary poverty. Peter believed that many Catholics were unable to embrace a program of meaningful social and economic reform because of their personal attachment to the material riches of the world which deadened the life of the spirit.

A bourgeois is a man
who tries to be somebody,
by trying to be like everybody
which makes him a nobody.
Catholic bourgeois
try to be
like non-Catholic bourgeois
and think they are
just as good
as non-Catholic bourgeois.[11]

Peter Maurin was an insightful student of socio-economic conditions in American society in the decades of the 1930's and 1940's. Although he recognized the greed of those who were unwilling to concern themselves with the plight of their brothers and sisters, he believed that many people longed for new challenges to carry them beyond the alienation and superficiality of contemporary life. For this reason he repudiated class conflict as a way of achieving the creation of a new economic order. The rich, however, blinded by the bourgeois mentality which rendered them insensitive to the needs of others, were also in need of a new social order. In their own way they were also oppressed by many of the elements of industrial capitalism.

The wealth of Peter Maurin's thought and vision is more to be found in what he "announced" than in what he "denounced." However, an appreciation of his program for social and economic reform is best appreciated against the backdrop of his criticism of contemporary society and culture. What follows is a brief description of a few of the major social ills which characterized his analysis of American society.

Peter viewed the secularism of the modern age as the biggest obstacle to any effort to build a society based on Christian principles. Secularism divorced the material realm of human life both personally and socially from its foundation in the spiritual realm. American society reflected the disunity which resulted when the realm of the spirit and the realm of the material were pulled asunder. Political, social, and economic life, and all the impulses which derive from the human creation of culture, were divorced from their origin in God's creative act. "Maurin's great concern was secularism, the separation of the spiritual from the material, of the Church from political, economic and social life. Society, he felt, by definition required a 'unity of thought,' a common belief in what underlay its life. He aimed at a new synthesis, a restoration of unity to the chaotic modern world by means of an integral Catholicism. The size, complexity, and impersonality of modern life preoccupied Maurin, particularly mass production, which brutalized man. The conditions of modern society destroyed what he regarded as the heart of Christianity, personal responsibility, the need to recognize in every man the image of God and to treat him accordingly."[12] Because of the nature of contemporary society modern man was thrown into a search for meaning which could not be found apart from the life of the Spirit. Capitalist economics treated men like objects of manipulation. It was not an economics grounded in a proper understanding of God's plan for material creation. Peter rejected the secular notion that a just society could be built independently of religious faith. When man strives to build a society independently of his origins in God's creative love only chaos and confusion can result. The privatization of Christian faith apart from the structures of social, economic and political life offered additional evidence of the power of secularism to distort the meaning of the Christian Gospel and faith. Peter saw all Christian faith as social faith. The privatization of Jesus' love represented the corruption of Jesus' love. Unless the redemptive power of Christ's action in human history was experienced in the social realm, the power of Christ's redemption was muted. When Christian faith is privatized so that it no longer has its moorings in the structural life of society it is trivialized. Combating the secularism of American culture requires nothing less than a new socialized Catholicism seeking to imbue the social order with the values of the Gospel. In a new social order Christians would once again take seriously their obligation to care for the poor, to nourish the common good and to foster solidarity among peoples. A socialized Catholic faith will give birth to a politics of service, not domination and manipulation; an economics of sharing, not greed and selfishness; and a social life based on cooperation, not competitiveness and individualism.

The three tragic isms of the modern age—capitalism, totalitarianism and fascism—represented dramatic examples of the consequences which follow when culture and society are torn from their moorings in Christian faith and belief. These three modern evils presented themselves as pathways to man's salvation when in reality true salvation personally and socially could only be found in Jesus Christ. The privatization of Christian faith had contributed to the rise of these modern social evils, and conversely the rise of capitalism, totalitarianism and fascism had accelerated the privatization of Christian faith. Peter saw modern man trapped in a vicious circle. Man's alienation from the transcendent source of his creation had contributed to the rise of capitalism, totalitarianism and facism. These evils now rendered man's divorce from the sacred even more profound.

Maurin regarded man's slavery to capitalism in American society as the greatest source of his alienation. Industrial capitalism was not only an economic system but a mentality, a social imagination which rendered individuals insensitive to the needs of others. By enthroning money as the measure of a person's worth, capitalism undermined the inherent dignity of the human person. Capitalism rendered the poor and the powerless vulnerable to the power of those who refused to recognize the inherent dignity of the human person. The poor became a by-product of a capitalist economy and the rich grew richer as they presided over the exploitation of their fellow human beings.

Peter distinguished between the fact of capitalism, that is, how it operated in the realm of economic production and exchange, and the spirit of capitalism which was bred by the system and contributed to its further entrenchment in society. The characteristic marks of capitalism included a rugged individualism which counseled people to look after their own needs without regard for the needs of their brothers and sisters; a rigid competitiveness which pitted people against one another in the quest for material prosperity regardless of the consequences for others; and its materialism which suggested that the acquisition of material goods was the highest of all human values. In Peter's eyes the failure of capitalism was self-evident in the plight suffered by the poor in American society. Capitalism generated a class of people of no use to the economy. In a capitalist bourgeois society the creation of wealth took precedence over the dignity of human labor. People were expendable in the service of realizing increasingly greater profits. The plight suffered by the non-working poor was only different in degree from the plight suffered by the poor working-class. The poor working-class was similarly made subservient to the production of wealth because capital always took precedence in economic affairs. Throughout his life Peter remained ambivalent about the value of labor unions. He certainly did not share Dorothy's passionate support for the labor movement as an avenue for realizing fundamental economic and social reforms. He regarded the labor movement in America as a by-product of an economic system which was wrongheaded in its very foundations. The labor movement tried to correct some of the gross imbalances between capital and labor, but it was not able to deal with the fundamental causes of the alienation and injustices suffered by the laboring class. This could only be addressed properly by a complete repudiation of capitalism and the creation of a new socio-economic order founded on Christian principles.

> When the workers
> sell their labor
> to the capitalists
> or accumulators of labor
> they allow the capitalists
> or accumulators of labor
> to accumulate their labor.
> And when the capitalists
> or accumulators of labor
> have accumulated so much
> of the workers' labor
> that they do no longer
> find it profitable
> to buy the workers' labor
> then the workers
> can no longer sell their labor
> to the capitalists
> or accumulators of labor.
> And when the workers
> can no longer
> sell their labor

to the capitalists
or accumulators of labor
they can no longer buy
the products of their labor.
And that is what the workers get
for selling their labor.[13]

Often Peter felt that a continuing support for the labor movement, however justified on pragmatic grounds, only served to obscure the real inadequacies of capitalism. Furthermore, it only increased the level of class conflict, further fragmenting the members of society.

Another sign of the moral bankruptcy of industrial capitalism was the growing size of the welfare state and the increasing power of the state in all aspects of social and economic life. The growth of the welfare state enabled the members of society to abandon the poor and the needy, and to throw their personal responsibility for the poor onto the shoulders of an impersonal bureaucracy. Peter looked on the emergence of the welfare state as a dramatic sign of the deterioration of community and concern for the common good. Citizens, even Catholics, were willing to direct the needy to the care of an impersonal state. What could be more in contradiction to Jesus' admonition in the Gospel to practice the works of mercy. In American society the state had become the mercy-worker. Particularly troubling was the fact that Catholics ignored the needs of the poor without realizing that their actions violated their obligations as Christians. This corruption of the Christian imagination represented a sin as grievous as the plight suffered by the poor. To the extent that Catholics were not even willing to support the services provided for the poor by the state, the scandal was only compounded.

In all Peter's writings few themes were more the subject of his analysis than the nature of bourgeois culture. Bourgeois culture represented the consequences of a society which was secularist and capitalist in orientation. Bourgeois culture embodied the shallowest understanding of human life. It was characterized by forms of elitism which reduced millions of people to second-class status; by levels of economic competitiveness which reduced economic life to a jungle affording survival to the fittest alone; by displays of such rigid individualism and self-centeredness that people found it increasingly difficult to think in terms of community and cooperation; and by styles of acquisitiveness which tolerated the impoverishment of the many so that a few could live in affluence. Bourgeois culture was the cultural form of the anti-Christ. In Peter's eyes the greatest tragedy of bourgeois culture was that people, even Catholics, became so caught up in its destructive tendencies that they did not realize it posed an enormous threat to Christian life. It drew people into a form of moral amnesia which rendered them unable to address the needs of their brothers and sisters.

Maurin's Program for Social and Economic Reform

Peter Maurin never harbored the thought that his vision for social and economic reform was uniquely his own. He considered himself more a spokesperson reaffirming the principles of Catholic social teaching than an innovator. A solution to the present economic crisis did not lie in discovering new principles, but in re-establishing the Christian values trampled on by the rise of industrial capitalism.

> The Catholic Worker believes
> in the gentle personalism
> of traditional Catholicism.
> The Catholic Worker believes
> in the personal obligation
> of looking after
> the needs of our brother.
> The Catholic Worker believes
> in the daily practice
> of the Works of Mercy.[14]

A remedy to the existing economic injustices was to be found in a return to the source; a return to Jesus' model in the Gospel; a return to the socio-economic principles extolled by St. Thomas; embracing Christian personalism; and in a return to the teachings of the Popes, especially Leo XIII and Pius XI.

Peter believed that many Catholics were caught off-guard by the rise of secularism and industrial capitalism. As a result of a desire to enjoy the benefits of capitalism, Catholics had severed their ties with the moral principles of the Catholic social tradition. Now Catholics had to reappropriate this rich social tradition and bring its moral insights to bear on existing social and economic structures in American society. Charges that Peter was an anti-intellectual and romantic seeking to flee from the present into an idealized vision of medieval society deserve little credence. He was convinced that industrial capitalism was tragically flawed. By severing itself from its moorings in a Christian understanding of economic life, modern society had taken a fateful turn. This error had to be corrected. The Catholic tradition provided the resources to rebuild the moral foundations of social and economic life.

In describing Peter's program for socio-economic reform a distinction must be made between the principles which shaped his vision and the practical program he proposed. The former requires an understanding of his philosophy of Christian personalism and the relationship Peter envisioned between economic reform and voluntary poverty. The latter requires some attention to his proposal for a threefold program of round-table discussions to stimulate a renewed appreciation of the Catholic social tradition, the creation of houses of hospitality to serve the needs of the poor, and the establishment of farm communes to re-establish the proper relationship between individuals, work and the land. His moral vision and his practical program were interdependent. However, they can be analyzed independently of one another.

Christian personalism was the key to Peter's vision of economic reform. At a time when many economic reformers advocated the need for structural and systemic reforms, Peter's vision seemed naive at first glance. But careful examination reveals its radical implications. The practice of Christian personalism engages each individual in the struggle for economic reform. It does not originate in some abstract realm, but in the lived experience of each individual. The radical transformation of society begins with the radical transformation of each individual.

A personalist
is a go-giver,
not a go-getter.
He tries to give
what he has,
and does not
try to get
what the other fellow has.
He tries to be good

by doing good
to the other fellow.
He is altro-centered,
not self-centered.
He has a social doctrine
of the common good.
He spreads the social doctrine
of the common good
through words and deeds.
He speaks through deeds
as well as words,
for he knows that deeds
speak louder than words.
Through words and deeds
he brings into existence
a common unity,
the common unity
of a community.[15]

What were the main elements of Peter's understanding of Christian personalism? The most fundamental element held that economic reform had to begin with each individual. No effort to build an economic order embodying Catholic values could succeed unless Catholics began to live out these values in their personal lives. If I am anxious to build an economic order which cares for the needs of the poor and the needy, I must care for the poor and the needy. If I want to love Jesus, I must love my neighbor, especially my neighbor in need. Jesus' witness in the Gospels was the model for Peter's Christian personalism. It does not allow me to delegate my Christian responsibilities to others. I must assume personal responsibility for being my brother's keeper.

Christian personalism is not asocial. On the contrary, it is radically communal. As each individual assumes responsibility for the suffering Christ who stands before him, a social environment is created which differs dramatically from an economic order characterized by the individualism, competitiveness and bourgeois spirit of capitalism. The economics of Christian personalism envisions a cooperative economic order which understands that the bounty of God's material creation needs to be placed in the service of the entire community. An economics of Christian personalism re-establishes the proper relationship between the material and the spiritual and it recognizes the primacy of the worker in economic affairs. An economics of Christian personalism places the productive wealth of society in the service of the common good.

In his writings Peter repeatedly underscored the tragic moral flaw of secularism because its spirit severed economic activity from its moorings in Christian faith. An economics of Christian personalism seeks to re-establish the relationship between the religious and the secular in all realms of economic activity. The person is not an instrumental means intended to serve the end of wealth creation. The person is at the center of all the processes of economic life. Peter's vision of Christian personalism had its roots in the Gospel. Jesus offered the model for economic and social life. This conviction was the foundation for his advocacy of voluntary poverty as an appropriate means for achieving the economic transformation of society. The Gospel could not be followed in the abstract. It had to be lived in the concrete. Jesus comforted the poor and made himself one with them in order to demonstrate God's love for all his people. Nothing less is obliged of Jesus' followers today.

The practice of voluntary poverty also frees Christians from an inordinate attachment to the material goods of creation. Voluntary poverty frees the individual from an entrapment to economic goods at the expense of the life of the spirit; it gives rise to the growth of the spirit. At the very least, it provides an opportunity to share the economic goods of creation with others in need.

The world would be better off
if people tried to become better.
And people would become better
if they stopped trying to become better off.
For when everybody tries to become
better off,
nobody is better off.
Everybody would be rich
if nobody tried to become richer.
And nobody would be poor
if everybody tried to be the poorest.
And everybody would be what he ought to be
if everybody tried to be
what he wants the other fellow to be.[16]

In light of Peter's advocacy of voluntary poverty, it is not hard to understand why he abhorred displays of Christian affluence. He was especially troubled by Catholics who attempted to rationalize the discrepancies between the rich and poor in society. Displays of Catholic wealth in the midst of so much human poverty were a source of scandal. Although he affirmed Catholic teaching on the right of private ownership in principle, he was deeply troubled by the fact that many Catholics had lost sight of their stewardship responsibilities. Consequently, wealth was stored up in the hands of a few, even Catholics, at the expense of the common good.

From Peter Maurin's commitment to Christian personalism and voluntary poverty flowed his threefold program for the reconstruction of the economic and social order. The first element of the program is found in his call to establish round-table discussion groups among Catholics throughout the United States in order to give rise to a new awareness of the relationship between Catholic faith and the economic conditions existing in society. Peter was concerned about the crippling power of the bourgeois ideology generated by capitalism. It had the power to corrupt the moral consciousness of Catholics and undermine their ability to understand the relationship between Catholic belief and the socio-economic conditions in society. The establishment of round-table discussions would provide a new vehicle enabling Catholics to break through the prevailing bourgeois ideology. These discussions, attended by lay people, priests and religious, could create a new sense of Christian solidarity in the struggle for economic and social reform in American society. Even non-Catholics, radicals and communists would be invited so that they could appreciate the social program available within the Catholic tradition.

The second element of Peter's program involved the establishment of houses of hospitality in parishes across the country. He regarded this as a new idea, although it was rooted in the medieval church. Houses of hospitality created in order to respond to the needs of the poor, the outcasts of industrial capitalism, would provide an opportunity for the practice of Christian personalism, and they would accord Catholics with an opportunity to serve the needs of the poor.

We need Houses of Hospitality
to give to the rich
the opportunity to serve the poor.
We need Houses of Hospitality

122

to bring the Bishops to the people
and the people to the Bishops.
We need Houses of Hospitality
to bring back to institutions
the technique of institutions.
We need Houses of Hospitality
to show what idealism looks like
when it is practiced.
We need Houses of Hospitality
to bring social justice
through Catholic Action
exercised in Catholic institutions.[17]

At one point Peter wrote a letter to all the Catholic bishops in the United States encouraging them to establish houses of hospitality in every diocese and parish in the country. Although this request never materialized, the Catholic Worker established houses of hospitality in several cities across the United States providing a refuge for the outcasts of society and giving witness to the principles of Christian personalism.

The third element of Peter's program was least realized. It involved the establishment of farm communes. Except for the few farm communes which were established by the Catholic Worker, this element of his program never really developed in a significant way. Peter saw urban life as basically a threat to Catholic life. The growth of large urban industrial centers was a by-product of industrial capitalism. American cities were ill-designed to offer people an opportunity to live the Christian life.

We need Communes
to help the unemployed
to help themselves.
We need Communes
to make scholars out of workers
and workers out of scholars,
to substitute a technique of ideals
for our technique of deals.
We need Communes
to create a new society
within the shell of the old
with the philosophy of the new,

which is not a new philosophy
but a very old philosophy
a philosophy so old
that it looks like new.[18]

Urban life was a symbol of the anti-Christ. Salvation could best be safeguarded by a return to the land. Farm communes not only offered people an opportunity to escape the moral ills posed by urban life, but also they provided an environment fostering the cooperative bonds between people. Peter viewed the individualism of modern society as life-threatening. Communes would offer a new experience of solidarity, a solidarity in keeping with a Catholic understanding of social life.

In addition to freeing people from the ills of urban life farm communes could also re-establish the proper relationship between human life and work. Peter held that human labor should enhance the person's understanding of human life. On farm communes people would work to live and not live to work. Work would be designed to foster solidarity, cooperation, community and a growth in the life of the spirit. Contrary to existing economic conditions, workers on farm communes would not become cogs in a machine. They would be engaged in more creative and fulfilling labors. With few exceptions Peter's hopes for the establishment of farm communes in the United States were never realized. Even his most ardent supporters, including Dorothy, came to see this venture as the most impractical idea of the peasant-dreamer. But Peter himself never abandoned belief in the idea. Perhaps it was his peasant roots which fueled his convictions about the morally transformative power of the land. Perhaps it was simply his inability to see anything positive in urban life. From the perspective of a half century removed, Peter's plan may seem all the more unrealistic. Nonetheless, it continues to attract the attention of those who perceive a close connection between rural and farm life and the rhythms of the Spirit removed from the depersonalizing forces of industrial society.

The Church's Mission

Peter Maurin's relationship with the institutional Church was paradoxical. He was a loyal son of the Church and drew his own vision for social and economic reform from the Catholic tradition. However, at times he was disappointed at the Church's unwillingness or inability to live up to her own rich social tradition. In his relationship with the institutional Church he both loved and cajoled. To those who criticized the Church, he defended her rich social tradition. At the same time he was willing to expose the inconsistencies between what the Church proclaimed and how she lived in society.

> Christ drove the money changers
> out of the Temple.
> But today nobody dares
> to drive the money lenders
> out of the Temple.
> And nobody dares
> to drive the money lenders
> out of the Temple
> because the money lenders
> have taken a mortgage
> on the Temple.
> When church builders build churches
> with money borrowed from money lenders
> they increase the prestige
> of the money lenders.
> But increasing the prestige
> of the money lenders
> does not increase the prestige
> of the Church.[19]

Peter was sustained in these times of trial by his own experience of the Church which he found alive in the life of the Catholic Worker movement and in other efforts of Catholics to live in fidelity to the Gospel.

He repeatedly stated that the Church had no need to develop a new social program in order to address the social and economic ills of modern society. The message was already present in the treasury of the Church's tradition. What was needed was the courage to live the message and tradition. In one of his most well-known Easy Essays Peter spoke about the need for the Church to act courageously.

> Writing about the Catholic Church,
> a radical writer says:
> "Rome will have to do more

than to play a waiting game;
she will have to use
some of the dynamite
inherent in her message."
To blow the dynamite
of a message
is the only way
to make the message dynamic.
If the Catholic Church
is not today
the dominant social dynamic force,
it is because Catholic scholars
have failed to blow the dynamite of the Church.
Catholic scholars
have taken the dynamite
of the Church,
have wrapped it up
in nice phraseology,
placed it in an hermetic container
and sat on the lid.
It is about time
to blow the lid off
so the Catholic Church
may again become
the dominant social dynamic force.[20]

In the past the Church's economic vision had been incorporated in the life of society. The witness of the early Christians provided the model of a Christian community which believed in the works of mercy and actually practiced them in society. Likewise, during the Middle Ages the social and economic life of society was imbued with Christian principles. Peter argued that his program for economic reform was not a novel effort in the history of the Church. Christian history demonstrated the Church's historical ability to shape economic life in harmony with the values of the Gospel. Modern society was under the curse of the ideology of bourgeois capitalism which severed the bonds between economic life and Christian faith. In addition to the economic injustices resulting from the rise of industrial capitalism, Peter saw an equally ominous threat from the bourgeois mentality it generated among Catholics. This imagination stood in contradiction to the Gospel and the Catholic tradition; however, many Catholics were unable to perceive the danger it posed for Christian faith. Through the use of round-table discussions Peter hoped to generate both a new consciousness and a new spirit for economic reform in harmony with Catholic belief and principles.

As an educated Christian Peter was not entrapped in a literalist interpretation of the Scriptures; however, he refused to dilute the values proclaimed by Jesus in the Gospel. Jesus' love for the poor imposed a moral imperative on Christians today which could not be satisfied by the creation of an impersonal state welfare bureaucracy. Jesus' admonitions about the dangers inherent in the accumulation of excessive wealth had to be taken seriously by Catholics. Jesus' willingness to suffer and sacrifice on behalf of those who were exploited and oppressed needed to find re-affirmation in the life of the Church today.

What we give to the poor
for Christ's sake
is what we carry with us
when we die.[21]

When the Gospel message is muted, the Church loses her ability to promote meaningful social and economic reform.

Peter viewed with equal seriousness the Church's obligation to promote the teachings of St. Thomas on economic life. He almost despaired at times because the Church's rich tradition concerning the common good had been abandoned by a Church entrapped in the rigid individualism generated by industrial capitalism. Likewise, the Church's teaching about the responsibilities associated with private ownership of property had to be reaffirmed.

All the land
belongs to God.
God wants us
to be our brother's keeper.
Our superfluous goods
must be used
to relieve the needs
of our brother.
What we do for our brother
for Christ's sake

127

is what we carry with us
when we die.
This is what the poor are for,
to give to the rich
the occasion to do good
for Christ's sake.
To use property
to acquire more property
is not the proper use
of property.
It is a prostitution
of property.[22]

All too often the Church had exercised enormous energies in defending the right of private ownership without being equally concerned about the obligations of Christian stewardship imposed on owners of private wealth. This shortcoming tended to undermine the credibility of Church teaching. He also saw the need for a more forceful presentation of the economic thought of Leo XIII and Pius XI in American society. Peter often expressed dismay that the American Church exerted so much energy in condemning communism and totalitarianism while remaining almost silent about the Church's criticism of capitalism. It was not enough for the Church to condemn the evils of the existing economic order. The Church had a parallel responsibility to propose a new vision of a just economic order.

Whether with respect to the power of the Gospel and Jesus' witness, the vitality of the Church's rich social tradition, or the economic thought of Leo XIII and Pius XI, Peter remained convinced that the Church held the seeds for the social revolution which was so desperately needed in American society. Catholics had no need to look to the wisdom of the secular sages for a vision of social reform. It was already present in the life of the Church. What was needed was for Catholics to be living anew the vibrancy of the social message already in their hands.

Notes

1. William D. Miller, *A Harsh and Dreadful Love* (New York, 1973), p. 17.
2. Peter Maurin, *Easy Essays* (Chicago, 1961), pp. 110–11.
3. Ibid., p. 58.
4. See Arthur Sheehan, *Peter Maurin: Gay Believer* (New York, 1959).
5. See William D. Miller, *Dorothy Day* (New York, 1982), chapter 9.
6. John Cogley, *A Canterbury Tale* (New York, 1976), pp. 11–12.
7. *Easy Essays,* pp. 109–10.
8. Jay P. Dolan, *The American Catholic Experience* (New York, 1985), p. 411.
9. David A. O'Brien, *American Catholics and Social Reform* (New York, 1968), pp. 19–20.
10. *Easy Essays,* p. 45.
11. Ibid., p. 90.
12. O'Brien, p. 195.
13. *Easy Essays,* p. 40.
14. Ibid., pp. 76–77.
15. Ibid., pp. 116–17.
16. Ibid., p. 37.
17. Ibid., p. 7.
18. Ibid., p. 36.
19. Ibid., p. 3.
20. Ibid.
21. Ibid., p. 123.
22. Ibid., pp. 167–68.

PAUL HANLY FURFEY

⌣

Personalist Economics

Paul Hanly Furfey, priest and lifelong professor of sociology at Catholic University of America in Washington, D.C., has made a significant contribution to American Catholic economic thought. Regrettably few scholars have given his life the attention it deserves.[1] One reason which may partially explain this lack of interest was Furfey's unequivocal condemnation of capitalism. In 1936 he wrote: "All Christians must acknowledge that capitalism in its modern form is evil."[2] He held that Catholics had a moral obligation to reject the promises and rewards of an economic system built upon greed, selfishness, materialism and a denial of God's dominion over all creation. Throughout his career he challenged his fellow Catholics to join together in building a new economic order embodying the values proclaimed by Jesus in the Gospel. " . . . we have the power—through the insight which is ours by faith and through the supernatural graces which are ours—to build a new world, strong and clean and breathlessly beautiful, a world whose common purpose is but to aid man to his supernatural end, a world which shall be heaven on earth and which can find its perfect fulfillment and consummation only in the blessed society of the world to come."[3] At a time when a majority of Catholics either adopted a reformist attitude toward capitalism or proclaimed its superiority to any other economic system, Paul Hanly Furfey remained adamant about the evils of capitalism in America and its incompatibility with Catholic moral teaching.

The scope of Furfey's thought makes it difficult to offer a succinct summary. However, some principal concerns deserve particular mention. First, his commitment to the poor remained a constant throughout his labors. Decades before President Johnson's War on Poverty or the publication of Michael Harrington's *The Other America,* Furfey was a staunch advocate for the poor in America. He used his academic talents to identify the relationship between the plight of the poor and the inherent inability of capitalism to foster and protect the rights of the individual and the common good. Second, he analyzed how the spirit of capitalism bred a destructive individualism into the social fabric of American culture, rendering citizens insensitive to the needs of the common good. He always thought in terms of community. Without an enriching community life the well-being of the person is jeopardized. And, finally, the danger of social conformism was a concern which frequently drew his attention. In *The Mystery of Iniquity* (1941) he expressed alarm about the growing number of Catholics who proclaimed allegiance to the Church and her teachings and yet ignored the moral imperatives of the Gospel in social and economic life. "Catholics can never make their rightful contribution to social reform until they set a high price on the dogmatic truths which are theirs. These are the truths which Christ himself brought to the world. These are the truths which countless martyrs lived so well that they died rather than abandon the smallest of them. Without these truths a basic cure for the ills of society is impossible. To overlook them, to abandon them even in part, or to underemphasize them is to render ourselves ineffective against the mystery of iniquity. To hold them uncompromisingly, without conforming to the spirit of the world to the slightest degree, is a sure road to success."[4]

Paul Hanly Furfey's ability to combine a life of scholarship with advocacy for those who suffered economic injustice made his career special. In 1934 he became one of the earliest supporters of Dorothy Day, Peter Maurin and the Catholic Worker movement. And he defended their efforts against attacks from other Catholics. He joined with a colleague in the 1930's in establishing Il Poverello House and Fides House in the slums of Washington, D.C. as hostels for the poor and the homeless of that city. He supported Baroness Catherine de Hueck in her work at Harlem Friendship House in New York City. And he gave encouragement to those involved in efforts to promote the Cooperative Movement. In the 1960's he founded Emmaus House in Washington, D.C. as a center for Catholic resistance to the war in Vietnam. These activities afforded him an opportunity to balance his intellectual pursuits in theology and sociology with efforts to promote social and economic reforms designed to better the conditions of the oppressed poor in American society.

Msgr. Furfey's scholarly work should also be given proper recognition. Between 1936 when he wrote *Fire and Earth* and the 1978 publication of *Love and the Urban Ghetto* he published several other books including *Three Theories of Society* (1937), *The Mystery of Iniquity* (1941), *The Morality Gap* (1969) and *The Respectable Murderers*

(1972), as well as numerous scholarly articles in the *American Catholic Sociological Review, Theological Studies* and the *Catholic Biblical Quarterly*. Prior to 1936 he published several scholarly sociological studies and in the 1960's his articles on poverty were applauded as significant contributions to urban studies in America.

As is frequently the case with scholars whose work spans more than half a century, Furfey's thought underwent a series of developments. This growth reflected a blend of continuity and change. In 1926 he earned his doctoral degree in sociology from the Catholic University of America. Between this time and the mid-1930's he regarded himself as a liberal sociologist and social reformer. He was confident that the empirical tools available to the sociologist could eradicate the most glaring social ills in society. After 1932 he no longer regarded himself as a "liberal" nor was he as confident about the ability of the social sciences to reform society. From this point forward Furfey espoused the cause of Catholic radicalism. He viewed the existing socio-economic order as morally bankrupt. Only the creation of a new economic order built on Christian faith could alleviate the social and economic problems in American society. In his final book published in 1978, *Love and the Urban Ghetto,* Furfey described himself as a Christian revolutionist. He issued an urgent call to all Americans to use their social and political power to dethrone capitalism and create a new economic order.

In his movement from Christian liberalism to Christian radicalism, and finally to Christian revolutionism, Furfey's thought changed and developed, and yet a number of his primary concerns remained constant. These elements represent the core of his contribution to American Catholic economic thought. He never wavered in his conviction that capitalism was morally bankrupt. Unless checked the ethos of self-centered individualism and materialism generated by modern capitalism would continue to undermine the social fabric of American society and fragment the bonds of human solidarity. Catholic teaching offered a vision for social and economic reform. If Catholics in America were willing to boldly embrace Jesus' Gospel and the social principles of the Church and model their lives after the example of the saints of the Christian tradition, meaningful social and economic reforms would follow. The moment for decisiveness was at hand. Catholics in America faced a fundamental choice. One course obliged fidelity to the Gospel and Jesus' love for the poor. The other represented a surrender to the allure of riches and worldly security. According to

Furfey the proper choice was clear enough. St. Matthew's Gospel revealed the challenge. " . . . it is clear that the famous eschatological passage in the twenty-fifth chapter of St. Matthew's Gospel is not a literary extravagance but a highly exact dogmatic text. When Christ shall say in the last day: 'I was thirsty and you gave me to drink; I was a stranger and you took me in; I was in prison and you came to me' (Mt 25:35–36), He will be speaking a literal truth, since acts performed for the love of God in our neighbor are also acts of love of God himself."[5]

Monsignor Furfey's Community

Appreciating Furfey's criticism of American society, especially his condemnation of capitalism, requires an examination of the influences which shaped his life and thought. He has assisted us in this regard with the publication of three autobiographical essays. The first appears in a chapter of his book *The Morality Gap* (1969) entitled "Experience with Personalism,"[6] the second "From Catholic Liberalism to Radicalism"[7] appeared in *The American Ecclesiastical Review* (1976), and the third is an unpublished essay entitled "The Light at the End of the Tunnel."[8] Some additional autobiographical reflections can also be found in his last book, *Love and the Urban Ghetto.*[9]

Early in his career Furfey was deeply influenced by his colleagues at Catholic University of America, especially Msgr. John A. Ryan, author of *The Living Wage*, William Kerby, author of *The Social Mission of Charity*, and Thomas V. Moore. He worked closely with these men at the university and the National Catholic School of Social Service. Although he eventually came to differ with Ryan and others in his own approach to social and economic reform, their presence accorded Furfey the experience of a vibrant community of scholars deeply committed to social and economic justice based upon Catholic faith and teachings. His own words tell the story: "In the 1920's and during the early 1930's the most important focus of Catholic social thought was undoubtedly on the Catholic University campus. It was an exciting place to be. There was present a group of men who combined a deep faith in the Church's social ideal with an expertise in the behavioral sciences. The ends were supernatural, but they knew how to use natural means. They had a deep faith, coupled with a keen perception of current reality."[10]

In 1932 Furfey traveled to Germany to study medicine for a year.

This experience changed his life. On his departure for Germany he was confident that the social sciences would enable sociologists to address and remedy the social problems which plagued American society. His outlook was optimistic. He considered himself a liberal social reformer. His experience in Europe undermined the optimism which previously had characterized his thought. No longer was he as confident that the social sciences held the key to eradicating the social ills which plagued American society. Furfey later wrote of the experience: "In the meantime, something else was going on inside me, something more subtle and difficult to describe. I was becoming conscious of beauty in a strange, new way. Whenever I could get away from that exciting medical school, I immersed myself in concerts, operas, art museums. I came to realize that beauty was a reality. Moreover, it was a reality that could not be explained in scientific terms. I felt that I was becoming acquainted with a whole new order of reality. And of course this new order included ethical beauty. It was something beyond science. Great deeds cannot be explained in terms of neurology and endocrinology. In 1932, I returned from my wonderful year in Europe, somewhat confused, but perhaps with more insight into reality."[11]

The next significant event in his life was his encounter with Dorothy Day, Peter Maurin and the Catholic Worker in New York. "The thing that overwhelmed me about Dorothy Day, Peter Maurin, and their colleagues was their conviction that the New Testament ought to be taken literally. Christ had warned against the danger of riches, so the Catholic Worker group lived in voluntary poverty. Their house was rundown, shabby, and less than spotlessly clean. Their food and clothing were very plain and simple. Christ had said that it was the Christian's strict duty to give food and drink to the hungry and the thirsty, to clothe the naked, to harbor the harborless; and these were precisely the things the group was doing. Christ preached universal love. We must find him in all men, even the most humble. It was touching to see the tenderness, utterly unmixed with any trace of condescension, with which the Catholic Worker staff treated the pathetic, broken-down, rejected men and women who came to them for help."[12]

Furfey's first meeting with Dorothy and Peter was the beginning of a lifelong friendship. He considered the Catholic Worker movement one of the most viable means available to promote the social and economic reforms so sorely needed in American society. Shortly after first meeting Dorothy he assisted a colleague at the university, Gladys

Sellew, in establishing Il Poverello House in Washington. The house served the needs of the city's poor and homeless. He actively engaged in the work of the house by serving meals and preparing lodging for those in need. "Living down there gave insights that could never be learned from books. And it was an unforgettable experience in Christian charity. It was very beautiful."[13] He was also attracted to the work of Fr. Virgil Michel, O.S.B., the Benedictine liturgist and social activist. Michel's writings about the relationship between the liturgy and social reform, and his description of the social significance of the Church as the mystical body of Christ, pointed in the same direction as Furfey's own thoughts about social and economic reform.

As his interest in the Catholic Worker movement increased, and his work in Washington's ghetto took on more significance, Furfey became increasingly interested in the Christian personalism espoused by the French philosopher Emmanuel Mounier. He was especially attracted to its emphasis on the need for voluntary poverty as a pathway to economic reform. It profoundly shaped his own thinking. "The prudent, easy way of reaching Heaven, therefore, is to be really poor. This does not necessarily imply destitution, but it does imply a willingness to put aside whatever interferes with man's true end. This is a hard saying, indeed, but it is an ordinary condition for success in supernatural social reform."[14] He was also encouraged by the work of Catholic journalists like Norman McKenna and Richard Deverall whose publication *Christian Front* advocated fundamental social and economic reforms in American society. In 1938 Furfey's continuing interest in Christian personalism and its application to social and economic reforms in America led him to Europe once again. He visited the headquarters of the Young Christian Workers in Brussels and he observed the work of the Compagnes under the direction of Abbé Remillieux in Lyons, France. After his return to the United States, his collaborator at Catholic University, Mary Elizabeth Walsh, decided to purchase a house in Washington, D.C. to serve the poor and give witness to the Christian obligation to care for those in need. He assisted her in this effort and in 1941 Fides House was opened. In 1949 Archbishop Boyle was so impressed with the work of Fides House that he donated a larger house to increase the efforts of the members of the Fides House community. Furfey continued this work until 1958 when other responsibilities obliged him to resign his position.

His admiration for Pope Pius XI's encyclical *Quadragesimo Anno* (1931) led to Furfey's interest in the Cooperative Movement. He traveled to St. Francis Xavier University in Antagonish, Nova Scotia, a training and educational center for the cooperative movement. In Reserve Mines he met with Fr. James Thompkins who had already begun to apply the principles of *Quadragesimo Anno* to farming, fishing, small industries and grain cooperatives. The work he observed convinced him of the possibility of creating an economy based upon cooperation and solidarity between people. Writing about the possibility of creating a cooperative economic order Furfey said: "This is, of course, a very radical proposal. It would involve the abandonment of modern capitalism in its present form, but it is a plan very familiar in Catholic economic thought, being, in a sense, the Church's official program."[15]

In 1968 Paul Hanly Furfey was already seventy-six years old. However, his career as a social activist was not over. He founded Emmaus House in Washington, D.C. as a center for Catholic resistance to the war in Vietnam. The war was a dramatic example of the consequences which result when society's social priorities were distorted by economic interests. In 1974 at the age of eighty-two he traveled to Latin America to learn more about liberation theology and the efforts of Catholics to promote economic justice and alleviate the economic oppression of the Latin American people. Impressed with the work of "liberation theology" and the formation of "base communities," he proposed that the American Church had much to learn from her sister Church in Latin America.

Few scholars in the history of the American Catholic Church have shown such an ability to combine a life of scholarship with social activism. A few commentators have pointed out that Furfey had two careers: one in the classroom and library, another in the streets. No other description of his life is more appropriate. The vibrancy of his thought was rooted in the fact that he never allowed himself to grow old intellectually. Although he never abandoned his interest in sociology, or his commitment to the philosophy of Christian personalism which inspired him in the 1930's, he welcomed with equal enthusiasm the Second Vatican Council. In his own work emphasizing the primacy of Scripture, the importance of the Church's social teachings and the relationship between the liturgy and social reform, he anticipated many of the achievements of Vatican II. Today the National Conference of Catholic Bishops is regarded by many people as a moral force for social and economic reform in American society, especially with respect to its recent pastoral letters on war and peace and the need to create a more just economic order. More than half a century ago Paul Hanly Furfey was advocating this posture as the proper role of the Church in the midst of society.

Furfey's Critique of Capitalism

In the mid-1930's Paul Hanly Furfey was one of the harshest Catholic critics of capitalism in America. His condemnation was unequivocal. He paid particular attention to the consequences of capitalism on the poor and the powerless members of society. A condemnation of capitalism was a major theme in his first book *Fire on Earth* published in 1936 and it remained an important theme in his last book published four decades later, *Love and the Urban Ghetto*. The year 1937 saw the publication of his second major book, *Three Theories of Society*. Here he outlined the reasons for his moral condemnation of capitalism. He likened the nature of capitalism to a Positivist Society and found its spirit deeply ingrained in American culture. The economic ethos of American society promotes an understanding of personal and social life at odds with the values of the Christian Gospel. In a Positivist Society the success-ideal becomes the sole object of people's worship and the meaning of human life as intended by the Creator is distorted.

Furfey identified a number of characteristics of Positivist Society, revealing its incompatibility with a Catholic understanding of social and economic life. First, Positivist Society is essentially materialistic in nature. The accumulation of wealth is looked upon as the highest goal in human life. "To begin with, it is clear that by and large the success-class has an irrational love of money."[16] Members of a Positivist Society place their economic self-interest above any other values. Second, American Positivist Society nurtures ego-centeredness. People look upon others as instrumental means to serve their own ends. Relationships are viewed in terms of expediency. When they no longer serve economic interests they are discarded. In a Positivist Society the intrinsic value of the person has no place. Third, Positivist Society is built upon an ethos of competitiveness. It proclaims the "survival of the fittest" and defends this philosophy as the law of economic life. "The result is that the young man who wishes to 'succeed' must put out of his life everything which would interfere with his efficiency as a money-making machine."[17] In this highly competitive environment human rights must be earned. Those unable to protect their own interests ought not look to others for assistance. Finally, Positivist Society is morally untenable because it is rooted in a secular philosophy which denies man's transcendent nature and the existence of a benevolent God who invites people to participate in building the kingdom of God.

The success-ideal generated by the spirit of capitalism is the idol of American Positivist Society. It is the most obvious sign of its moral bankruptcy. The worship of the success-ideal is a logical consequence of a capitalist economy which rewards people on the basis of their economic worth. In a Positivist Society those with material wealth are valued. Those without economic power are disposable. "The modern success-class looks down on the lower socio-economic groups and despises them as shiftless, unambitious, degraded, criminal; but can the morals of the success-class stand close inspection?"[18] The success-ideal generated by capitalism produces a spirit as destructive as the economic system itself. This spirit has the power to capture the social imagination of the people and to exercise a power convincing people that the values of the Positivist Society are pre-eminent in social life. "It is this class with its meanness and its courage, its selfishness, its altruism, and its complicated etiquette, from which our modern civilization takes its character. For not only does the success-class regulate its own life according to the success-culture, but by its power of controlling society it tends to direct the whole trend of modern civilization towards this same mass culture. This directive process is partly unconscious; for by acting as an ideal to the rest of society, successful men diffuse from their own customs, their own scale of values, their own principles, through the rest of society. Thus, the success-class gives society its telos."[19] Furfey even identified the ability of this spirit to capture the minds of Christian religious leaders and distort their ability to preach the Gospel of Jesus Christ in word and deed. The bourgeois spirit of American capitalism can corrupt the moral conscience of a people. It can lead the selfish to regard themselves as benevolent and the godless to think of themselves as devoutly religious.

Paul Hanly Furfey was especially concerned about the impact of capitalism on the poor and the powerless in society. Positivist Society, as demonstrated by the Great Depression, subjected millions of people to deprivations of every sort. The existence of a sub-proletariat in American society was neither an accident nor an aberration. It was the logical consequence of an economic system devoid of the ability to recognize the inherent worth of the human person. In Positivist

Society the poor are not deserving of consideration because they have failed to achieve success in the economic realm. Members of a Positivist Society do not have the ability to feel empathy for those in need. "The success-ideal by its very nature involves the desire to have more than the next man."[20] At times the economic elite may throw crumbs to the poor, but they will never make room for the poor at their table of affluence. "These Men of Measured Mercy control our economic system. They take more than their proportional share of the profits."[21] The existence of a permanent class of poor is a characteristic mark of capitalism in America.

Positivist Society is hostile to the creation of meaningful community in a manner faithful to the Christian Gospel. The rich may tolerate a shadow of community in order to calm those who are denied access to economic well-being, but they will never agree to temper the pursuit of their own economic self-interest for the sake of the common good. Communities are devoid of real substance. "The success-class is unidealistic: Its members confer benefits on society, but insist on being well paid for doing so. The success-culture as a whole is merely an unheroic *via media* between virtue and vice."[22] A commitment to the creation of true community in the economic realm is an admission that the goods of material creation are intended by God for the enjoyment and benefit of all. American Positivist Society cannot agree to this proposition. The lack of community in American life increases alienation, despair and brokenness in people's lives. Only the creation of a new economic order will overcome these afflictions.

Furfey consistently refused to align himself with those in the Catholic community who held out hope for the reformability of capitalism. Here he differed with his friend and colleague Msgr. John A. Ryan. Unlike most other social critics of American society Furfey did not look upon the Depression in the 1930's as an aberration to an otherwise acceptable economic system. He saw the Depression as a natural consequence of the materialism, individualism, competitiveness and secularism of Positivist Society. He believed that reformist Catholics were only fooling themselves in thinking that capitalism could be brought into harmony with Catholic teaching and principles. Among the sources for his own economic vision Furfey looked to Pope Pius XI's *Quadragesimo Anno* (1931) as a support for his own social and economic vision. He found in Pius' encyclical arguments which supported his contention that the nature of modern capitalism was too far removed from the tenets of Catholic teaching to be worthy of support. Economic justice required a transformation of the present order and the creation of a new economic order.

Sources of Transformation

Furfey's encounter with Dorothy Day and Peter Maurin in 1934 represented a significant turning point in his life, and it profoundly influenced his approach to social and economic reform. Two years earlier his studies and travel in Europe had undermined his confidence in the ability of the social sciences alone to cure the ills of society. Although he never abandoned his respect for sociology and its empirical methodology, he reached the conclusion in 1934 that a transformation of American society, and the eradication of its social evils, required something more profound than what the social sciences alone could offer.

He believed that the transformation of society and the creation of a just economic order had to be built upon the foundation of Christian faith. The great tragedy of Positivist Society was its failure to understand the transcendent meaning of human life. The shallowness of Positivist Society was demonstrated by its inability to focus the attention of people on anything more than the most mundane values. "When we examine the pleasures implied by the success-ideal, money, power, prominence, we find that they characteristically lead to attainment satisfaction than to post-attainment satisfaction. We conclude therefore that the success-ideal is only superficially satisfactory. It is not satisfying in the deepest sense."[23] Christian faith, on the other hand, offers the members of society an opportunity to reflect on the meaning of social life in light of man's transcendent nature. The creation of a just society requires an act of faith. Christian symbols reveal the mystery of man's redemption and provide insight into the meaning of social life. They disclose the communal nature of man's existence. "In a society founded on Christian faith cooperation and common love become infinitely deep . . . such a society is welded together by the fire of divine love."[24] He argued that unless the members of society embrace a supernatural understanding of social life no meaningful economic reforms were possible. Belief in the Gospel of Jesus Christ can inspire the members of society to overcome selfishness, materialism and greed in favor of the creation of a just social and economic order.

Furfey looked to a variety of sources for inspiration in the work of building a just society. The Scriptures held a special place, especially the witness of Jesus in the Gospels. Catholics in America, dedicated to the struggle for economic justice, had to see in Jesus' life a model for the work that lay ahead. "I think we can never meditate enough upon the fact that He chose to be born in a stable. What an insult this was to the standards of the privileged classes. He conspicuously chose those things which they despised. He conspicuously rejected those things which they loved, those things which they spent their lives to get. He chose to be born poor, to live poorly, to be known as a peasant, an artisan, a man of the poor."[25] The example of the early Christians who held material goods in common for the sake of the kingdom also deserved attention. And the saints who shaped their lives in faithfulness to the Gospel offer insight into the proper path to social reform. "If we wish to see ideal social Catholicism in action, then we should turn to the lives of the saints. The lives of these men and women have been approved by the Church, after mature consideration, as examples of the practice of Christian virtue to a heroic degree. Their lives form the textbook of Catholic social action, just as the sources of Revelation form our textbook of Catholic social theory."[26] Finally, the social teaching of the Church offers a significant program for social and economic reform, and yet all too often it was ignored by Catholics in America. Furfey believed that the Scriptures, the example of the saints, the model of the early Christians and the social principles of Catholic teaching offered the supernatural basis for the creation of a just society. Catholics simply needed the courage to embrace the social teaching available to them.

In Part III of *Three Theories of Society* Furfey described Pistic Society as a model of a society built on faith in Jesus and his Gospel. Pistic Society differs dramatically from Positivistic Society. The members of Pistic Society accept the transcendent meaning of personal and social life and shape their lives accordingly. "When God reveals a truth to man, this truth often is one otherwise unattainable by the human mind. Divine faith is thus a wholly new approach to reality, and a Pistic society, one founded on divine faith, is a wholly new type of society."[27] The members of Pistic Society seek to mold social and economic life in fidelity to the truths available through the rich symbols of the Christian tradition. Such a society foreshadows the coming of the kingdom of God and it stands in opposition to the rule of Satan revealed in Positivist Society. All the members are valued as children of God and treated accordingly.

The fabric of Pistic Society influences every aspect of social life, but no aspect more profoundly than the economic realm. It infuses economic activity with a supernatural meaning. In a Pistic Society the place of materiality is transformed in order to serve the purpose intended by the Creator. In a Positivist Society, characterized by American capitalism, the economic realm is given priority in human life. In a Pistic Society economics is made subservient, designed essentially to enhance the dignity of persons and foster communal bonds between people. In a society grounded in Christian faith economics becomes a cooperative economics in service of building up the kingdom of God. The materialism, individualism and competitiveness which characterize Positivist Society are replaced with a new economic order based upon human solidarity and respect for the common good. The Eucharist is the central symbol of a new economic order in Pistic Society. "The Mass re-presents the Sacrifice of Calvary. The devout faithful who assist in the proper spirit must unite themselves with this sacrifice, must repeat, in a sense, the act of Christ by offering their own personal sacrifices and sufferings also for the love of man. Thus, in the bold words of St. Paul, they supply what is wanting in the sufferings of Christ, not, of course, in the sense that anything was lacking in the perfect sacrifice of the Cross, but in the sense that by participating actively in this sacrifice, they become fit instruments to spread the benefits of the Cross to their fellow citizens."[28] The celebration of the Eucharist should flow into the structure of economic relationships; it should become the measuring rod in evaluating the quality of economic relationships.

How does Furfey propose to create Pistic Society in the midst of American society? Some ambivalence can be found in his response. In a certain sense Pistic Society is already present in American culture through the presence of the Catholic Church. " . . . the Church constitutes a Pistic Society within the larger Positivistic Society of the modern world."[29] As a Pistic Society in the midst of American culture the Church has the responsibility to act as a leaven transforming culture and awakening others to God's intentions for society. Furfey recognized that at times the Church's mission as a Pistic Society within the larger society has been compromised. In some instances the Church has even taken on the face of a Positivist Society. "It is vain to seek a logical explanation for the existence of Catholic conformism. The phenomenon cannot be explained by logic. It can be explained only in terms of cowardice. It requires unusual courage the conformist lacks, so he tries to run with the hare and hunt with the hounds."[30]

142

Despite these occasional failures, Furfey believed that Christ sustains the Church and invites her members to participate in the transformation of society.

Furfey's attraction to the Catholic Worker movement was linked in part to his belief that the movement itself represented a kind of Pistic Society calling both the Church and American culture to a new faithfulness to the Christian Gospel. "Association with the Catholic Worker group was a very stimulating experience. We felt that Catholic thought was being reinterpreted in a more valid way, a way closer to the spirit of the New Testament. Then, too, we were conscious of being part of a new sort of movement, a personalist movement, which seemed a much better vehicle for social action than older Catholic mass movements, which now appeared to us dull and flaccid. The atmosphere of our talks and meeting was exciting and we were shipmates on a common voyage of discovery."[31] Recurring frequently in Furfey's writings is an awareness that the Church can easily lose sight of her vocation to be a leaven in society. This led him to speak frequently about the danger of Catholic conformism which threatens the vitality of Christian faith in America. The Church fails to fulfill her vocation when she surrenders to the seductions of the world. In his book *The Mystery of Iniquity* Furfey paid particular attention to the struggle underway between the kingdom of God and the kingdom of Satan. Too frequently, he asserts, the Church loses sight of the fact that Satan lurks in society intent on building obstacles to the realization of the kingdom of God. The struggle between the kingdom of God and the kingdom of Satan should not be underestimated or ignored. The Church, as a Pistic Society in the midst of culture, can also fail in her vocation by placing too much emphasis on the world to come. When the Church acts in a way which is perceived as apolitical and asocial, important economic relationships are ignored, and the Church fails to correctly understand the intensity of God's interest in the dynamics of human history. When this occurs the Church compromises her ability to bring society into harmony with the truths of Christian faith. This failure is no less grievous than when the Church surrenders to the values of Positivist Society.

Paul Hanly Furfey's theological vision anticipated many of the reforms of the Church at the Second Vatican Council. Clearly this was the case in his understanding of the place of Scripture both in the life of the Church and in the struggle to create a just society. Here again he was influenced in his own thinking by the place accorded the Scriptures in the theology of the Catholic Worker. The creative literalism of the Catholic Worker opened his eyes. If we want a blueprint for a just society, we need only look to the Scriptures. The Gospels tell us about our Christian obligations toward the poor, and we have the example of Jesus as our model. The Scriptures give us a model of community in which the common good takes precedence over the whims and excesses of those who claim the right to control the destiny of others. Jesus tells us about the danger of riches which all too often blind us from seeing the face of God in the needy who surround us. The Scriptures offer us a moral vision which can provide the foundation for a just society. People of faith need the confidence to turn to the Scriptures as a model for personal and social transformation. In 1974 Furfey traveled to Latin America in order to better understand the scriptural foundations of its "liberation theology." Four decades earlier, however, he was already exploring the foundations of a "liberation theology" for American society.

Furfey recognized that the transformation of American society required more than simply a renewed reliance on the Christian Scriptures. The philosophy of Christian personalism, as presented by Emmanuel Mounier and others, made available important insights into the creation of a just society. Personalist action works as a leaven promoting the transformation of society. It invites Catholics to live the Gospel in a simple, yet dramatic fashion. If I choose to be a follower of Christ, I will place myself in touch with the poor as Jesus did. I will embrace a life of voluntary poverty both to express my solidarity with the poor and to give witness to my own awareness that riches can blind me from seeing God's intentions for society. Furfey considered people like Dorothy Day, Peter Maurin, Fr. James Thompkins and Catherine de Hueck to be models of Christian personalist action. They were models of men and women building a Pistic Society in the midst of American culture. Personalist action, however, was not restricted to those who lived the Gospel in heroic fashion like Dorothy Day. It was the vocation of every member of the Church. Personalist action was an invitation to live the religious meaning of every kind of work and profession. Its aim was to disclose the religious meaning of all social, cultural, political and economic activity.

In 1943 Pope Pius XI issued his famous encyclical, *The Mystical Body of Christ.* Earlier in 1936 Furfey dedicated an entire chapter of *Fire on Earth* to exploring the social meaning of the Church as the mystical body of Christ. For Furfey the mystical body provided a central Christian symbol revealing the face of Christian economics. "If the fact of the mystical body constitutes an intimate bond between Christ, the Head, and ourselves, the members, it must also unite us most intimately with each other . . . as a matter of fact, St. Paul explicitly declares that this mutual relationship exists. 'If one member suffers anything, all the members suffer with it; or if one member glory, all the members rejoice with it' (1 Cor 12:26)."[32] An economic order built on a belief in the mystical body of Christ reflects an economic system which respects the dignity of every person. It regards the economic activity as a way of fostering human solidarity. It is an economics which places the natural resources of God's creation in the service of social justice. It is an economics which looks upon economic activity as a way of giving praise to God the Father. In Positivist Society the reality of the mystical body of Christ is denied. In Pistic Society the mystical body is affirmed and becomes the basis for the organization of economic life.

In his writings Furfey never offered a detailed blueprint for the transformation of society or for the creation of a just economic order. He was more interested in promoting a theological vision which could serve as the foundation for a new socio-economic order. However, he was very supportive of Pope Pius XI's encyclical *Quadragesimo Anno,* and he was especially encouraged with the emphasis which Pius placed on the creation of a new cooperative economic order. Although he did not commit himself to this approach to the exclusion of other alternatives, he did have special sympathy for the values which provided the basis of the cooperative movement. They complemented the values of his own Christian personalist philosophy.

Strategies for Transformation

A careful review of Furfey's work reveals an ambivalence in his thought about how Catholics in American society can best contribute to the creation of a new socio-economic order. Occasionally his thought even seems contradictory. Sometimes he appears to counsel Catholics simply to separate themselves completely from all aspects of social life which threaten and undermine the values which Jesus proclaimed in the Gospel. In these instances we hear him saying that although Catholics are in the world, they should not be a part of the world. At other times he contends that political action can significantly advance the goals of the Gospel. In these instances he suggests that

Catholics should become involved in the political process. In his later writings Furfey seems to emphasize this approach more consistently but the ambivalence remained nonetheless. Although he insisted that Catholics not become involved in the world to the detriment of their religious vocations, he certainly did not counsel a posture of despair or an attitude of passive resignation to the evils of the world. In this context he spoke about the value of witness bearing, non-participation and separation in his book *The Morality Gap* published in 1968.

Furfey's commitment to Christian personalist action was the foundation-stone for his program of socio-economic reform in American society. Personalist action enables Christians both individually and communally to take control of their destinies in an increasingly hostile social environment. "Every individual, even the most humble, controls the tiny segment of society which consists of his own interpersonal relations, and he can strive to make this tiny segment as perfect as possible."[33] Furfey repeatedly pointed to Pius XI's advocacy of Christian personalism in *Quadragesimo Anno*. Although personalist action is only a first step in the transformation of society, it enables the believer to say "no" to those forces in society which violate the values of the Gospel. He considered witness bearing as an important aspect of personalist action. "When the Christian actionist has attained clear insight into a problematic social situation and when he has judged it in the light of the New Testament moral code, there still remains the duty of proclaiming publicly what he has discovered. This, of course, is the essence of witness bearing."[34] Furfey frequently turned to an example of voluntary poverty as a way of pointing out the significance of witness bearing. When a Christian makes a judgment in conscience that the present economic order gives rise to a destructive materialism, he is then called to embrace voluntary poverty as a way of placing himself in solidarity with the poor who are the victims of the existing economic structures and institutions. If a Christian truly believes that excessive material prosperity holds a relatively low place on the scale of Christian values, he should witness to this conviction by the life-style he leads. Christian beliefs should be put into action in the social order. Furfey believed that voluntary poverty was possible for all Catholics. Voluntary poverty does not require one to live a life of material deprivation in any extreme sense, but it does require witnessing to the conviction that an exaggerated concern for the material can be detrimental to Christian life and faith. Similarly, if a Catholic shares the moral judgment that the present economic order perpetuates a class of poor people, faith obliges the believer to establish solidarity with the poor in opposition to the present order. A Catholic does not give witness to a belief that the poor deserve justice if he ignores their plight. "If Christianity is to be socially effective, there must be an abundance of witnesses, both lay and clerical, who are willing to speak up 'out of season'. They must be willing to alienate persons in high places who might otherwise have been helpful to them. They must be willing to endure storms of criticisms, name-calling and the imputation of unworthy motives. It is only thus that the gospel message can become relevant."[35] If the poor are victims of economic injustices in society, then Christian actionists must demonstrate their solidarity with them and express their moral outrage publicly.

Non-participation is another form of Christian personalist action designed to bring about the transformation of society. In discussing non-participation Furfey argued that there were some "professions" which were simply incompatible with Christian life. For example, he argued that Catholics should not be involved in the stock market which epitomized the willingness of capitalism to put the production of wealth above human needs. "Non-participation can be a very effective technique of social action. By separating oneself and adopting a special way of living, one dramatizes one's rejection of the current mores."[36] Because Furfey believed that capitalism was fundamentally at odds with the Christian Gospel, he counseled Catholics to refuse to foster its development. There were no reformist sentiments in Furfey's thought here. He insisted that reformist sentiments in the past had not curtailed the evils of capitalism. On the contrary, reformist sentiments simply diluted the power of the Gospel's condemnation of capitalism and contributed to the spread of greed, individualism, competitiveness and materialism in American society. Reformism has not worked and it will not work. Adopting a posture of non-participation with the evils of capitalism will entail some sacrifices, but Catholics should not expect to be able to live the Gospel without sacrifice.

Furfey also counseled separation from the world and its influences as a way for Catholics to maintain their Christian integrity in the face of an economic order rooted in the exploitation of workers and the poor. He encouraged Catholics to join together in building "communities of opposition" to the status quo. "The Christian living in a worldly society can cooperate as long as the mores do not contradict his principles. He can cooperate, for example, in programs for crime control or for the improvement of public health. However, it is practically inevitable in such a society that sooner or later he will be asked to follow certain mores which contradict his code of Christian love. When this happens, his duty is clear. He must proudly refuse his co-operation. He must follow St. Paul's mandate to the Corinthians: 'Come out from among them, and be ye separate.' "[37] In his earlier writings Furfey suggested that Catholics were obliged to separate themselves even from other Christians. As the years passed and he embraced the spirit of the Second Vatican Council, he became less insistent on this point and agreed with the need for ecumenical co-operation in opposition to capitalism in American society.

Witness bearing, non-participation and separation were not easy challenges which Furfey proposed to Catholics who wished to stand against the evils of capitalism. Nor were they easy roads to follow. However, he thought they were a necessary course for Catholics committed to the transformation of socio-economic life. Social transformation begins with personalist action; it begins with personalist resistance; and it begins with personalist non-participation in those aspects of social and economic life which threaten the dignity of people and violate justice. The most important concern of Furfey's was that Catholics dedicated to socio-economic reform realize that the transformation of society had to be grounded in Christian faith and the values of the Gospel of Jesus Christ.

The Legacy

Paul Hanly Furfey's repudiation of American capitalism was absolute. He rejected the thought of those who argued for capitalism's reformability. American capitalism contradicted the fundamental values of the Christian Gospel by giving primacy to wealth and profits over human needs. Because Furfey's repudiation of capitalism was unequivocal, his thought has at times unsettled even those who are dedicated to economic justice. Today many Catholics may also be disturbed by his thought because it poses a challenge to so many Catholics who enjoy the rewards of capitalism. There may be no better reason why Furfey's thought deserves renewed attention today. His radical critique of capitalism can help American Catholics break through the moral complacency which frequently paralyzes those who enjoy the fruits of an economic system which treats others in society so harshly.

Few Catholics of equal prominence have so carefully balanced a life of academic scholarship and a life of social activism. His intellectual pursuits brought him into association with the poor in Washington, D.C., Catholic Workers, trade unionists, and others intent on building a more cooperative economic order. His associations with these dedicated men and women inspired his scholarship. When his work is understood in this context it adds significance to his theological and social analysis of American society. His approach to the transformation of society was not fragmented. It was grounded in an intellectual analysis which was continually open to "the signs of the times" he experienced in the lives of men and women involved in the work of justice.

In a certain sense Paul Hanly Furfey was a traditionalist in his approach to social and economic reform. His debt to the social thought of St. Thomas Aquinas and a rather traditional ecclesiology are evident in his writings. However, under the surface he was a visionary in both his theological and social thought. A careful reading of his work today reveals that he anticipated many of the reforms of the Second Vatican Council. His understanding of the Scriptures as the foundation for personal and social transformation, his emphasis on the Church as community and the importance he placed on the role of the laity in building up the kingdom of God are evidence of this. When Vatican II arrived he embraced it with vigor and discovered a new energy to bring his own ideas, born decades earlier, to bear on an understanding of the role of the Church in society.

Paul Hanly Furfey's probing intellect has never retired. Long after any respectable standard would have him relaxing and enjoying the peace of old age, Furfey was traveling through Latin America studying "liberation theology" so he could bring its message to the Church in the United States and apply its principles to a socio-economic analysis of American society. In his last autobiographical essay Furfey described himself as first a liberal, then a radical, and finally a revolutionary. He never allowed himself to think that he had all the answers. He was always on pilgrimage to a better understanding of the Gospel. He was constantly seeking better ways to bring the Gospel of Jesus Christ into the life of American society.

Throughout his life Paul Hanly Furfey was a priest. His priestly vocation was the starting point of his Christian spirituality. In an age when the need for social activism often diminished the need for a vital spiritual life, Furfey overcame this temptation. He frequently said that his prayer life, especially his celebration of the Eucharist, fed his social activism. His social activism, in turn, fueled his prayer life. His spirituality never became a means of escaping the world, or a justification for ignoring those who stood before him in need. On the contrary, it became the source which enabled him to act so consistently on behalf of the transformation of society.

For those today who are committed to the work of justice in American society, Paul Hanly Furfey's life and thought continue to offer vital instruction. His work deserves renewed attention. Neither Catholics nor others should allow his unequivocal condemnation of capitalism to lessen his appeal. There is nothing lukewarm about Paul Hanly Furfey. He saw evil for what it was. Because his thought is unsettling, it can be refreshing for those who have become complacent beneficiaries of an economic system which too often ignores those most in need.

Notes

1. See Charles Curran, *American Catholic Social Ethics: Twentieth-Century Approaches* (Notre Dame, 1982), pp. 130–71.

2. Paul Hanly Furfey, *Fire on Earth* (New York, 1936), p. 119.

3. Paul Hanly Furfey, *Three Theories of Society* (New York, 1937), p. 119.

4. Paul Hanly Furfey, *The Mystery of Iniquity* (Milwaukee, 1944), p. 41.

5. Furfey, *Fire on Earth*, p. 35.

6. Paul Hanly Furfey, "Experience with Personalism," *The Morality Gap* (New York, 1968), pp. 99–113.

7. Paul Hanly Furfey, "From Catholic Liberalism to Catholic Radicalism," *The American Ecclesiastical Review*, 166, June 1972, pp. 678–86.

8. Paul Hanly Furfey, "The Light at the End of the Tunnel," unpublished autobiographical essay (Archives, Catholic University of America, Washington, D.C.).

9. Paul Hanly Furfey, *Love and the Urban Ghetto* (New York, 1978).

10. Furfey, "From Catholic Liberalism to Catholic Radicalism," p. 678.

11. Ibid., p. 683.

12. Paul Hanly Furfey, *The Morality Gap* (New York, 1968), p. 100.

13. Furfey, "The Light at the End of the Tunnel," p. 6.

14. Paul Hanly Furfey, "Five Hard Sayings," *America*, 56, April 3, 1937, p. 604.

15. Furfey, *Three Theories of Society*, p. 39.

16. Ibid., p. 19.

17. Ibid., p. 23.

18. Ibid., p. 32.

19. Ibid., p. 14.

20. Ibid., p. 42.

21. Ibid., p. 31.

22. Ibid., p. 35.

23. Ibid., pp. 52–53.

24. Ibid., p. 54.

25. Furfey, *Fire on Earth*, p. 72.
26. Ibid., p. 9.
27. Furfey, *Three Theories of Society*, p. 160.
28. Paul Hanly Furfey, "The New Social Catholicism," *Christian Front*, vol. III, 1936, p. 184.
29. Furfey, *Three Theories of Society*, p. 214.
30. Furfey, *The Mystery of Iniquity*, p. 31.
31. Furfey, *The Morality Gap*, pp. 102–03.
32. Furfey, *Fire on Earth*, p. 47.
33. Furfey, *The Morality Gap*, p. 133.
34. Ibid., p. 133.
35. Ibid., pp. 134–35.
36. Ibid., p. 122.
37. Ibid., p. 114.

DOROTHY DAY

᧖

A Catholic Worker

Dorothy Day, co-founder of the Catholic Worker movement, died on November 29, 1980 in her eighty-third year. Shortly after her death historian David O'Brien wrote: "Dorothy Day, in my view, was the most significant, interesting and influential person in the history of American Catholicism."[1] Commenting on O'Brien's assessment of Dorothy's life Robert Ellsberg, editor of *Little by Little: The Selected Writings of Dorothy Day*, later wrote: "Such a statement is all the more extraordinary considering that it refers to someone who occupied no established position of authority, and whose views, after all, met with virtually universal rejection, throughout most of her career."[2] Any intelligent discussion about the relationship between Catholic faith and capitalism in American society is impossible without examining the life and thought of Dorothy Day. No other person in the history of American Catholicism committed so much energy and time to analyzing the moral fabric of American economic life against the measure of the Gospel of Jesus Christ.

Dorothy Day was born in Brooklyn, New York on November 8, 1897. Her father was a journalist by profession and the family moved frequently during Dorothy's youth, traveling between New York, Chicago and California. For the most part she enjoyed a normal childhood and adolescence. However, a careful examination of her early years reveals the seeds of Dorothy's later interest in religious faith and social reform. As a child she was baptized into the Episcopal Church, although her family apparently didn't regard religious faith with a great deal of seriousness. As a young girl Dorothy took comfort in her belief in God's benevolent concern for people and she experienced God's protective presence in her life. Her early travels also exposed her to the human misery and deprivation of the poor. She wondered aloud how a benevolent God could abandon people to such circumstances. Years later in her autobiography, *The Long Loneliness*, she wrote: "I felt at fifteen, that God meant man to be happy, that He meant to provide him with what he needed to maintain life in order to be happy, and that we did not need to have quite so much destitution and misery as I saw around me and read in the daily news."[3] At an early age Dorothy was already pondering the relationship between religious faith and social justice.

In 1914 she enrolled at the University of Illinois in Urbana. Initially Dorothy found the experience exhilarating. It offered freedom from an overly protective family environment and an opportunity to explore questions of importance to her. Dorothy's interest in social issues, especially the plight of the poor, soon brought her into contact with the Socialist Party in Urbana and she became an ardent supporter. She was inspired by the writings and speeches of Eugene Debs who focused her attention on the need for radical social change in America. After a few years at the university a combination of homesickness and a desire to begin implementing a program of social and economic reform brought Dorothy back to New York City. She soon found a job as a reporter for the socialist paper, *The Call,* and for a brief period became a supporter of the Industrial Workers of the World. The Wobblies, as they were called, were intent on a fundamental restructuring of the American economy. During this time period Dorothy also wrote for the communist newspaper, *The Masses.* Dorothy's association with the Socialist Party and with Marxism was more principled than doctrinaire. They appeared to her to be the only people in America committed to improving the conditions of the poor and the victims of bourgeois capitalism. " . . . the Marxists, the I.W.W.'s who looked upon religion as the opiate of the people, who thought they had only this life to live and then oblivion—they were the ones who were eager to sacrifice themselves here and now, they were doing without now and for all eternity the good things of the world which they were fighting to obtain for their brothers. It was then, and still is, a paradox that confounds me. God love them! And God pity the lukewarm of whom St. John said harshly (though he was the disciple of love) that God would spew them out of His mouth."[4] Throughout her lifetime Dorothy frequently expressed frustration that the Christian Churches frequently seemed to defend the status quo in economic life and quickly condemn those who advocated fundamental social and economic change in society.

During the early 1920's Dorothy lived in Greenwich Village associating with a variety of literary figures who shared her anguish about existing economic conditions. Eugene O'Neill was one of her frequent companions during this period. While in his company Dorothy first heard Francis Thompson's "The Hound of Heaven." She offered this reflection. "The idea of this pursuit by the Hound of Heaven fascinated me. The recurrence of it, the inevitableness of the outcome made me feel that sooner or later I would have to pause in the mad rush of living and remember my first beginning and my last end."[5] Throughout the early 1920's Dorothy continued her writing in support of radical causes while experiencing a rebirth of the religious sentiments which had touched her childhood. She frequently found herself drawn to quiet churches for prayer and reflection. She was not sure about what was happening to her, but she was clearly in search of something which could give greater meaning and direction to her life. The tension was apparent to those around her. She continued to espouse the need for radical social and economic changes in American society, and yet she longed for a personal life less unsettling and more deeply rooted. Could religious faith provide her with an anchor enabling her to carry on her struggle for social reform? During this period she was arrested while participating in a protest demonstration in Washington, D.C. Her words from jail are instructive: "I clung to the words of comfort in the Bible, and as long as the light held out, I read and I pondered. Yet all the while I read, my pride was fighting on. I did not want to go to God in defeat and sorrow. I did not want to depend on Him. I was like the child that wants to walk by itself. I kept brushing aside the hand that held me up. I tried to persuade myself that I was reading for literary enjoyment. But the words kept echoing in my heart. I prayed and I did not know that I prayed."[6] With her quest already underway Dorothy entered into a common law marriage with Forster Batterham. In the late summer of 1925 she was pregnant.

The birth of Tamar Teresa in March of 1926 afforded Dorothy a dramatic opportunity to confront the transformation which had been underway in her life for some years. Her own religious quest convinced her to have Tamar baptized in the Catholic Church. In hindsight she confessed that she had acted more out of instinct than out of any dogmatic considerations. Tamar's life would not be subjected to the turmoil which had characterized her own. The Church would be an anchor. Tamar was baptized shortly after her birth despite Dorothy's knowledge that this would rupture her relationship with Forster. She saw no other alternative. In *The Long Loneliness* she wrote: "Yet always those deep moments of happiness gave way to a feeling of struggle, of a long silent fight still to be gone through. There had been the physical struggle, the mortal combat almost, of giving birth to a child, and now there was coming the struggle of my own soul. Tamar would be baptized, and I knew the rending it would cause in human relations around me. I was to be torn and agonized again, and I was all for putting off the hard day."[7] Tamar was baptized in July of 1926 and in 1927 Dorothy followed her daughter into the Church. The next few years represented one of the most troubling periods in Dorothy's life. Her entry into the Church ended her relationship with Forster and with many people who shared her commitment to social reform. However her conversion did not place her in the company of others who seemed especially concerned about the plight of the poor or the need to address the glaring social evils in American society. Dorothy was caught in a time of uncertainty. "If I could have felt that Communism was the answer to my desire for a cause, a motive, a way to walk in, I would have remained as I was. But I felt that only faith in Christ could give the answer. The Sermon on the Mount answered all the questions as to how to love God and one's brother."[8] In the years immediately after her conversion she accepted some writing assignments for the Catholic journal *Commonweal*. In December of 1932 she traveled to Washington, D.C. to cover the Hunger March on Washington. While in Washington she visited the National Shrine of the Immaculate Conception and uttered a pleading prayer that God provide her with some direction about how she could fulfill her mission in the Church while remaining faithful to her commitment to social and economic reform. "I had visited the national shrine at Catholic University in Washington to pray for the hunger marchers. I felt keenly that God was more on the side of the hungry, the ragged, the unemployed, than on the side of the comfortable churchgoers who gave so little heed to the misery of the needy and the agony of the poor. I had prayed that some way would open up for me to do something, to live my life on their side, to work for them, so that I would no longer feel that I had been false to them in embracing my new found faith."[9] On her return to New York a few days later Dorothy found Peter Maurin on her doorstep ready to share his plan for the social and economic reform of American society based upon the Gospel and Catholic social principles. Dorothy's prayer had been answered.

To Live the Works of Mercy

From the moment of their first meeting in December of 1932 until his death in 1949 Dorothy Day and Peter Maurin were almost inseparable. During most of his adult life Peter had been at work formulating a new Christian synthesis for the moral and religious transformation of western society. In Dorothy he found a soulmate and a co-worker. "He was a man of tremendous ambition, in spite of his simplicity, or perhaps because of it. He wanted to make a new synthesis, as St. Thomas had done in the Middle Ages, and he wanted to enlist the aid of a group of people in doing this."[10] During the early months and years of their relationship Peter was the teacher and Dorothy was the willing, if sometimes reluctant, student. Peter presented and explained his threefold program of Cult, Culture and Cultivation. In Dorothy he found someone with the enthusiasm and the determination to implement his social program based upon the cornerstone of Christian personalism. Soon Dorothy and Peter shared a common vision for the transformation of American society and the creation of a new society out of the shell of the old. A new socioeconomic order would be built on the counsels of the Gospel of Jesus Christ.

Peter Maurin's threefold program for Christian social reconstruction entailed the establishment of houses of hospitality to serve the poor and the dispossessed, the creation of round-table discussions to educate others about the importance of Catholic social philosophy, and, finally, the development of farm communes to enable alienated workers to return to the land and discover anew the proper relationship between man and his labor. From the outset Dorothy embraced Peter's threefold program. As a journalist, however, she also saw the need to launch a publication which would spread the word about their new Catholic social movement and counter other social philosophies which denied the need for radical social reform or encouraged social reform through the use of violence. On May 1, 1933 the first issue of *The Catholic Worker* appeared. Initially twenty-five hundred copies were printed and sold for a penny a copy on the streets of New York City. In the first edition Dorothy offered this description of the social conditions which prevailed in 1933. "We were in the third year of the depression. Roosevelt had just been elected President. Every fifth adult American—12 million in all—was unemployed. No smoke came from the factories. Mortgages on houses and farms were foreclosed, drawing more people to the city and loading them on the already overburdened relief rolls. In New York long, bedraggled breadlines of hatless men wound along city streets. On the fringes, by the rivers, almost every vacant lot of a Hooverville, a collection of jerry-built shanties where the homeless huddled in front of the fires."[11] Until her death in 1980 Dorothy continued to serve as the editor of *The Catholic Worker*. Today it continues to have an enormous impact on the social conscience of many Catholics in America.

Dorothy relied on *The Catholic Worker* for forty-seven years to spread her message of Christian social and economic reform in the United States. Over the years it has not only published Peter Maurin's "Easy Essays" which outlined his program for the social reconstruction of the social order, but the writings of most of the significant, and some of the not so significant, figures in the history of twentieth century Catholicism. For more than five decades *The Catholic Worker* has remained consistent in its call for radical social and economic reforms in America and in its commitment to Christian pacifism as the only Christian way of saying "no" to the violence and insanity of contemporary society. To read *The Catholic Worker* from 1933 to the present is to understand the Christian social philosophy of Dorothy Day, Peter Maurin, and those who joined them in the struggle to reform American society. "What we would like to do is change the world—make it a little simpler for people to feed, clothe, and shelter themselves as God intended them to do. And to a certain extent, by fighting for better conditions, by crying out unceasingly for the rights of workers, of the poor, of the destitute—the rights of the worthy and unworthy poor, in other words—we can to a certain extent change the world."[12] What follows is a summary of some of the most salient aspects of Dorothy's thought and her efforts to evaluate the moral fabric of American society in light of the Gospel.

Any examination of Dorothy's criticism of American society is distorted if it obscures the simplicity of her thought. Dorothy Day remains a challenging figure today because of the single-mindedness with which she pursued her Christian responsibility to practice the works of mercy. The starting point of her social theology was a recognition of the dignity of each person as a child of God. She saw the presence of God in the life of every person. She never wavered in this conviction. This insight was the basis of all her works. "We *are* our brother's keeper. Whatever we have beyond our own needs belongs to the poor. If we sow sparingly we will reap sparingly. And it is sad but true that we must give far more than bread, than shelter."[13] As children of God created in the likeness of the Creator all people deserve to be treated with dignity. Without justice in America there can be neither respect for human dignity nor the enjoyment of fundamental human rights. The measure of the moral fabric of American society was how well it protected human dignity and social and economic justice. A society which marginalized millions of people didn't deserve the name Christian. The moral quality of any society must be judged on the basis of how well it protects the rights of those least able to care for themselves. "We can talk about Christ's Mystical Body, about the vine and the branches, about the Communion of Saints. But Christ Himself has proved it for us, and no one has to go further than that. For He said that a glass of water given to a beggar was given to Him. He made heaven hinge on the way we act toward Him in His disguise of commonplace, frail, ordinary humanity."[14]

A special feature of Dorothy's theology was its balance between a personal concern for the individual person and a call for the transformation of the social order. Traditional Catholic social theology, articulated by St. Thomas Aquinas, recognized the intimate relationship between the individual good and the common good. Dorothy Day gave new life to traditional Catholic social teaching in the context of American society. She was determined to demonstrate the relationship between Christian personalism and socio-economic reform. She was continually in combat against the rigid individualism she found in American society. As a young woman she had come to appreciate the social nature of the human person. "I always felt the common unity of humanity; the longing of the heart is for this communion."[15] People simply need one another. Social institutions must foster meaningful human relationships. Without the support of a nurturing community people are frustrated in their ability to flourish and develop as human beings. When people are deprived of a vibrant community life the quality of justice suffers. Dorothy advocated both a radical Christian personalism and the creation of a new socio-economic order. She consistently refused to choose between justice and charity. She rejected both the individualistic philosophies of those who advocated charity toward the poor without showing any serious concern about the social and economic inequities in society, and the collectivist philosophies of those who advocated fundamental social reform without demonstrating any interest in those who stood before them in misery and deprivation. Dorothy wanted a society both charitable and just. "Together with the Works of Mercy, feeding, clothing, and sheltering our brothers, we must indoctrinate. We must give reason for the faith that is in us. Otherwise we are scattered members of the Body of Christ, we are not 'all members one of another'. Otherwise our religion is an opiate, for ourselves alone, for our comfort or for our individual safety or indifferent custom."[16] This was the cornerstone of Dorothy's legacy. With Peter Maurin she rejected the dominant social philosophy of her day and encouraged a return to traditional Catholic social thought which consistently advocated a balance between the rights of the individual and the good of society.

When we examine the lives of men and women who have embraced Catholicism and then gained some measure of prominence in the Church or society there is always a temptation to simply date the significant change in their lives with the point of their conversion. Adopting such an interpretation of events often distorts the record. This is certainly true in the life of Dorothy Day. Long before any mature religious sentiments had developed in her life, Dorothy had read the works of Upton Sinclair, Jack London and others who vividly described the extent of man's inhumanity to man in America. "I read Jack London's books . . . and his essays on the class struggle, his journeys through America and England. When I read *The Jungle* by Upton Sinclair I began taking long walks toward the West Side rather than going to the park or the lake."[17] As a young woman Dorothy belonged to the Socialist Party and she credited Eugene Debs with awakening her social conscience. Well before her entry into the Church she saw the need for radical social and economic change in American society. It was not her conversion which gave rise to her concern for the poor or the need for a more just society. "Since I had been a Socialist in college, a Communist in the early twenties, and now a Catholic since 1927, I had a very definite point of view about poverty, unemployment, and my vocation to try to do something about it."[18] Why then was she willing to suffer the loss of her lover and many friends by entering the Church? Her own words are not terribly instructive. She tells us that conversion came to her as something she had to do. Her decision to have Tamar baptized was certainly a factor but there was more. My own analysis suggests that Dorothy's conversion to Catholicism, although rooted in a leap-of-faith, was in large measure due to her realization that the Church offered her a place where she could more profoundly understand and live the truth she had known for years. From an early age she experienced an affinity for the poor and those afflicted by oppression. She found in the mystery of Catholic faith a better understanding of why the poor were so deserving of her concern. Faith revealed the poor as the children of a benevolent God. From an early age she understood the importance of community and the intimate relationship between the well-being of the individual and the well-being of the community. Belief in the mystical body of Christ enabled Dorothy to more deeply appreciate the bonds which exist between all people. And Dorothy knew about the sufferings endured by those who assist others in need. However, the mystery of the cross enabled her to better understand the meaning of the suffering of those who struggle for the sake of justice. A primary goal of Christian education is to introduce the believer to the symbols of Christian faith, the dignity of human persons, the mystery of suffering and redemption and the solidarity all people share with one another. For Dorothy this dynamic was in a sense reversed. It wasn't the Church which awakened her to the poor, to the meaning of suffering or the need for community. However, her conversion enabled her to understand the meaning of her convictions more profoundly. Dorothy's conversion carried her concern for the poor and for the creation of a just society to a new level. It enabled her to see more clearly what she had only glimpsed before. "One reason I feel sure of the rightness of the path we are traveling in our work is that we did not pick it out ourselves. In those beautiful verses in the twenty-fifth chapter of St. Matthew, Jesus tells us that we must feed the hungry and shelter those without homes and visit the sick and the prisoner. We cannot feel too satisfied with the way we are doing our work—there is too much of it; we have more than our share, you might say. Yet we can say, 'If that's the way He wants it.' "[19]

When the significance of Dorothy's conversion to Catholicism is properly understood it is easier to appreciate the affinity she had for the Church's liturgy, especially the celebration of the Eucharist. She found in the Eucharist both a powerful symbol of God's love for the world and the solidarity God intended between all people. It has often been said that Dorothy was a traditionalist with respect to the Church's liturgy. However, it should also be noted that she found more in the Eucharist, especially in understanding its social and economic implications, than most of her contemporaries in the Church. In the Eucharist she found the model for the creation of a new socio-economic order in which all people come together to share the bread of life. The celebration of the Eucharist is the school for the creation of a new moral consciousness in every new age. In the Eucharist the believer experiences the meaning of Jesus' suffering for the sake of all humankind. As Jesus suffered and sacrificed his life for the redemption of all, the Eucharist invites Christians to a life of sacrifice and suffering for the sake of others. Dorothy was fond of quoting a line from Guardini which observed that a Christian cannot have Christ without the cross. There can be no real love of Christ without a willingness to suffer on behalf of those who have been denied their rightful share of God's generous bounty. Dorothy knew that the truth of the Gospel could only be demonstrated by action. Love for Christ required nothing less than love for one's neighbor. "It is by the Works of Mercy that we shall be judged."[20]

Those who have carefully read the writings of Dorothy Day have correctly observed that she never developed a coherent synthesis of her theological or her socio-economic thought. However, it would be incorrect to assume that her analysis of American society and her vision of a new society were not grounded in basic Christian values. Dorothy repeatedly stated that Jesus' Sermon on the Mount provided her life with sufficient direction. It was her synthesis for a new social order. When she was accused of advocating biblical literalism in her understanding of the Sermon on the Mount she responded by saying that Jesus had literally invited his followers to feed the poor, to clothe the naked and to shelter the homeless. She was only trying to live out her Christian vocation. Performing the works of mercy was a Christian obligation to be fulfilled in the concrete. Fidelity to the Sermon on the Mount and the works of mercy were the measure of salvation for the Christian. At times she expressed disappointment with the institutional Church because it preached the Sermon on the Mount but was not always willing to live it in the concrete. "I loved the Church for Christ made visible. Not for itself because it was so often a scandal to me. Romano Guardini said the Church is the Cross on which Christ was crucified; one could not separate Christ from his Cross, and we must live in a state of permanent dissatisfaction with the Church."[21] She considered hypocrisy a bitter price to pay for preserving a comfortable station in life.

Dorothy brought a special wisdom to the Church's understanding of the poor in American society. Her starting point was simple, direct and biblically grounded. The poor are a special expression of Christ's continuing presence in human history. Long before "an option for the poor" became a part of the popular theological language of the Church Dorothy advocated an "option for the poor." To love the poor is to love Christ. "The mystery of the poor is this: that they are Jesus and what you do for them you do for Him. It is the only way we have of knowing and believing in our love. The mystery of poverty is that by sharing it, making ourselves poor in giving to others, we increase our knowledge of and belief in love."[22] Her theological understanding of the poor did not lead her to adopt a sentimental view of the poor or their poverty. Nor did she harbor any sentiments that God had created the poor in order to give the rich an opportunity for the practice of virtue. The poor were no more created poor by God than were the socio-economic conditions which perpetuated their poverty. "I am sure that God did not intend that there be so many poor. The class struggle is of our making and by our consent, not His, and we must do what we can to change it. This is why we at the Worker urge such measures as credit unions, cooperatives, leagues for mutual aid, voluntary land reforms and farming communes."[23] The conditions of the poor were the work of human hands and it was the responsibility of men and women to create a new social and economic order which could free the poor from their misery and deprivation.

As a way of demonstrating her solidarity for the poor Dorothy lived a life of voluntary poverty as did the other members of the Catholic Worker. The practice of voluntary poverty not only allowed for a greater identification with the poor but it freed Christians from an inordinate attachment to material goods. "Over and over again in the history of the Church the saints have emphasized voluntary poverty."[24] Dorothy recognized that an inordinate desire for material prosperity undermined the life of the spirit. The practice of voluntary poverty established a proper relationship between materiality and spirituality. It placed material goods in the service of building up the kingdom of God. Dorothy was always fond of quoting Peter Maurin's writings. She rejoiced in the simplicity, yet the power of his words. He often said: "We need to make the kind of society where it is easier for people to be good." Dorothy hoped for the creation of a new socio-economic order which would embody a better balance between the material and the spiritual. And she believed that the practice of voluntary poverty would foreshadow the creation of the new social order.

Building a New Economic Order

No aspect of Dorothy Day's thought was more passionately argued than her repudiation of industrial capitalism. Although her condemnation of capitalism was well articulated prior to her conversion to Catholicism, Dorothy's entry into the Church afforded her a new opportunity to analyze the incompatibility between the Christian Gospel and capitalism. William Miller, Dorothy's biographer, offered the following summary of her critique of capitalism in his book *Dorothy Day:* "The heart of the problem was economic. The problem was that contemporary people worked for wages and were so bound by the wage system that they could not offer their work to their fellows as a gift. The logical end of the money economy was the ultimate reduction of existence to a price-tag accounting. An economy in which the wage was the ultimate criterion of value left nothing for human values. Money became the 'truth' by which people lived, and this, in turn, opened the way for the development of the non-productive class: those who lived by the manipulation of money, mainly through charging interest, and who, because of their fortunes, were able to exercise a lien on the work of others and condemn them to servile labor."[25] Her writings do not offer a systematic critique of capitalism as much as they offer the vision of a new cooperative economic order beyond capitalism. Dorothy shared Peter Maurin's belief that more energy should be dedicated to building a new social order than in condemning the old order which was in a state of moral collapse. Capitalism divorced economic activity from the Christian vocation to build up the kingdom of God. At best it was amoral in its understanding of the relationship between economic activity and human life.

Although Dorothy never developed a comprehensive analysis of capitalism, her writings do identify a number of specific moral flaws. A review of these is appropriate here. First, capitalism is wrong-headed because it defends the primacy of capital over labor. Within a capitalist economy the dignity of the human person takes second place to the creation of wealth. Men, women and children who labor to create wealth are often regarded as little more than instruments of production. When more efficient means are found to increase production and create wealth, people become disposable. "Let us be honest, let us say that, fundamentally, the stand we are taking is not on the ground of wages and hours and conditions of labor, but on the fundamental truth that men should be treated not as chattel, but as human beings, as 'temples of the Holy Spirit'. When Christ took on our human nature, when He became man, He dignified and enobled human nature. He said: 'The Kingdom of God is within you.' "[26] Second, capitalism fragments community. It pits people against one another in the quest for greater productivity and wealth. It introduces a highly individualistic spirit into the life of the community. In capitalistic societies people often experience themselves alone and against one another in the struggle for economic advantage. "The entire industrial world has so little to offer what with its cannibalism and its competition."[27] The importance of community and human solidarity becomes an afterthought in the normal course of economic activity. Third, the competitive spirit generated by capitalism makes it difficult for people to focus on the needs of the common good. Both economic and social reality are viewed in terms of self. The ability to nurture personal sacrifice for the sake of the common good is hard to foster. "So many sins against the poor cry out to high heaven. One of the most deadly sins is to deprive the laborer of his hire. There is another: to instill in him paltry desires so compulsive that he is willing to sell his liberty and his honor in order to satisfy them."[28] Fourth, capitalism is materialistic. Although it may give lip service to other values, it essentially focuses on material productivity and the creation of wealth as the highest values in social life. Because of its materialistic nature, capitalism embodies no real respect for the life of the spirit or spiritual goods. It reduces value to the material order. Finally, Dorothy observed a tendency within capitalism toward violence and a legitimation of violence in the pursuit of the goals of capitalism. Because of capitalism's denial of the inherent dignity of workers, its materialistic philosophy and its highly competitive spirit, it often generates violence in an effort to secure economic advantages.

In her criticism of industrial capitalism Dorothy was not unmindful of the facade of civility it could create in society. However, she repeatedly insisted that a careful analysis of capitalism, and its impact on personal and social life, revealed its inherent destructiveness. By its very nature capitalism is unable to nurture the spirit of Christian personalism in the conduct of economic activity. In a capitalist society people are less caring toward one another because economic advantage is promoted as the highest value in social life. Countering this philosophy Dorothy said: "We believe in an economy based on human needs, rather than on the profit motive."[29] Because of the insidious power of capitalism to corrupt moral imagination people fail either to show their concern for the poor, the victims of capitalism, or they look to the state to redress the grievances created by capitalism. When this happens the natural solidarity which exists between people as children of God is torn asunder. Millions of men, women and children are assigned to the care of an impersonal state bureaucracy. "It is a strange and terrifying business, this all embracing state, when it interferes to such a degree in the personal practice of the works of mercy. How terrible a thing it is when the state takes over the poor."[30] Although Dorothy was confident that the inequities in capitalism would eventually become abundantly clear, she realized that the material rewards it made available to some, and the hope of sharing in these rewards which it instilled in others, would make the effort to create a more equitable and cooperative economic order a long and tedious struggle continuing long after her lifetime.

Dorothy was Peter Maurin's eager student. She ardently supported the need to establish houses of hospitality to care for the poor and farm communes in order to provide more appropriate forms of human labor. However, this was not the limit of her economic vision for the future. In many ways she was more of a pragmatist than Peter. She frequently spoke favorably about the Distributist Movement in England championed by G.K. Chesterton, Hilaire Belloc and others. The Distributists favored more decentralized and cooperative economic relationships between people as a means of focusing greater attention on the needs of the common good in the conduct of economic affairs. When Dorothy carefully studied the social encyclicals of Pope Leo XIII, and especially Pope Pius XI's *Quadragesimo Anno,* she found additional support for her own sentiments about the need for greater decentralization of ownership in economic affairs. "We oppose the misuse of private property while we uphold the right of private property. The Holy Father says that 'as many as possible of the workers should become owners', and how else in many cases except by developing the cooperative ideal?"[31] She also embraced Pius' sharp criticisms of industrial capitalism and its inherent inability to respect the primacy of labor over capital. While most of her fellow Catholics in the United States seemed preoccupied with Leo's and Pius' condemnation of socialism, Dorothy was more intent on giving voice to the concerns about capitalism which both Leo and Pius had expressed. She frequently looked to Pius XI to give credence to her own criticisms of capitalism much to the consternation of her fellow Catholics in America. She observed that it was hypocritical for Catholics in America to simply parrot Pius' condemnation of socialism without giving any voice at all to his severe judgments about the inequities of industrial capitalism. "Most Catholics speak of Communists with the bated breath of horror. And yet those poor unfortunate ones who have not the faith to guide them are apt to stand more close in the eyes of God than those indifferent Catholics who sit by and do nothing for 'the least of these' of whom Christ spoke."[32]

Dorothy's attraction to the cooperative spirit of the Distributist Movement and her affinity for the the socio-economic thought of Pius XI led her to support the pioneering work of Fr. James Tompkins in Nova Scotia. Fr. Tompkins established a host of cooperative experiments which brought people into cooperative ownership of the economy including farming, small manufacturing, craft work, etc. The supporters of this movement struggled to place economic activity within a larger context of personal and social well-being. When she visited Nova Scotia she found a model which she hoped could be duplicated in American society. She was also attracted to the work of Virgil Michel of St. John's, Collegeville, whose interest in the relationship between the liturgy and social reform led him to advocate new forms of cooperative economic arrangements among people. Dorothy recognized the difficulties which were involved in promoting a more cooperative economic order in the face of the power of industrial capitalism. However, she remained hopeful that a movement which was grounded in firm moral foundations would eventually attract the support of the American people.

One of the most significant aspects of Dorothy's work was her adamant support for the right of workers to form labor unions. At times her support for organized labor has been misunderstood and misinterpreted. Dorothy looked to the creation of a more cooperative economic order in America because she had no faith in the reformability of capitalism. However, she understood the need to be practical. She realized that a new economic order could not be created overnight. In the interim workers had a right to protect those economic rights which were essential for their personal well-being, the well-being of their families and the well-being of society in general. "While we are upholding cooperatives as part of the Christian social order, we are upholding at the same time unions as organizations of workers wherein they can be indoctrinated and taught to rebuild the social order."[33] As a Christian personalist Dorothy continually found herself caught in the tension of addressing both the concerns of those who stood before her in need and the creation of a new economic order. However, she never allowed her dedication to the latter goal to distract her from her Christian obligation to care for the Christ who stood before her in need.

Her activities long before her conversion to Catholicism in 1927 already demonstrated Dorothy's support for working men and women and their right to form labor unions to protect their economic rights. Before reading Pope Leo XIII's *Rerum Novarum* and Pope Pius XI's *Quadragesimo Anno* she had sung: "Workers of the world, unite." However, as she became more familar with the writings of Leo and Pius, she found all the more reason to champion the rights of workers. She frequently chided her fellow Catholics for not reading the encyclicals of Leo or Pius. If they had studied the social encyclicals they would not have taken such offense at the support of workers and their right to strike which she so frequently defended in the pages of *The Catholic Worker*. In addition to the pragmatic considerations which motivated Dorothy's support for the right of workers to form labor unions, she also saw in union activities the opportunity for workers to experience solidarity in their support for one another in a common struggle. "We have lived with the unemployed, the sick, the unemployables. The contrast between the worker who is organized and has his union, the fellowship of his own trade to give him strength, and those who have no organization and come to us on a breadline is pitiable."[34] Labor unions, if properly organized, could foster the seed of solidarity and cooperativeness in economic affairs which were key to Dorothy's vision of a more cooperative economic order in the future. Labor unions and the workers who formed them could provide a model of what could be realized if individuals were willing to temper self-centered economic interest for the sake of the common good. She was not foolish enough to think that her support for labor unions would lead to a transformation of capitalism overnight. But these activities could provide a starting point. "As Christian masters freed the slaves who had converted them, because they recognized their dignity as men made in the image and likeness of God, so the industrial slaves of today can find their freedom through Christianity."[35] In the midst of one of her last labor crusades Dorothy uttered this prayer on behalf of the farm workers of the United States. It eloquently expressed her hopes for the labor movement. "Dear Pope John—please, yourself a campesino, watch over the United Farm Workers. Raise up more and more leader servants throughout the country and stand with Cesar Chavez in the nonviolent struggle with Mammon, in all the rural districts of North and South, in the cotton fields, beet fields, potato fields, in our orchards and vineyards, our orange groves—wherever men, women and children work on the land. Help make a new order wherein justice flourishes, and as Peter Maurin, himself a peasant, said so simply, 'where it is easier to be good'."[36]

As I have indicated Dorothy did not develop a comprehensive new synthesis for the creation of a new economic order in American society. Although she was convinced of the inevitable decline of capitalism, she was not prepared to outline with any definitiveness the form of the new economic order. Her singular goal was to re-establish the proper relationship between material and spiritual well-being on both the personal and the social level. Capitalism had for too long heralded the primacy of the material over the spiritual. As a result, economic relationships had become divorced from the common good, and man's relationship with God had been undermined. Dorothy never denied the legitimate role of the material in human life. However, she protested vehemently those forms of social and economic relationships which placed excessive emphasis on the material to the detriment of the spiritual. The creation of a new economic order would create a proper balance. Without this no meaningful economic reform was possible.

The Legacy

The life and thought of Catholic Worker Dorothy Day offers itself as a continuing challenge to American Catholics who are anxious for a better understanding of the intimate relationship between the Christian Gospel and the socio-economic conditions in American society today. One of the most appealing aspects of Dorothy's social thought was its simplicity. Although she was extremely well read in theological and religious thought, as well as in economic and political theory, she consistently refused to obscure her thought and message in a language few could understand. Her challenge was extended to all God's people and not simply to a learned few. Because of the simplicity of her style, her thought remains accessible to all people of good will.

Dorothy centered her life on the Sermon on the Mount. She frequently said that once she discovered the Sermon she no longer needed to search for a blueprint for the social and economic transformation of American society. It was already present in Jesus' own challenging words. She rejected those theological arguments which lessened the challenge found in the Sermon. Although she criticized biblical literalism as a methodology for understanding the Scriptures, she remained insistent that Christians had to incorporate the message of the Sermon in the concrete affairs of their personal lives and in the socio-economic fabric of society. To do less was to distort Jesus' challenge and the Christian vocation.

Although Dorothy's conversion to Catholicism was a momentous event in her life, it did not temper her desire to better understand the meaning of her Christian vocation. She never rested intellectually. She continually struggled to understand the meaning of the Gospel in light of personal and social life. Her passion in this task was contagious. It deeply affected not only the lives of other Catholic Workers, but the lives of those who observed her from afar. Even as she grew older Dorothy maintained the ability to be gently critical and chide those in the Church who seemed inattentive to the social implications of the Christian faith.

Throughout her lifetime Dorothy was frequently labeled a radical because she focused so much personal energy and attention on the social and economic structures of American society. However, a sensitive and thoughtful reading of her work reveals that her attention to socio-economic realities did not lessen her attentiveness for the individual person who stood before her in need. She continually focused on the natural tension between the personal and the social. Her social imagination reflected the classical thought of St. Thomas Aquinas more than the thought of many of the radical reformers she admired. This was the challenge offered by Catholic social thought: to balance the rights of the individual and the rights of the community. This aspect of her thought continues to offer food for thought to Catholics who are engaged in the work of building up the kingdom of God.

The Eucharist was the center of Dorothy's life. In her abiding love for the Eucharist we find a testimony to her concern for the individual and the community. Participation in the liturgy was the source of her own religious and moral transformation. At the same time the Church's liturgy, especially the Eucharist, provided her with a model of the community which Christians were called to build in society. The Eucharist foreshadowed the coming of the kingdom of God. As believers participate in the Eucharist, their moral imaginations are enriched, and they are accorded a vision of life in the kingdom. The Eucharist was the model for the transformation of society. Through the celebration of the Eucharist Christians become more attentive to the needs of the poor and the powerless, and more conscious of the work necessary for building up the kingdom of God.

No aspect of Dorothy's life and thought is more compelling than her attitude toward the poor. Her own words tell the story: "The mystery of the poor is this: they are Jesus." Her understanding of the Gospel was always concrete in nature. Christ is present in the lives of poor men, women and children; and the poor are a special revelation of Christ's presence in society. Dorothy agreed with Peter Maurin when he said that it is the good works done for the poor that we take with us when we die. She consistently rejected efforts to diminish the obligation of Christians to care for the poor. She was particularly annoyed when these arguments came from her fellow Catholics. Her dedication to the poor is best seen in the life she lived. Voluntary poverty was the hallmark of her life as a Catholic Worker. She often insisted that in order to love the poor we must be with them in their sufferings. When she fed, clothed and sheltered the poor Dorothy knew she was in the company of the Lord.

In decades to come American Catholics will better understand and appreciate the life and thought of Dorothy Day. Her life is at once inspiring and unsettling. She has much to offer Catholics in the United States who are committed to building a society with liberty and economic justice for all. Because of the encompassing nature of her vision she speaks to us about the foundations of an American Catholic spirituality which perceives and understands the relationship between the Gospel of Jesus Christ and the transformation of society. In her thought we find the seeds for a non-violent social revolution; one that aims at building up the kingdom of God.

Notes

1. David J. O'Brien, "The Pilgrimage of Dorothy Day," *Commonweal,* December 19, 1980, p. 711.
2. Robert Ellsberg, editor, *By Little and By Little: The Selected Writings of Dorothy Day* (New York, 1983), p. xv.
3. Dorothy Day, *The Long Loneliness* (New York, 1963), p. 38.
4. Ibid., p. 63.
5. Ibid., p. 84.
6. Ibid., p. 81.
7. Ibid., p. 138.
8. Ibid., p. 141.
9. Ibid., p. 142.
10. Ibid., p. 170.
11. Dorothy Day, *Loaves and Fishes* (New York, 1952), p. 4.
12. Day, *By Little and By Little,* p. 98.
13. Day, *Loaves and Fishes,* p. 88.
14. Day, *By Little and By Little,* p. 97.
15. Ibid., p. 29.
16. Ibid., p. 91.
17. Ibid., p. 37.
18. Day, *Loaves and Fishes,* p. 8.
19. Ibid., p. 192.
20. Day, *By Little and By Little,* p. 100.
21. Day, *The Long Loneliness,* p. 150.
22. Day, *By Little and By Little,* p. 330.
23. Day, *Loaves and Fishes,* p. 70.
24. Ibid., p. 80.
25. William Miller, *Dorothy Day* (San Francisco, 1982), p. 29.
26. Day, *By Little and By Little,* p. 241.
27. Ibid., p. 249.
28. Ibid., p. 111.
29. Ibid., p. 271.
30. Day, *Loaves and Fishes,* p. 199.
31. Day, *By Little and By Little,* p. 244.
32. Ibid., p. 63.

33. Ibid., p. 244.

34. Ibid., p. 239.

35. Dorothy Day, *Houses of Hospitality* (New York, 1954), p. 259.

36. Day, *By Little and By Little*, p. 257.

CESAR CHAVEZ

Economic Justice for All

Cesar Chavez, a Catholic of Mexican-American heritage, is credited with establishing the first successful union of farm workers in the United States. For decades organizing efforts to bring farm workers together in common cause to advance their social and economic well-being had been unsuccessful. When the National Farm Workers Association was founded in an abandoned movie theater in Fresno, California in September of 1962 Cesar Chavez was determined to succeed where so many others before him had failed. During the past three decades Chavez has continued the struggle he began in the early 1960's. Today he remains a symbol of hope for the millions of farm workers in the United States who continue to bear the burden of economic exploitation and injustice.

The contribution of Cesar Chavez to American society cannot be limited to the narrow focus of a union organizer who succeeded where so many others had failed. His vision was always much broader. By raising the issue of economic justice for farm workers Chavez provoked a renewed national debate in American society about the meaning of economic justice. He repeatedly rejected assertions that his efforts were limited in nature. By heralding the cause of farm workers who were exploited by ruthless growers and the octopus of agribusiness, Chavez hoped to expose economic injustices of every kind. At the heart of his struggle was his passionate dedication to the dignity of farm workers. "Cesar Chavez—more than anything else—is a symbol; the very essence of the energy of a drive; the catalytic agent that has crystalized the sufferings of a people forgotten and almost excommunicated by society from its benefits, and who has been able to rally around him by some inner strength uncharted the kind of devotion only conscience can capture and which money has never been able to buy."[1] The National Farm Workers Association became a means for securing the fundamental human rights of men, women and children who labored in the heat and the cold to bring food to the tables of their fellow Americans.

Cesar Chavez became a symbol of the aspirations of Mexican-American people. He did not join with farm workers from outside their experiences simply to improve their economic well-being. On the contrary, he rose from within their experiences to articulate their deepest human hopes and aspirations. "Chavez's ideas did not come from union headquarters in the East; they came from his own experience in the orchards, vineyards and the cotton and vegetable fields of the West, from his own daily life. Inspiration came from his fellow campesinos; he was, like them, the victim of the injustice pressed down on the poor and the unorganized."[2] At times Cesar perplexed other labor leaders in the United States because of the simplicity of his style. However, he never wavered in his determination to be with the workers in the fields so his advocacy on their behalf would be grounded in the reality they experienced day to day. As a young man Cesar Chavez tasted first-hand the exploitation and injustices suffered by farm workers. With his parents, brothers and sisters he worked the fields in California and the American northwest. In his early years he attended more than thirty different schools because his family was continually forced to move to new fields and regions where work could be found. "My family became migrants during the Depression, when my father lost his land in Arizona. I went to school whenever I could—30 different ones, because we moved so much—but I never got past the seventh grade: there was work to do."[3] He not only felt the economic injustices leveled against farm workers but the racial discrimination which treated Mexican-Americans as second-class citizens. Cesar has frequently said that his personal experiences afforded him a reservoir of experiences which shaped his moral imagination. In his late twenties and early thirties Chavez began a program of self-study which enabled him to understand the reasons that led farmers and growers to exploit farm laborers. This education was only possible because Cesar knew intimately the economic injustices which shaped the early years of his life. In becoming a spokesperson for his people Cesar was able to speak from within their experience. As the National Association of Farm Workers grew through the decade of the 1960's he worked hard to maintain the simplicity of his own life-style so that he would not become divorced from the reality of those for whom he struggled to serve.

No study of the life and contributions of Cesar Chavez is complete without examining the role his Catholic faith played in his efforts to protect and enhance the dignity of farm workers. Few American Catholics in the twentieth century have so vibrantly lived the social message of the Gospel of Jesus Christ. Again the reader needs to understand that Cesar's dedication to economic justice did not flow primarily from an intellectualized understanding of his Catholic faith. It was only later in his life that Cesar developed a broader appreciation for the social theology of the Church. His familial experiences and the deep and abiding faith of his parents, especially his mother, awakened in Cesar a keen awareness of the relationship between God's love for his people and the rightful claim of farm workers for a life of justice and dignity. Long before it became theologically fashionable Cesar Chavez understood God's special concern for the poor and the victims of oppression. This understanding enabled him to articulate a Catholic theology of liberation in word and deed. Cesar's deep religious faith was frequently a source of consternation to other labor leaders who failed to understand the rhythm of the relationship he found between prayer and penance and the creation of a union for farm workers. Without an understanding of Cesar's religious faith an adequate appreciation of his life is impossible.

Cesar Chavez's approach to organizing farm workers and building a more cooperative economic order did not lead him to write a great deal or to develop an elaborate theoretical exposition of his vision. The scope of his social, economic and moral vision is found principally in the speeches and letters he addressed to his supporters and his antagonists. Again the simplicity of his style and the straightforwardness of his message are more than evident. Because he was convinced that the truth of his message was simple, Cesar never gave in to the temptation to use rhetoric few could understand. He spoke a simple language and counseled others to do the same. In the following analysis of Cesar Chavez's work I will focus primarily on the early life experiences which shaped his social vision, the formative years of the National Farm Workers Association, his understanding of economic injustice, and finally, the religious and theological vision which provided the moral substance of his struggle to realize economic justice for farm workers.

Formative Years

On March 31, 1927 Cesar Chavez was born in Yuma, Arizona. He spent the first ten years of his life on his family's small farm until it failed in 1937. Although the farm only provided a meager existence for the large family, it offered a level of security and permanence which Cesar spoke of fondly in later years. The year 1937 marked the beginning of Cesar's migrant wanderings. At first the family worked the crops in Arizona, traveling back and forth across the state. In 1939 they arrived in California, choosing San Jose as a settling place. From here Cesar worked the fields and orchards of the San Joaquin Valley and in other regions where work could be found. One writer offered this description of these difficult years. "Chavez grew up in a series of labor camps where home was invariably a tar paper shack, and he attended more than thirty elementary schools scattered along the family's itinerary. When he dropped out of school he was theoretically a seventh grader, but in practice he could barely read and write. Only later did he master the three R's through self-study."[4] During his adolescence Cesar experienced all the indignities visited upon farm workers, and he wondered about the enormous disparities in life-style between the growers who lived in affluence and farm workers who labored long into the night with little to show for their labors. Frequently he suffered the brutalizing effects of racial discrimination, encountering signs which read "No Dogs or Mexicans Allowed."[5]

Between 1944 and 1945 Cesar served in the U.S. Navy on a destroyer in the Pacific. After the war he returned to California and resumed his labors in the fields and orchards. The year 1947 marked the beginning of Cesar's union activities when he picketed for the National Farm Labor Union. Unfortunately he watched the union fail that same year. In 1948 he married Helen Fabela who became one of his most trusted colleagues in his struggle to establish the National Farm Workers Association. Two years later they moved to San Jose, California and found shelter for themselves in a Mexican-American barrio named "Sal Si Puedes" which is loosely translated "Escape if you can." The move to Sal Si Puedes proved to be providential because here Cesar met Fr. Donald McDonnell and Fred Ross. Both played an enormous role in the formation of his vision of economic justice for farm workers.

In the early 1950's Saul Alinsky, a community organizer and head of the Industrial Areas Foundation in Chicago, sent one of his most trusted associates, Fred Ross, to southern California in the hopes of building a grass roots organization to address a variety of social and economic issues which perpetuated the poverty and exploitation of farm workers. Soon after arriving in California Ross was given Cesar's name by Fr. Donald McDonnell, who had already recognized Cesar's passion for bettering the plight of his fellow Mexican-Americans and his ability as a leader and organizer. McDonnell believed that Cesar could give focus to the solidarity that Mexican-Americans, especially farm workers, felt for one another. Fr. McDonnell was not to be proved wrong in this assessment. At first Cesar avoided meeting Ross, thinking that he was just another "Anglo" intent on imposing a social agenda on Cesar's people. However, after their initial meeting Chavez recognized that Ross was different from the others. He reflected this when he said " . . . the first practical steps I learned from the best organizer I knew, Fred Ross. I first met him in Sal Si Puedes. He changed my life."[6] Ross' aim was to empower Mexican-Americans so that they could shape their own social and economic agenda in accordance with their own desires and aspirations. In 1952 after developing his own skills as an organizer under the tutelage of Fred Ross, Cesar accepted a position with Ross' organization, the Community Service Organization.

After recommending that Fred Ross enlist Cesar in the work of the Community Service Organization, Fr. McDonnell did not lose interest in Cesar's intellectual and religious development. He first introduced Cesar to the social teachings of the Catholic Church, especially the modern social encyclicals, and encouraged him to study more carefully Jesus' message in the Gospels and the thought of St. Thomas Aquinas, Gandhi and others who could provide a focus for Cesar's own conviction that the injustices suffered by the farm workers were contrary to the tenets of Christian faith and belief. While Fred Ross schooled Cesar in the techniques of community organizing, Fr. McDonnell provided him with the moral substance for his socio-economic vision. He not only introduced Cesar to a number of religious writers who heralded the cause of economic and social justice, but he helped him to understand some of the basic principles of economics, as well as the relationship between the exploitation of farm workers and the affluence of rich growers and farmers. It was Fr. McDonnell who introduced Cesar to the appropriate role of labor unions from the perspective of Catholic teaching. Cesar later said: "Actually my education started when I met Fr. Donald McDonnell, who came to Sal Si Puedes because there was no Catholic church there, no priests, and hundreds of Mexican-Americans."[7] For Cesar the decade of the 1950's was characterized by enormous intellectual development and the emergence of a new consciousness about the nature of the problems confronting farm workers. This educational process supported by both

Ross and McDonnell provided Cesar with the foundation he needed when in the early 1960's he decided to take the bold step of trying to successfully organize the first union of farm workers.

During the 1950's while his education was underway Cesar held a series of positions with the Community Service Organization. Between 1952 and 1958 he served in a staff position with the CSO, traveling to a number of areas in California where he established local chapters of CSO and built a coalition of farm workers across the state. In 1958 Cesar became the General Director of CSO. While assuming overall responsibility for the organization throughout California, he continued local organizing efforts from his base in Los Angeles. During this same year he focused considerable time and effort on the "bracero" program which enabled farmers and growers to import Mexican laborers into the United States. Chavez and CSO opposed this program because it led to a gross exploitation of the Mexicans involved, and it enabled farmers, growers and representatives of large agribusinesses to ignore the legitimate demands of Mexican-American farm workers.

There is no question that Cesar's work with the Community Service Organization was fruitful and that it contributed a great deal to his own education as an organizer. However, as the 1960's approached Cesar became convinced that the traditional approach of providing social services to Mexican-Americans was alone inadequate. By the late 1950's he began to urge the leaders of the CSO to commit the energies and resources of the organization to the formation of a legitimate labor union for farm workers. He was convinced that unless farm workers were empowered to exert economic self-determination in the fields their hopes of achieving social and economic justice would continue to be frustrated. By early 1962 Cesar convinced the leadership of CSO of the reasonableness of his plan to put CSO in service of establishing a labor union for farm workers. However, when a showdown came with the membership of the organization, Cesar lost the battle. Convinced more than ever that a union was essential, Cesar resigned from CSO in March of 1962. With only $1,200 in savings Cesar set out to fulfill a dream. He knew that if he stayed with CSO because of the security it offered him and his family, he would eventually regret that he did not have the courage to follow through on his conviction that a farm worker union was absolutely necessary. When Chavez broke with the CSO he was convinced that it was out of touch with farm workers. He understood his commitment to the rural man when he wrote in a letter to boycott supporters in late

September 1968: "Our movement is a militant beginning of a new hope for American farm workers."[8] Only such an effort would enable his brothers and sisters to escape the economic injustices visited upon them by men without conscience.

The National Farm Workers Association

After resigning his position with the Community Service Organization Cesar moved his family to Delano, California in the midst of the San Joaquin Valley. This decision served both practical and tactical ends. Other Chavez family members were already living in Delano and they provided Cesar's family with some support as he launched his organizing efforts. Secondly, due to the large number of grape vineyards in the San Joaquin and Imperial valleys the migration of farm workers was less here than in other areas, because the vineyards required attention during most of the year. If Cesar hoped to organize farm workers into a viable union, his prospects were best among farm workers who had a continuing and consistent stake in the union. He expressed his hopes in the following words: "I had some ideas on what should be done. No great plans; just that it would take an awful lot of work. A gamble? Sure it was. But I had seen *so much* injustice, and I knew that organizing was the key to changing it. *Someone* had to do the organizing."[9]

Between March and September of 1962 Cesar traveled throughout the region. He visited approximately eighty different towns, talked to the farm workers about their concerns and encouraged them to see their own self-interest in the formation of a strong union for farm workers. During this early period he encountered a number of roadblocks and often found his efforts frustrated by the people he hoped to serve. Despite these trials he never wavered in his commitment. Throughout the most difficult periods Cesar turned to his family and extended family for emotional support and encouragement.

September 1962 represented a turning point in Cesar's efforts. The National Farm Workers Association (NFWA) held its first convention in Fresno, California. More than two hundred and fifty farm workers from several communities attended. The delegates approved a constitution for the NFWA, adopted a symbol for the new union and elected Cesar Chavez its first president. Cesar drew much of the organizing philosophy for the NFWA from Pope John XXIII's *Mater et Magistra* which detailed the rights of workers to form labor unions.[10]

During the next few years Cesar and the other leaders of the union, including Richard Chavez and Dolores Huerta, continued their methodical organizing efforts in the Delano area. In addition to soliciting membership, the NFWA established a credit union, founded a newspaper, offered counseling services to farm workers and attempted to intervene with farmers and growers with respect to grievances raised by the workers. These efforts were slow and progress was often hard to see, but Cesar and his supporters remained firm in their convictions. Patience was a necessary virtue. Time would eventually reveal the justice of the farm worker struggle.

By September of 1965 the development of the NFWA reached another important turning point. On September 8 more than five hundred farm workers associated with the Agricultural Workers Organizing Committee (AWOC) walked off the fields in an area near Delano in a strike which sought a minimum wage of $1.40 per hour. After much debate the NFWA agreed to support the AWOC strike and more than one thousand of its members walked off several Delano area farms. From this point on the struggle was engaged. Within days the AWOC and the NFWA established a joint strike committee, and Cesar issued several letters to area growers outlining the goals and objectives of the strike. Throughout the next several months members of the AWOC and the NFWA were engaged in those activities required for the success of a strike. Cesar encouraged other workers to leave their fields and join "La Huelga." In October a number of farm workers were arrested as it became more evident that although *right* might be on the side of the farm workers, *might* was on the side of the farmers and growers who had the support of the local government and law enforcement officials. Cesar was arrested in November on a charge of using a bull horn without a permit. He was encouraging farm workers to leave their fields and join the strike. In December Walter Ruether, head of the AFL-CIO, visited Delano and expressed his support for the activities of the NFWA and the AWOC. Shortly afterward the NFWA announced a nationwide boycott of Delano grapes because of the refusal of the growers to negotiate with the union.

On March 17, 1966 Cesar and members of the NFWA announced their intention to begin a three hundred mile march from Delano to the state capital in Sacramento. A number of reasons motivated this course of action. It became increasingly clear to Cesar that the success of the NFWA efforts, and the Delano strike in particular, rested on their ability to bring the general public to see the justice of their cause and support the boycott. Secondly, Cesar saw the need to keep his followers focused on the significance of the strike and the boycott. While economic issues were very much at the heart of NFWA activities, even more significant concerns were at stake. Cesar's was a struggle to achieve basic justice for farm workers and to restore their dignity as human beings, as children of God. Speaking of the farm worker Cesar said: "He is not a pawn, slave or agricultural tool. He is a person."[11] The march to Sacramento required enormous sacrifices on the part of all who were involved, but if the struggle for justice and dignity was to be won suffering and sacrifices would be required. Cesar envisioned the march as an opportunity for moral transformation. Farm workers would be purfied in their cause, the general public would see the righteousness of their struggle, and the farmer and growers would see the determination in the eyes of the farm workers.

On Easter Sunday April 10 Cesar and his supporters reached Sacramento and were joined by nearly 10,000 supporters. The rally which followed drew national attention to their struggle and it gave new momentum to the NFWA. Indeed, shortly before they reached Sacramento the Schenly Company announced its intention to begin negotiating with the NFWA. During the next few years union organizing continued. In June of 1966 NFWA won an election at the DiGiorgio Farm, one of the largest in the area. And on June 21 the Schenly Company signed a contract with the NFWA in Los Angeles. This represented a milestone because it was the first successful contract negotiated by the NFWA. In August of 1966 the NFWA and AWOC formally merged into one organization, the United Farm Workers Organizing Committee, AFL-CIO. In early 1967 Dolores Huerta, a UFWOC vice president, met with representatives of the DiGiorgio Farms to begin discussing the terms of the contract. This was significant because DiGiorgio's action would influence other farmers and growers in the Delano area. Later in the year the union called a strike against Giummara Vineyards and shortly afterward announced a boycott of all Giummara products. In the following months the UFWOC held representational elections on dozens of farms throughout the region and won more and more support to negotiate contracts with local farmers and growers. But difficulties were also a part of the mosaic of activities. As strikes dragged on and the boycott seemed to yield only mixed results, a number of farm workers became disgruntled and occasionally violence erupted on both sides of the struggle.

Cesar again recognized a new need to center the efforts of the

UFWOC and to reawaken his followers to the justice and the significance of their cause. He feared that some were losing sight of the fundamental values of justice and dignity which were at the heart of the struggle. On February 14, 1968 Cesar Chavez began a fast which lasted no fewer than twenty-five days. He stated that his reasons for the fast were both personal and public. On the other hand, he saw the need to create an environment within which he could purify his own thinking about the goals and objectives of the UFWOC and the many strikes and boycotts which were underway. He sensed the significance of his leadership responsibilities and wanted an opportunity to clarify his own intentions as president of the union in order to give faithful service to its members. On the other hand, Cesar was equally conscious of the deeply religious implications of the struggle and looked upon the fast as an opportunity to understand more clearly the religious meaning of the struggle for liberation which UFWOC was engaged in. Public goals were also apparent. Cesar realized that the philosophy of non-violence which he made a part of the UFWOC organizing strategy was not always an easy burden to bear. Violence had occurred on both sides and he wanted to provide a public reaffirmation of his philosophy of non-violence. He saw the need to do penance so that the violence perpetuated by the farm workers would be curtailed and the farmers and growers would realize that the union would not go away. Its struggle was rooted in a fundamental longing for justice and human dignity. Cesar ended his fast on the advice of his doctors on March 10, 1968. He announced his decision at a rally and liturgy attended by thousands of his supporters in Memorial Park in Delano. Due to the physical weakness resulting from his fast Cesar was not able to personally address those assembled; however a colleague delivered his brief remarks. This speech has come to be regarded as one of his most powerful public statements. Although simple in tone and style, it eloquently set forth the moral determination of Cesar and the UFWOC to win the struggle for economic justice for farm workers. In the speech he said: "It is my deepest belief that only by giving our lives do we find life. I am convinced that the truest act of courage, the strongest act of manliness, is to sacrifice ourselves for others in a totally non-violent struggle for justice. To be a man is to suffer for others. God help us to be men."[12]

In July of 1968 Cesar took the unprecedented and bold step of announcing a nationwide boycott of all California table grapes throughout the United States. Soon the boycott took on an international focus with the refusal of some dock workers in some European countries to unload shiploads of California table grapes. The UFWOC established dozens of boycott teams which were sent to large cities across the United States and Canada in order to coordinate the boycott. On Good Friday, April 4, 1969 Cesar issued his now famous Good Friday letter from Delano which called on representatives of agribusiness across the United States, especially in California, to recognize the moral righteousness of the farm worker cause and begin negotiations. In the letter Cesar said: "As your industry has experienced, our strikers here in Delano and those who represent us throughout the world are well trained for this struggle. They have been under the gun, they have been kicked and beaten and herded by dogs, they have been cursed and ridiculed, they have been stripped and chained and jailed, and they have been sprayed with the poisons used in the vineyards. They have been taught not to lie down and die or to flee in shame, but to resist with every ounce of human endurance and spirit. To resist not with retaliation in kind but to overcome with love and compassion, with ingenuity and creativity, with hard work and long hours, with stamina and patient tenacity, with truth and a public appeal, with friends and allies, with mobility and discipline, with politics and law, and with prayer and fasting. They were not trained in a month or even in a year; after all this new harvest season will mark our fourth full year of the strike and even now we continue to plan and prepare for the years to come. Time accomplishes for the poor what money does for the rich."[13]

On September 7, 1969 Cesar, the leadership of the UFWOC and the National Liturgical Conference sponsored a rally in Washington, D.C. in order to bring additional public attention to the UFWOC struggle and to celebrate the fourth anniversary of the strike against the California growers. Shortly afterward he joined with other UFWOC leaders and traveled to a number of major cities in the United States and Canada to gain additional support for the union and its efforts. The year 1970 marked the most dramatic turning point for the young union. On April 1, 1970 the UFWOC signed the first in a series of contracts with the table grape growers in California. Throughout the year several other table grape growers signed contracts or entered into negotiations with the union. By July of 1970 approximately eighty percent of the table grape growers in the Delano area had signed agreements with the UFWOC. Cesar Chavez summoned up the spirit behind La Causa and the reason for its success with these eloquent words:

"Today in Delano we have a group of men and women who have done outstanding work to try to liberate themselves through their collective action to get things in life that other workers have had so long. They have gone to great personal expense and personal selfless dedication and work just to stay alive as a group. We ourselves frequently ask: What causes a man to give up his pay check for forty-eight months for the right to have a living? Or what would cause a woman striker to picket and demonstrate, peacefully and non-violently, and then be arrested as a common criminal? Or what would cause men and women in the struggle to suffer the painful separation from family and be sent across the country to all the major cities and Canada, to bring the word of the boycott and the struggle of the farm workers? We often ask ourselves: What would cause teenage boys and girls to go to school without a new pair of shoes or to go to school with the same old clothes and do without noon lunch? What causes this great personal sacrifice? Why are they going insane? Or what would cause still little children, who are too small to understand the struggle, to do without milk, to do without the basic necessities of life because their parents are involved in what is getting to be perhaps the longest and, perhaps, we hope, the most successful strike of farm workers ever in the history of our country? We say that what causes this is what causes other people in our country and in other parts of the world—a spirit of independence and freedom—the spirit that they want to change things and that they want to be independent and they want to be able to run their own lives. This is the cause why these workers are so willing to bear the sacrifices and all the personal suffering that go with the strike and the boycott."[14]

Building a Cooperative Economic Order

From the outset of his work Cesar Chavez saw his efforts on behalf of farm workers in much broader terms than simply the organization of a farm workers union. He understood himself as the leader of a movement. His goal was to bring his people out of the misery and oppression which characterized their lives. Cesar defined his mission with these words: "We make a solemn promise: to enjoy our rightful part of the riches of this land, to throw off the yoke of being considered as agricultural implements or slaves. We are free men and we demand justice."[15] The N.F.W.A. offered a means of achieving this goal in the economic realm. But La Causa was not limited to this.

When he spoke of "La Causa" he wanted to awaken farm workers to a new awareness of their rightful claim to lives of human dignity. If the movement was successful, more than economic rewards would result. Here he spoke of the need for not only an economic revolution, but a revolution of the heart and mind as well. People had to begin thinking about farm workers as human beings. A revolution was also necessary in the minds of farmers and growers so that they would cease looking upon farm workers simply as instruments of agricultural production. Cesar was always involved in a twofold struggle. On the one hand, he wanted to instill a new confidence and hopefulness in the lives of farm workers. And, on the other hand, he recognized the need to develop a strategy enabling farmers and growers to see the economic and social injustices which were inherent in the present system of farm labor.

A commitment to fundamental moral principles is often characteristic of people who seek to achieve social change in society. This was certainly true in Cesar's case. His early life and experiences led him to the conviction that all God's children should have a rightful share in the bounty of God's creation. The land and the fruits thereof belong to all God's children. Although he did not offer any detailed blueprint how God's bounty should be distributed, he was convinced that the present plight of farm workers was evidence enough that changes were needed. His call for economic justice in the fields and on the farms was basically a call for the creation of a new economic order in accordance with God's plan for all his people. Continuation of the present system represented a violation of the order intended by God. Closely allied with Cesar's belief that justice required a more equitable distribution of the goods of the earth was his belief that respecting the dignity of each person was a minimal obligation within the human community. The right to be treated with dignity was God-given, and no elaborate excuses, however rationalized by past practice, could lessen this obligation. The cause of the farm workers was right in the eyes of the Lord because it was a struggle to restore the dignity proper to every farm worker. La Causa was about the restoration of the fundamental human dignity essential for the proper development of every man, woman and child.

Cesar had little tolerance for those who saw a more equitable treatment of farm workers in terms of the charity extended by farmers and growers. The fair and just treatment of farm workers whose labors filled the coffers of large agribusiness interests was not an option linked to charity. It was an obligation required by justice. Without justice, and in particular economic justice, the dignity of farm workers was violated. The economics of farm labor had to be subjected to a moral evaluation. Cesar held up the experiences of farm workers and argued that present conditions did not pass the test. No proof of the inequities of the present system was more evident than in the enormous disparity between the affluence and luxuries enjoyed by farmers and growers and the dehumanizing conditions which subjected farm workers to lives of misery and deprivation. Statistics painted a very sad picture. "We have accepted child labor, because otherwise our families couldn't live. We have accepted poverty and handouts or hunger during the off-season, because we don't know what unemployment insurance is. We have accepted all these things because we were powerless to defend ourselves. The deathrate of migrants' babies is 125% higher than the rest of the country. So is the deathrate among mothers. We are three times more likely to be injured at work. We are twice as likely to get flu or pneumonia; TB is even more frequent. The average American lives to be 70. The average migrant dies at 49."[16]

In his efforts to organize the National Farm Workers Association Cesar took no particular interest in developing a comprehensive analysis of the inadequacies of capitalism in American society. As a strategist he realized that this would not enhance his efforts to gain public support for the cause of the farm workers. However, a profound distaste for America's brand of capitalism is evident to those who reflect carefully on his economic philosophy. The protection of human dignity and economic justice were fundamental to his economic vision. These values had to be the foundation-stone of economic relationships between people. He saw the need for a more cooperative economic order in American society in order to overcome the self-interested individualism and materialism which continually pitted people against one another in the quest for economic advantages and rewards. He repeatedly rejected the suggestion that his intention was to establish a brown capitalism for Mexican-Americans in order to confront the power of white capitalism on equal terms. Such a strategy would only increase the already existing problems. What he hoped for was the emergence of a new way of understanding the cooperative nature of economic relationships among people. "I am not advocating black capitalism or brown capitalism. At the worst it gets a black to exploit other blacks, or a brown to exploit others. At the best, it only helps the lives of a few. What I'm suggesting is a cooperative movement."[17] The logic of the present system has resulted in the exploitation of farm workers because it embodies an understanding of economic relationships in terms of power. A new imagination is necessary which will enable all the participants in economic life to see the benefits of an economic order designed to enhance the common good of all the people.

Within the Mexican-American experience the family represents a central value. This is abundantly clear in Cesar's own life. The value of the family in his own experience enabled Cesar to better understand the proper nature of economic relationships. He proclaimed the importance of solidarity among his supporters. By supporting one another in a common cause to achieve dignity and economic justice, the needs of each individual are served. Solidarity among farm workers accorded them the opportunity to confront the power of agribusiness interests. "It is our belief that in working together we are going to be able to bring justice to an important group in our land. In working together, whether white or black or brown, it really doesn't matter because we really are just one people. In working together we will be able to bring justice to all of these people who suffer the pains of injustice. In working together as one people, we will one day be proud to know that it was our generation who was responsible for eliminating the inhuman treatment of workers and other minorities and other poor people. In working together, we know that we will be able to accomplish much more than that because the farm worker is not organized today, and if the farm worker ever gets organized, he is going to become a powerful force in our society, whereby he will work with you in those things we all share so dearly like peace."[18] Cesar's convictions about the importance of solidarity were not limited to its value in the family or among farm workers. He envisioned a new solidarity which would not only bind farm workers together, but which would bring workers and owners together in a common endeavor. An economics of solidarity stands against an economics which applauds "the survival of the fittest" in economic life. Just as human dignity and justice are essential for human well-being, solidarity is a necessary element for a just society.

After a careful examination of the life of Cesar Chavez few could argue that he lacked patience. From the outset of his struggle Cesar realized that achieving fundamental economic changes for farm workers would be a slow and plodding process. However, he remained ever hopeful that "La Causa" would eventually have its day in the sun. "Time accomplishes for the poor what money does for the rich."[19] In order to appreciate Cesar's patience and hopefulness, one has to understand his thoughts about the transforming power of moral truth. He believed that time would eventually vindicate the cause of the just man. The moral truth of their cause was mightier than the power of farmers and growers who remained comfortable in their exploitation of farm workers. Moral truth—the truth of human dignity, economic justice and solidarity—had its foundations in a reality more profound than existing conditions. If farm workers were given the opportunity to reveal the plight and injustices they suffered, their struggle for liberation would be greatly enhanced. Despite the fact that Cesar frequently felt discrimination at the hands of "Anglo-Americans," and although farm workers were exploited at the hands of their fellow Americans, Cesar remained confident that the American people were basically committed to justice and that they would rise up in support of those whose rights and dignity were so systematically violated. He was convinced that if confronted with an obvious moral evil most Americans would rise up in righteous indignation in support of the oppressed.

Cesar was a master at understanding the power of symbols and their ability to awaken people to new challenges. The labors of farm workers put food on the tables of the American people. The moral equation was simple enough in his mind. The nourishment of the multitude was purchased at the expense of farm workers. Justice could not tolerate such a circumstance. It violated basic and fundamental human rights. The children of God were created in order to live in harmony and in community with one another. Existing conditions violated this right order and pitted people against one another so that the riches of an economic elite were a by-product of the exploitation of farm workers. Cesar believed that the decent people of America would come to the defense of farm workers if they realized that their own nourishment was purchased by violating the dignity and rights of farm workers.

A Theology of Economic Justice

On March 10, 1968 Cesar Chavez ended the twenty-five day fast which he began on February 14. On the same day he attended a liturgical celebration and rally in Delano. Since Cesar was too weak to speak himself, one of his supporters delivered an address on his behalf. Cesar concluded the address with these words: "It is my deepest belief that only by giving our lives do we find life. I am convinced that the truest act of courage, the strongest act of manliness, is to sacrifice ourselves for others in a totally non-violent struggle for justice. To be a man is to suffer for others. God help us to be men."[20] No words more dramatically reveal the deep religious sentiments which shaped Cesar's activities on behalf of farm workers in the United States.

I have already indicated the impossibility of understanding Cesar's life without appreciating the influence of his Catholic faith on his activities. The more his life is examined the more apparent this becomes. Although his faith was simple, it was not simplistic. As he assumed more and more responsibilities on behalf of farm workers, he became increasingly interested in the relationship between his Catholic faith and the struggle for economic justice. Cesar's family experience imbued him with a deep faith in God and his benevolent concern for his people. As a young boy he learned this from his parents, and especially his mother who was always concerned about those in need. He frequently spoke of this influence in later life. One must also appreciate the role of the Catholic faith in Mexican-American culture. Belief in God and Jesus Christ was not an intellectualized theology but a part of daily life. It enabled the people to understand the meaning of their experiences and to endure the sacrifices and hardships they had to bear. More importantly it was a faith which proclaimed the value of each and every person in God's eyes, and the importance of caring for people and looking after one another. As Cesar matured and became more interested in a fuller understanding of the intellectual content of his Catholic faith, he had a powerful experiential foundation on which to build. He was already deeply aware that the central symbols of his Catholic faith, especially Christ's suffering on behalf of others, were intimately connected to his own experiences and the experiences of his people. His more formal reflection enabled him to unfold the meaning already present in his heart.

Cesar's introduction to a more formal understanding of the relationship between his Catholic faith and his struggle on behalf of farm workers came under the direction of Fr. Donald McDonnell. McDonnell recognized Cesar's leadership abilities and encouraged him. In the 1950's he introduced Cesar to the Church's teaching on economic justice through an examination of the encyclicals of Pope Leo XIII and Pope Pius XI. Cesar was particularly interested in these writings as they applied to the rights of workers and unions. But McDonnell also encouraged Cesar to read more broadly in religious matters, and his pupil responded enthusiastically. He turned to the Gospels and read them with a new awareness of Jesus' own commitment to the poor and the oppressed. He found in Jesus' life a dedication to justice and the promotion of justice through non-violent means. Cesar was also introduced to the writings of St. Paul whom he described as a tremendous organizer on behalf of the kingdom of God. He found in the life of St. Francis of Assisi a champion for his cause. He read some of the works of St. Thomas Aquinas and was particularly attracted to Thomas' analysis of the relationship between the individual good and the common good. In his studies he didn't limit himself exclusively to Catholic authors. He read the works of Henry David Thoreau and the writings of Gandhi who led a non-violent struggle for the liberation of the Indian people from British colonial rule. In the 1960's as he became more involved in the struggle to organize the NFWA he returned to the writings of Gandhi, and here he found a tremendous resource for the development of his own vision and strategy.

A further appreciation of the role Cesar's Catholic faith played in his life and his activities to organize the NFWA can be achieved by examining some of his more important speeches and letters. The most relevant of these include: a letter which outlined the purpose of the three hundred mile march to Sacramento in 1966; a letter he wrote to the National Council of Churches during his twenty-five day fast; the address he prepared at the end of the fast; and the "Good Friday Letter" which he wrote to representatives of agribusiness interests in California in April of 1969. I will briefly review these documents in an effort to summarize the social content of Cesar's Catholic faith.

I indicated earlier that Cesar was a keen student of the power of symbols to clarify for his supporters, the general public and his antagonists the meaning of the struggle which engaged farm workers. He was particularly alert to the significance of religious symbols as a way of promoting the cause of farm workers. I do not mean to imply that he distorted these symbols in order to serve the strategic purposes of the union. On the contrary, he simply wanted all the participants involved in this drama to realize that the meaning of their struggle was greater than what met the eye of the casual observer. This was the case of the march to Sacramento in 1966. In this event the traditional role of the pilgrimage in Spanish cultures, especially Mexican culture, was linked to a contemporary need of the poor, the downtrodden and the oppressed to give public witness to their plea for freedom, dignity and justice. The religious pilgrimage in the form of a march voiced the cry of the oppressed. "In the march from Delano to Sacramento there is a meeting of cultures and traditions; the centuries-old religious tradition of Spanish culture conjoins with the very contemporary cultural syndromes of 'demonstration' springing from the spontaneity of the poor, the downtrodden, the rejected, the discriminated-against baring visibly their need and demand for equality and freedom."[21] But the meaning of the march was broader than protest alone. The march was also linked to a religious need, deeply rooted in the Catholic faith, to do penance for the sins which have been committed by those engaged in the struggle for justice for farm workers. "The penitential procession is also in the blood of the Mexican-American, and the Delano March will therefore be one of penance— public penance for the sins of the strikers, their own personal sins as well as their yielding perhaps to feelings of hatred and revenge in the strike itself. They hope by the March to set themselves at peace with the Lord, so that the justice of their cause will be purified of all lesser intentions."[22] And it was an opportunity to understand the sacrifices required of those who commit themselves to the struggle for economic justice. In this letter Cesar indicated his belief that every struggle for liberation is essentially a religious struggle because it seeks to establish the right relationships which should exist among people in accordance with God's plan. The farm worker movement is a movement grounded in the Gospel of Jesus Christ because it seeks the liberation of God's people in a non-violent way. Catholic faith and social change are not at odds with one another. On the contrary, social change expresses the deepest sentiments of the Gospel when it seeks to free people from the bondage of economic oppression. Speaking of the transforming power of Christian faith Cesar said: "For me, Christianity happens to be a natural source of faith. I have read what Christ said when he was here. He was very clear in what he meant and knew exactly what he was after. He was extremely radical, and he was for social change."[23]

In February of 1968 Cesar was invited to attend the annual convention of the National Council of Churches. Due to the fact that he was weakened by his fast, he was unable to attend. However, he sent a letter to the National Council of Churches in which he outlined the goals of the farm workers' struggle and the role Christian churches could play. He wrote: "My fast is informed by my religious faith and by my deep roots in the Church. It is not intended as a pressure on anyone but only as an expression of my own deep feelings and my own need to do penance and to be in prayer. I hope that you understand and that you will pray for me . . . we cannot be faithful to this responsibility without the participation of the Christian community. You can help us survive and win new victories; but because of who you are you can also help us to stay true to our intention to serve our fellow farm workers."[24] Cesar was aware that the struggle would be longer than many of his supporters anticipated. And he also realized that frustration could lead to violence and jeopardize the success of "La Causa." The fast was a religious act of penance for the wrongs which had been committed by farm workers. It was also an act of sacrifice. Jesus' life was a model. Cesar saw the need for sacrifice so that the cause of the farm workers would remain pure. At the conclusion of the letter he asked the help of the Christian churches in the struggle. The Christian Gospel stood on the side of those who promoted justice, and clearly this was so in the struggle of farm workers.

I have already quoted from the address prepared by Cesar at the end of his fast on March 10, 1968. It deserves repeating here because it contains the essence of his understanding of the relationship between Christian faith and the struggle for economic justice. "It is my deepest belief that only by giving our lives do we find life. I am convinced that the truest act of courage, the strongest act of manliness, is to sacrifice ourselves for others in a totally non-violent struggle for justice. To be a man is to suffer for others. God help us to be men."[25] I do not know if it is possible to summarize Jesus' great counsel in the Gospel more succinctly and powerfully than the words I have just quoted, but I think not. Cesar's faith was not simplistic. He understood the intellectual content of the social message of the Gospel as presented in the Church's tradition and social teachings. However, the articulation of his faith was always simple in tone and style. To be a believer requires me to suffer on behalf of others in the cause of justice. Christ's message is not mystified. Nor is the reward of faith delayed to a world to come. History is the place of man's redemption and salvation.

On April 23, 1969 Cesar Chavez wrote a letter to Mr. E.L. Barr, Jr., President of the California Grape and Tree Fruit League. It was simultaneously published in *Christian Century* and the *National Catholic Reporter*. In the letter Cesar once again outlined the goals of the UFWOC and the strategy of militant non-violence which he intended to employ in order to achieve the goals of the union. "Today on Good Friday 1969 we remember the life and the sacrifice of Dr. Martin Luther King,

Jr., who gave himself totally to the non-violent struggle for peace and justice. In his letter from the Birmingham Jail Dr. King describes better than I could our hopes for the strike and boycott. 'Injustice must be exposed, with all the tension its exposure creates, to the light of human conscience and the air of national opinion before it can be cured.' For our part I admit that we have seized upon every tactic and strategy consistent with the morality of our cause to expose that injustice and thus to heighten the sensitivity of the American conscience so that farm workers will have without bloodshed their own union and the dignity of bargaining with their agribusiness employers."[26] He also presented a vivid description of the suffering which farm workers were forced to endure at the hands of growers and farmers. "They have been under the gun, they have been kicked and beaten and herded by dogs, they have been cursed and ridiculed, they have been stripped and chained and jailed, they have been sprayed with poisons used in the vineyards."[27] The most moving aspect of the letter is Cesar's reaffirmation of the union's commitment to non-violence as a way of awakening the American people to the plight of farm workers. "We advocate militant non-violence as our means for social revolution and to achieve justice for our people, but we are not blind or deaf to the desperate and moody winds of human frustration, impatience and rage that blow among us. Gandhi himself admitted that if his only choices were cowardice or violence, he would choose violence. Men are not angels, and time and tide wait for no man. Precisely because of these powerful human emotions, we have tried to involve masses of people in their own struggle. Participation and self-determination remain the best experience of freedom; and free men instinctively prefer democratic change and even protect the rights guaranteed to seek it. Only the enslaved in despair have need of violent overthrow."[28] Although it is true that Cesar learned a great deal about non-violence from the writings of Gandhi, his own philosophy was deeply influenced by his reading of the Gospel and the life of Jesus. Non-violence was critical to Cesar's understanding of the best of the Catholic tradition. Only the advocacy of non-violence would enable farm workers to achieve the goals of their movement. And the strategy of non-violence would enable those who oppressed farm workers, as exemplified by Mr. Barr and his associates, to redeem their own humanity and participate in the creation of a just economic order.

No aspect of Cesar Chavez's economic thought or his program for economic justice for farm workers more adequately reflects the religious foundations of his efforts than his dedication to non-violence. Therefore it deserves special attention in summarizing his contributions to economic justice in American society. In the early 1950's Cesar first became familiar with Gandhi's thought, and he utilized it as he shaped an appropriate strategy for the NFWA. However, it was during his twenty-five day fast in 1968 that he came to a fuller appreciation of Gandhi's philosophy. From this point his commitment to non-violence deepened significantly and he made a more concerted effort to explain it to his colleagues in the union, the general public and his antagonists in the agribusiness industry. Much can be said about Cesar's commitment to non-violence but a few elements merit special attention. First, a philosophy and strategy of non-violence is essential in the struggle to achieve social and economic justice because it explicitly recognizes the inherent dignity and worth of every human person. It proclaims the humanity of those who struggle to free themselves from the yoke of oppression, as well as the humanity of their oppressors. In seeking to lift up the oppressed in a non-violent struggle, a philosophy and strategy of non-violence also seeks to free the oppressor from the bonds of an oppressed consciousness which denies the common humanity of all people. Secondly, Cesar was convinced that in the struggle to liberate farm workers from their misery and oppression the use of violence would only prove to be morally counter-productive. If the goals of farm workers could only be achieved through the use of violence, then they would have to compromise their dignity for a very meager economic return indeed. And finally, Cesar embraced Gandhi's convictions about the redemptive meaning of a non-violent struggle for economic justice. It is redemptive for the victims of injustice because it enables them to strengthen their moral character as they struggle for liberation. And it is a redemptive force for those who act unjustly because it affords them an opportunity to encounter the humanity of those they oppress. A philosophy and strategy of non-violence is redemptive because it offers an opportunity for new life to the entire community. It brings new light into the world.

The Legacy

Cesar Chavez has made a special contribution to American Catholic economic thought. During the past four decades he has embraced the values of the Gospel of Jesus Christ and the social teachings of the Church, and carried their wisdom and transformative power into the socio-economic life of American society. His labors have profoundly touched the lives of farm workers across the United States and they have reawakened the moral conscience of a nation. In his work Cesar Chavez is first and foremost a symbol of all farm workers—brown, white and black—who yearn for the simple justice America has always promised her people. Cesar has never asked for more than that farm workers be accorded the human dignity which God bestows on all people.

When Cesar Chavez's life is examined superficially his contribution can be reduced to the work of a union leader who sought only economic rewards for the workers he represented. Cesar's work and message are far more profound. Although he was unquestionably interested in an economic revolution for farm workers, his more fundamental concern was for a moral transformation in American society. He called farm workers to a keener awareness of their dignity as persons and workers; he called farmers and the leaders of agribusinesses to a keener appreciation of their moral obligations to treat their workers with justice and dignity; and he called all Americans to a deeper awareness of their moral obligation to live out America's promise of liberty and justice for all. In his work Cesar Chavez was the moral leader of a people speaking to the soul of a nation.

No aspect of Cesar Chavez's thought, and no element of his strategy, was more unsettling to people than his dedication to non-violence. As a labor leader Chavez was not unmindful of the use of violence in earlier labor campaigns in American society. However, he rejected the use of violence unequivocally. Under the guidance of Fr. McDonnell Cesar reflected on the life and words of Jesus in the Gospels. He read St. Francis of Assisi, and the modern thought of Henry David Thoreau and Gandhi. A campaign intent on moral transformation could not succeed if it was grounded in the use of violence. More than once Cesar almost abandoned his work because he felt he was unable to convince his followers to embrace non-violence. History tells us that his dedication to non-violence eventually played a pivotal role in the eventual success of his work. His commitment to non-violence, not unlike that of Dr. Martin Luther King, Jr., caught a nation off-guard and eventually contributed substantially to the popular support for his cause among the American people.

Historically the Christian tradition has struggled with the proper relationship between the virtues of charity and justice. This was an important focus of Cesar's own work. His mission was to convince the American people, and especially his fellow Catholics, that charity alone was not sufficient for farm workers. In fact, charity alone was morally inadequate. While farm workers welcomed charity from their employers, and were deserving of charity from Americans more affluent than themselves, they had a more fundamental right to justice. And no amount of charity could lessen this moral right. When men, women and children are treated justly, they can have access to those goods—material, social and spiritual—which are constitutive of human dignity and well-being. When people are treated unjustly no amount of charity can restore human dignity. Throughout his work Cesar's message was simple. He only asked that farm workers be accorded the basic social and economic justice which was a right due all God's children.

His Mexican-American experience, and his own familial experience, awakened Cesar to an abiding sense of the importance of community and human solidarity. His work nurtured community among farm workers, and he was equally anxious to awaken other Americans to the importance of community. His understanding of the Eucharist was intimately connected to his understanding of the importance of community. The Eucharist spoke of a common table long enough and wide enough to accommodate all the children of God. The Eucharist was the model for the economy. It had to be large enough and wide enough to accommodate all God's people. Cesar believed that economic activity should always foster the growth of community and human solidarity.

Cesar Chavez was not an economic theorist. He left this labor to others. Nor did he engage in elaborate debates about the relative merits of capitalism or socialism. He saw beyond these debates and talked instead about the need for a more cooperative economic order in American society. A careful reading of Cesar's work does reveal his feelings about how the material goods of God's creation should be distributed in society. He believed strongly that God did not intend that the fruits of creation be denied to some in society while others enjoyed these goods in abundance. Although he accepted the proposition that men and women have an obligation to work for their bounty, he rejected the proposition that some members of society have a right to steal the bounty of others in order to advance their own economic self-interest. God gives the goods of creation to all his people. The moral task in every society is to see to the distribution of these goods in a just and equitable fashion.

Today Americans are still struggling with the social and economic injustices which afflict farm workers and subject them to indignities of every sort. Cesar Chavez was the first American to successfully organize farm workers into a viable labor organization. But the work is not yet complete. At the heart of Cesar's work is a moral vision, the desire to create a social order where all men, women and children enjoy those rights endowed by the Creator and promised in the American pledge of liberty and economic justice for all. People today who continue the struggle begun four decades ago by Cesar Chavez can look to him for direction about the labors which still need attention. His labors awakened the moral conscience of a people. Today the work needs continued vigilance.

Notes

1. "Cesar Chavez: La Causa," *American Labor,* February 1970, p. 30.

2. Dick Meister and Anne Loftis, *A Long Time Coming* (New York, 1977), p. 110.

3. Cesar Chavez, "Nonviolence Still Works," *Look,* April 1, 1969, p. 56.

4. Joseph R. Conlin, *Cesar Chavez: The Rhetoric of Nonviolence* (New York, 1975), p. 23.

5. Meister and Loftis, p. 112.

6. Jacques Levy, *Cesar Chavez: Autobiography of La Causa* (New York, 1975), p. 23.

7. Ibid., p. 87.

8. Conlin, p. 32.

9. Meister and Loftis, p. 110.

10. Ibid., p. 110.

11. Conlin, p. 73.

12. Ibid., p. 47.

13. Ibid., p. 114.

14. Cesar Chavez, "Working Together for the Poor and for Peace," *Metanoia,* March 1970, p. 5.

15. Cesar Chavez, "The Little Strike That Grew to La Causa," *Time,* July 4, 1969, p. 17.

16. Chavez, "Nonviolence Still Works," p. 55.

17. Levy, p. 537.

18. Chavez, "Working Together for the Poor and for Peace," p. 7.

19. Peter Matthiessen, "Cesar Chavez: Organizer," Part II, *New Yorker,* June 21, 1969, p. 72.

20. Conlin, p. 47.

21. Ibid., p. 106.

22. Ibid., p. 66.

23. Levy, p. 27.

24. Conlin, p. 108.
25. Ibid., p. 47.
26. Ibid., pp. 112–13.
27. Ibid., p. 113.
28. Ibid., p. 115.